THE NEW MANAGER'S SURVIVAL GUIDE

THE NEW MANAGER'S SURVIVAL GUIDE

EVERYTHING YOU NEED TO KNOW TO SUCCEED IN THE CORPORATE WORLD

STEVEN HAINES

New York Chicago San Francisco Lisbon Athens London
Madrid Mexico City Milan New Delhi San Juan
Seoul Singapore Sydney Toronto

1 2 3 4 5 6 7 8 9 0 DOC/DOC 1 2 1 0 9 8 7 6

ISBN 978-1-259-58897-6
MHID 1-259-58897-1

e-ISBN 978-1-259-58976-8
e-MHID 1-259-58976-5

CONTENTS

FOREWORD

When I first read the manuscript for *The New Manager's Survival Guide*, I asked myself two questions:

1. Who exactly might benefit from this book?
2. Who exactly might *think* that they would benefit from this book?

Although these questions are separated by just a few choice words, the differences in their meanings are vast.

Having spent over 20 years in the corporate world with a variety of different companies and in a number of different leadership positions, I immediately knew the answer to my first question. In a word: Everyone. This may seem like a dramatically overarching response, but in truth, I can't think of a single person, inside business or outside of it, who couldn't benefit by knowing the ins and outs of how a company operates.

For anyone who works inside a company, the information that will be shared within these pages will serve as an invaluable resource that would take most business professionals decades to learn on their own—if it even gets learned at all. Throughout my career, I have witnessed far too many business people who fail to gain perspectives and understandings outside of their own job functions and, as a result, fail to fully grasp how to effectively collaborate and interact outside the boundaries of their own departmental walls. It takes time, patience, and an innate curiosity to learn about what other functions do and, perhaps more important, why they do it. As such, this knowledge tends to be coveted by those select few individuals whose job it is to deeply understand and interact with multiple different departments on a very regular basis, or by those people who actively seek out such opportunities on their own. In the grand scheme of things, neither of these scenarios is terribly common within large organizations and, as a result, internal misalignment and miscommunication can be something of the rule rather than the exception.

For those people working outside of companies, nary a day goes by without someone asking the question, "Why in the world did Company X, Y, or Z do that?" Whether this question is asked from the perspective of a frustrated customer, a concerned supplier, or an inquisitive investor, it is quite common for people outside of an organization to not fully understand what makes a certain company tick or, perhaps more commonly, not tick quite as steadily as maybe it should. Not that understanding the root of any particular company issue will automatically make it go away; but it will certainly lessen the frustration of not knowing, and clear the path for a smoother, more fruitful interface that all concerned parties can more effectively benefit from in the long run. Practically everyone on earth deals with companies at some point in his or her life, so understanding how they work can only make that interaction more meaningful.

This book provides the foundational knowledge that most people, both inside and outside of companies, don't always have ready access to. So, within this context, answering "everyone" in response to my first question doesn't seem so out of range.

My second question, on the other hand, is a bit more difficult to address. Let's face it, the reason I asked the question of how many people might *think* they need this book is because I have a sneaking suspicion that this number may not be very high—or at least not as high as it should be.

In my experience, I believe that most people in business instinctively know just how much they *don't* know about the way their companies operate. The problem is, some people in business might feel that they *should* know how a company operates and, therefore, they may be reluctant to fully admit when they don't. Couple that with the fact that deep learning takes time that may not always be in abundant supply, and you have a recipe for broad knowledge gaps not only to exist in business, but to actually widen as careers progress and responsibilities expand.

All of this brings me to my main concern, which is that new managers, or even aspiring ones for that matter, might be inclined to believe that they can learn everything they need to know "on the job" or, worse, that there might be some unwritten expectation of them to do just that. Of course, the fact that you have chosen to read this book indicates that you probably don't fall into this particular category. And it is for this very reason that I would like to ask for your help in two relatively simple ways as you work your way through the chapters that follow.

First, if you find the lessons in this book to be valuable, and you find that they provide you with insights that you did not previously have, then my first ask is simply that you apply whatever it is that you learn. I realize that many people will have picked up this book in order to advance their own careers, and, believe me, that is an honorable and worthwhile cause. But great careers also make great companies, which also happen to make great products. Applying the lessons you learn throughout this book will not only help you to enable your own career, it will also help you to enable this entire cycle. And the result of this is something that everyone can ultimately benefit from—employees, companies, investors, and consumers alike.

My second ask is even easier than the first, and that is that you proudly tell your colleagues about what you learn—and how you learned it. To be clear on this point, I am not directly asking you to promote this particular book (and I hope the fact that I am not the author of it helps to lend some credibility to this statement). Instead, I am asking you to promote the *idea* of this book.

Perhaps my view has been slightly jaded over the years, but I have heard far too much buzz within companies about management skills being something that can't really be taught. The result of this myth is not that the teaching won't exist but, instead, that it won't be embraced. And this is perhaps the most damaging scenario that can persist.

So, as you read this book, if you find that you're getting something out of it, be sure to tell your colleagues, your employees, and your friends that it's OK for them to use a business survival guide as well. Proudly display it on your bookshelf and openly discuss the exercises that appear throughout each chapter as you work your way through them. Despite what you may have been told, you weren't born to be a manager; you earned it. And now you need to learn it as well. This guide is just one of the tools that you will use along the way. And, hopefully, you will continue to refer back to this book and use it as a road map to help get you back on course if ever you should lose your way.

Which leads me to one last sentiment that I'd like to pass along to you—based on something my wife passed along to me the last time I drove nearly 50 miles out of our way before admitting that I had no idea where I was going.

Remember that there is no failure in being lost. The only real failure is in not knowing when to ask for directions.

My wife's version may have contained a few more exclamation points, but I'm sure you get the idea! In short, this book can serve as your directions. And just as important, the example you set by reading and utilizing all that it has to offer will almost certainly encourage other people to ask for their own directions as well. I can't think of a greater impact that this book can have on the business world. And I can't think of a better way to wish you well as you take the next step in your management career.

Bob Caporale
Author of *Creative Strategy Generation*

INTRODUCTION

I love business. Every day when I wake up, I switch on the TV to the business news channel, read through the *Wall Street Journal*, and scan the stories on Business Insider. I'm always trying to learn what business leaders think and how businesses achieve success—a mindset I'd like you to be able to adopt.

Many of you may be newer to the corporate world and find it a fascinating place to work. Based on my own experience and from what I learn in my research, challenges abound. You may be asked to work on projects that don't make sense or may witness business politics that just doesn't seem productive or logical. Business people who work in mid- to large-sized companies are often admonished by their bosses to deal with these issues, which is easier said than done. From my standpoint, it's easier to adapt and be productive when you know what you're working toward, expect the unexpected, and adopt a proactive mindset.

Business can and should be simple to understand, and that's why I've written this book. I've been involved with the world of business for decades and have accumulated knowledge, experience, and wisdom that I'd like to share with you. This is a book for you if you:

- Are newer in your business or managerial career and you need a concise guide that will show you how the gears of a business operate in any middle-to-large sized company
- Worked in a functional area of a company (e.g., engineering, operations) and will be taking on a business or management role
- Are in the process of entering the corporate world of business and will benefit from a resource to help you hit the ground running

Some people have an innate understanding of all things business, some do not, and others are somewhere in between. Some of you already work in a business role in a corporation, and others aspire to. Regardless of your role as a business person, I can tell you that leaders expect a lot. They want their newer managers to focus on the "big picture" of the business, cultivate great relationships across the enterprise, and contribute to the advancement of the firms' goals. In the overall scheme of things, managers are expected to understand how the business works, how to get things done, and how to influence others who don't work for them.

Business acumen is the term used to describe a person's understanding of various dimensions of a business that are "in play" as situations arise. This "business common sense" is built up over time, just like practitioners such as surgeons, musicians, or pilots get better with practice. My hope for you in this book is that you'll gain an appreciation for the interconnectedness of the parts of a business so that you can recognize the signals as various situations arise, and figure out what to do to get things done. My role as guide is to accelerate your journey. As you absorb what's contained in these chapters, some content will be familiar to you based on your own experience or what you learned in school. However, you'll derive the best benefit when you can see how to knit those areas together with new thoughts and ideas. This mindset will add to your expertise, resourcefulness, and confidence.

HOW TO USE THIS BOOK TO IMPROVE YOUR BUSINESS ACUMEN

I've written this book partially as a business practitioner's handbook, to help you view various dimensions of a company, and partially as a managerial development work tool, so that you can take direct action as required. How you use the book will depend on your experience and motivation. For you to gain the best perspective to start your work, I've summarized the 12 chapters contained in the book:

CHAPTER 1—STARTING OUT: ASSESSING YOUR BUSINESS ACUMEN

If you don't know where you are and where you want to go, how will you know what to do? This is the chapter where I'll define the key dimensions of business acumen and why they're so important. I'll also introduce you to a tool to help you assess your business acumen, which you can use to create a purposeful professional development strategy.

CHAPTER 2—FINDING YOUR WAY AROUND THE ORGANIZATION

Working in a company can be made easier if you know how the company makes money and how it's organized, the people who work there, and what makes them tick. While you may think it's simple to figure out who's who by looking at the organization chart, savvy business people need to figure out how to navigate the informal organization. They must create great working relationships while earning trust and credibility. This chapter will provide you with practical tools to help you chart your path.

CHAPTER 3—YOU CAN'T DO IT ALL YOURSELF

It's generally known that when people with different skills are brought together to work on a team, everyone benefits. This is easier said than done. I'll guide you by explaining various team structures and describing essential team operating paradigms. I'll then explain the importance of team leadership and collaboration, which is vital to business efficiency and competitiveness.

CHAPTER 4—MONEY IS NOT A FOREIGN LANGUAGE

In fact, money *is* the language of business, so I'll provide you with a basic overview of business finance so that you can get your bearings and establish a game plan to get your mind into the numbers game. To achieve this, I'll explain the fundamentals of finance and describe the key financial statements you'll need to know about. I'll also demonstrate why budgeting and financial planning is critical to aligning others in the organization, and in tracking progress.

CHAPTER 5—LEVERAGING PROCESSES TO GET THINGS DONE

Throughout your business career, whether you follow prescribed documentation or not, you will leverage processes to get work done. These processes lay out things to do, interdependencies between people, and results to be achieved. Some people feel that processes can be overwhelming and unwieldy. Fortunately, I'll show you how to understand how you might be able to focus your efforts on simplicity and efficiency so that business resources can be put to the best use.

CHAPTER 6—USING DATA TO SOLVE PROBLEMS AND MAKE DECISIONS

Businesses run on data. It's a premium fuel that gives everyone in the business the ability to make plans, uncover and solve problems as they arise, steer the business, and keep things moving and growing. After all, no one wants a stagnant business. This is a chapter that will offer you the tools and wherewithal to understand different types of data, where it comes from, and how it's used. Then, I'll introduce you to an interesting method to help you use data to find solutions to problems and make better business decisions.

CHAPTER 7—MASTERING MARKETS

Most people have an innate view of markets. You know this because, as a consumer, you're involved in markets every day. However, the simplicity on the surface masks the complexity of interactions between customers and competitors. Business people must be cognizant of market dynamics, so I'll make this topic easy to understand by characterizing the key aspects of markets and showing you how they're studied and how insights are derived—all of which contribute to the strategy of the company.

CHAPTER 8—SETTING DIRECTION WITH STRATEGY

People who work in a business, just like people who play on a sports team or perform in a show, need to know what they're working toward and why. Everyone needs a goal and a path to achieve that goal. This chapter supports you with the essential context required to understand the foundations of strategy and strategic planning so that you can contribute to the future direction of the company.

CHAPTER 9—UNDERSTANDING PRODUCTS

This chapter is designed to help you establish important linkages between market insights, strategies, and the ideas for innovative products. You'll learn that a product is anything that's sold—regardless of whether it's tangible or intangible. I'll show you how products are organized in a company and how they're brought to life with a business case—with recommendations on how you might pitch a product idea. Further, I'll share some areas that are important for business people to know about, including product design, make-versus-buy analysis, project management, and intellectual property. Who knows, you may be inspired to be a product manager one day!

CHAPTER 10—MARKETING: THE FULCRUM OF THE ORGANIZATION

As a consumer, you experience marketing every day. But what goes on in the marketing department of your company, and why is it so important? In this chapter, I'll explain the nuts and bolts of the marketing function in terms of what it does for the company. This includes inspiring dialogues with or between customers, attracting customers to your company and its products, creating a remarkable experience, and producing content to inform customers so they can make buying decisions. In the end, marketing helps bring the business strategy to life.

CHAPTER 11—ASSESSING BUSINESS PERFORMANCE

All the best plans and programs are rendered useless if a company cannot track how well it's doing. In this chapter I'll knit together much of what I covered in the book to place business performance center stage and in the front of your mind. Why? Because in business, everything boils down to execution on plans and profits earned. You'll learn that precision analysis and a keen eye allow business people to associate data-driven measurements that bring the state of the business into clear focus so that new plans can be imagined and put to work to keep the business growing.

CHAPTER 12—YOUR PROFESSIONAL DEVELOPMENT STRATEGY

In Chapter 8, I will explain the importance of business strategy. In the same vein, you will need to develop a purposeful professional development strategy to keep your business career on track. This brief chapter will provide you with the ability to integrate what you learned in the book with what you gleaned from your Business Acumen Assessment results. You'll be provided with a template to equate your goals with specific action plans!

You can use this book to take direct action as exemplified in the templates, exercises, and helpful hints in each of the chapters. I cannot emphasize this point enough: when you proactively take action, it means you seek out diverse job experiences to expand your portfolio of skills—which will contribute to your effectiveness as a business person. Also, when you are seen by your managers as an individual who takes on challenges and seeks out new experiences, you'll increase your chances of being promoted!

Also, to absorb what's contained in the book, you can certainly read it in a sequential manner to get the gestalt of the entire work. Then, you can refer back to various chapters when you encounter a specific situation and need a refresher. To contribute further to your knowledge, I've also provided a Glossary and Bibliography at the back of the book.

With this context, I want you, as a new manager, to develop your own sixth sense for business. I can safely say that leaders of organizations, large and small, are constantly on the lookout for new ways to do things. They have an insatiable need to get work done quickly and efficiently, and to remove as many obstacles as possible. They need employees whom they rely upon and trust to protect the interests of the organization—in other words, they need good managers! Even more, they want these managers to evolve into the leaders of the future. As you journey through this book, use the tools and suggestions to help you raise your game. My hope is that this book will offer you a set of lenses through which you can view business in a simple, practical way.

STARTING OUT: ASSESSING YOUR BUSINESS ACUMEN

After you read this chapter, you should be able to:

- Interpret the key dimensions of business acumen needed for business people to be successful.
- Evaluate your business acumen with a simple assessment.
- Define areas on which to focus to develop your business acumen.

The wise man will want to be ever with him who is better than himself.

—PLATO

Most managers say to their new hires that they have to "hit the ground running." I don't know about you, but most times I was advised to do this, I'd end up like a kid, falling down, scraping my knees, and feeling bad.

After I graduated college, I was hired as a management trainee at a company that distributed plumbing and heating products. I knew nothing about pipe, valves, fittings, toilets, or boilers. Nonetheless, I was told that I had to learn every job in the company by doing every job in the company. I thought that would be fun, although I was scared out of my mind.

When I started, I had to learn how the back office worked. Later, I was assigned to a distribution center to process orders, work the counter, and talk to customers. After that, I spent many months in the field as a salesperson. When I stumbled and thought I had learned my lesson, I'd make another error, but I eventually started to "get it." Luckily, my boss spent a lot time with me as a mentor and coach as I was brought more deeply into the business. During my three years at this company, I developed a tremendous understanding of how successful businesses worked.

During the early days of my career learning about business operations, I also attended graduate school on a part-time basis to earn an MBA in finance. Afterward, I held financial jobs in a variety of industries including defense electronics and medical products. In each of those roles, I always interacted with people in different functional departments. From these interactions, I realized that the organization was in a fluid state. Customer problems trumped daily plans and operational challenges delayed projects. Yet the big learning was this: *adaptability and flexibility are required characteristics for any business person to achieve success.* Furthermore, because of the shifting tides of markets and the adaption of companies to stay ahead of the curve, I realized why it is so important to become a student of business, and why it is vital to attain a well-rounded view of the business playing field.

What I learned then, and what I believe you will realize, is that you'll always have a host of urgent demands. They'll come in many different forms as e-mails lobbying for your attention, requests to attend an endless stream of meetings, and a barrage of things to do. When I was in the thick of things in any company where I worked, there were times that I felt like I was in a raft on a raging river of class 5 rapids, and that if I didn't handle a given situation correctly, I'd capsize and have to swim to the safety of the shoreline—and avoid the rocks at the same time! If you have sufficient preparation when you encounter the unexpected, you will be able to set the stage to deal with these issues. If you don't establish the proper context for the environment in which you work, others will set the context for you! When this occurs, you'll be a firefighter who battles a fire that just won't simmer down. This can put you and your business career at a major disadvantage.

To get started, I've designed this section to familiarize you with key skills that any business person should master. To do this, I will:

1. Present you with seven *groups* of business acumen, and a number of *characteristics* that are important to a business person's performance. Each will be defined for you.

2. Introduce you to a model and a tool to help you assess yourself and capture your current level of business acumen.

ALL ABOARD!

Imagine a roller coaster ride at an amusement park. The riders line up and then board the train. The safety bar is lowered, and the train takes you along the course. People who are frequent riders know the dips and curves and when they'll catch some air. In the world of business, the jobs we take may seem like we're on a roller coaster. Imagine how hard it would be to hop on the train while it was moving! It's not possible. However, when we start a new job or join a new company, it almost seems like we're boarding that moving train. From another vantage point, you may find that your business degree or experiences to date will not have prepared you to handle many of the unfamiliar situations you'll encounter. Yet you will still be expected to fulfill your responsibilities.

No matter where you start out (or started out) as a business manager, you've got to be able to determine where you are so you can figure out what to work on as part of your *purposeful professional development strategy*. (Note: In Chapter 12 and Appendix A, you'll have an opportunity to work on this professional development strategy with a helpful guideline, template, and online access to the Business Acumen Assessment.) As you create this strategy, I want you to be aware that there are some nonnegotiable characteristics that are required of all business people who aspire to become great managers. These include the following:

- Communicate clearly with people in all functional departments at all levels.
- Garner respect from people in those functional departments.
- Creatively collaborate with others in both recognizing and solving problems.
- Know the right processes to use to get things done and fulfill goals.
- Approach new opportunities with enthusiasm and passion.
- Focus on the achievement of business results.

As you gain experience from the work you do and the situations you encounter, your "state of experience" will shift—and you'll become better prepared to figure out what to do next!

ESSENTIAL ELEMENTS OF BUSINESS ACUMEN

Regardless of the type or size of company you work in, leaders want the same things from the business people they employ. This involves having sufficient familiarity with markets, the economy, and finance. They also want people to solve problems, make decisions, and contribute to positive business results.

As I mentioned in the Introduction, the term *business acumen* refers to the portfolio of characteristics employed by successful, productive business people. However, there's another dimension worth mentioning. It's the word *domain*, which is used to describe the environment of an industry or technology. For example, a business person who works in a bank should have sufficient knowledge of the financial services sector. This is crucial because the banking industry is strongly influenced by the state of politics, regulations, economics, and technology. This also involves staying up-to-date on customer behaviors and preferences in banking, which could include the fact that people are more mobile and bank online. People who might opt for a business role in a bank and stay current on activities in that domain would be more committed to that role, and may do a better job, than a person interested in consumer electronics.

I had an experience a number of years ago that illustrates an important perspective. While I was conducting an organizational research project, an executive explained to me that some business people needed a combination of domain (subject matter expertise) and business skills and understanding. This particular case had to do with the nuclear power generation market. He described how he had to evaluate prospective business managers for leadership roles based on their understanding of the industry, its relevant technology, and market dynamics. To further illustrate his point, he used his hands to form a *T* and said that a T-shaped manager with the combined breadth of business acumen and depth of domain was required to be a successful business person in his company.

Figure 1.1 The Intersection of Business Acumen and Domain Expertise

A lightbulb went off in my head! I took out a piece of paper and drew the T shape. Then, I thought to myself that there had to be a way to visualize the gradations of business and domain expertise—which is what I've visualized for you as Figure 1.1.

As I ventured through my own career, I subconsciously made choices about companies in which I could work based on my perceived level of business acumen and domain interest and expertise. Some roles were easy to get my mind around because I was interested and could more easily associate with them. In choosing one of my first financial positions, I opted for a job with a medical products manufacturer over a similar role in a bank. I learned the domain of those medical products because I was keenly interested and easily saw my way forward in learning that area. I had similar experiences in subsequent roles with computing hardware and business automation software.

In Appendix A, I'll explain the gradations of domain expertise and show you how to plot your "coordinates" on the chart shown in Figure 1.1.

I can safely say that you will immensely benefit from what's contained in this book as you expand your breadth of business knowledge and expertise. To help you do so, I'll provide information on those characteristics and a technique to conduct a self-assessment. The characteristics I describe in this chapter represent the superset of knowledge, skills, experiences, and behaviors that you should strive to attain, and that others expect you to embody. As you will discover, these relate to the actions you take and the outcomes you produce.

As you're guided through the definitions, and if you take the assessment (whether in this book or online), you will realize that you probably don't possess the entire portfolio of experience. I urge you to think of these characteristics from an aspirational point of view. Over time, you will learn what it takes to produce results that are visible and evident to yourself, your managers, and your peers.

To gain the best perspective, I'll ask you to read through the seven groups and the associated characteristics. I'd like you to approach these with the following points in mind:

1. These are career building blocks. Therefore, your understanding of them will sensitize you to what leaders want, what you'll need to exhibit to be recognized, and how success can be attained.
2. Discern what's relevant to you, whether it's in your current job or based on your aspirations, so you can concentrate on the areas that are most important.
3. Use these to set your own context and prepare yourself to assimilate what's contained in the chapters that follow.

Across the seven groups, there are a total of 38 characteristics. As you review the descriptions of each characteristic in each *group*, you may think they're obvious and, perhaps, somewhat oversimplified. Indeed, these descriptions are not highly nuanced or deeply detailed. However, I've interviewed many business leaders about these characteristics, and one of the things I've learned is this: *understanding a definition is one thing; living the definition is another.* The reason is simple. We all have blind spots. What we perceive as a strong ability may not be seen so by others, including your boss. On the other hand, it can mean that you have a strength that you're not fully aware of.

You may also notice some recurring patterns and connectivity among several of the characteristics. These can be interpreted as synergies. For example, when you read about problem solving, critical thinking, and decision making, you will see that each has its own definition, but you can't have one without the other. Further, when you see specific interconnections, you will be primed to understand the interconnectedness of business and why this perspective will help you see the big picture that is so important to your success. Most of these items are mentioned, either explicitly or tacitly, throughout this book. Therefore, I'll provide you with the ability to "check in" at the end of each chapter so that you can reinforce what you've learned, or to clarify your understanding about a characteristic. To reinforce my point made earlier, you'll be able to use these to focus on your purposeful professional development goals.

Group 1: General Business

- *Managing.* Managing involves the work of "getting things done" and is broken down into broad categories that include goal setting, planning, monitoring, and measuring work and its associated outcomes. Whether you're an individual contributor manager, or a manager of managers, "managing" is what you do to get things done every day.
- *Defining processes.* Processes involve the procedures that govern how work or information flows across an organization. They serve to define cross-functional work activities and clarify roles and responsibilities in the production of outcomes. In the definition and use of a process, there's an implication for business people who should be able to recognize and remove roadblocks that stand in the way of progress.
- *Making decisions.* Good decisions should be based on facts, data, and experience. Business people must be able to size up a problem or situation, collect and evaluate data, and surface alternatives. When you make a quality decision and follow through with a positive outcome, you'll know you're on the right path.
- *Being a self-starter.* The ability to identify and initiate work without supervision or direction is a sought-after capability.

If you are motivated to grow and be promoted, you shouldn't always have to wait for the boss's orders.

- *Managing time and being efficient.* Business people must keep their days organized by balancing meetings, work tasks, and administrative activities in order to produce expected outcomes. This also allows for the dynamic prioritizing that's needed every day.
- *Adapting to changing situations.* Business people function in a dynamic workplace with seemingly endless demands from others. They must flexibly adapt to each situation and understand that goals and associated plans may change from time to time. Staying cool and logical are the watchwords here.

Group 2: Business and Market Environment

- *Deriving market insights.* Businesses sell products to customers. Customers have choices among competitive offerings. The market is characterized by this dynamic interplay between customers and the competitors who vie for their business in any number of industry areas.
- *Understanding products.* All businesses sell a product of some kind. To get the best picture of how any company operates, you will need to understand the products being offered for sale by the company. This contributes immensely to the understanding of how any company makes money.
- *Evaluating the industry and domain.* A holistic perspective on the business environment means understanding a collective host of influences. These can include the political climate, regulations, economic activity, societal trends, and the evolving impact of technologies on your company and its products.
- *Experiencing business on a global level.* Many companies do business outside of their home markets. Whether you travel to other countries to transact business or do so through other means, business people should be able to understand the cultural dimensions of business in markets in which your company does business. This should not be taken lightly as

there are a number of cultural and other boundaries that separate people across the globe.

Group 3: Mindset and Orientation

- *Critical thinking.* Spending sufficient time to assimilate and evaluate business, market, financial, and environmental data yields vital conclusions that can help in the formulation of an insight and/or the derivation of a strategy. Critical thinkers tend to embrace ambiguity, uncover and solve problems, and make fact-based decisions.
- *Strategic thinking.* In ambiguous market environments, strategic thinking is used to consider and evaluate internal and external inputs and to envision future competitive solutions. Strategic thinkers therefore have deep knowledge of the market that is meshed with their understanding of the company's people, processes, and products. They are able to derive scenarios that identify business opportunities.
- *Systemic thinking.* This relates to the way in which you develop insights from the evaluation of complex interrelationships and the detection of patterns and/or trends and how those impact a business from a holistic perspective. Systemic thinkers have a great tendency to make connections. Think of how doctors utilize diagnostic procedures; they have to think systemically about the human body.
- *Solving problems.* Problem solvers are able to assess a situation and use a logical analysis to determine the source of the problem. They also engage others in analysis of solutions so that an appropriate decision can be made.
- *Entrepreneurial thinking.* As business people evolve in an organization, they are often expected to look for opportunities outside the current affairs of the firm. Leaders look for people who keep abreast of market trends, propose innovative products, and conceive of new ways of doing things.
- *Developing organizational instinct.* Business people improve their effectiveness over many years and through encountering various situations. These experiences lead to the development of organizational instinct. Thus, this instinct is usually acquired

rather than innate. It develops like a sixth sense in the minds of business people and matures with experience.

- *Exercising political judgment.* Business people must be able to recognize, analyze, and reconcile incompatible interests or agendas on a team or across an entire organization. Although you must act in the best interest of the company based on its goals, you may need to persuade others to examine different perspectives using thoughtful suggestions that may help people find common ground. As relationships are developed with key influencers across your organization, political judgment may also be driven through an understanding of the implicit or unspoken words of others.

Group 4: Communication

- *Listening attentively.* This skill is important not only for interacting with the people you work with, but also for hearing the voice of the customer—especially when you are observing or speaking with customers. Active listening may include asking open-ended questions, paraphrasing, reflecting, and summarizing what was said.
- *Observing actively.* Closely related to active listening, this capability is used by business people to evaluate operating environments. For example, active observation is an often-used technique for teaching medical students in a clinical environment. Active observation techniques include understanding organizational work flows and operating models used by the company.
- *Writing clearly and concisely.* This is the ability to assemble your thoughts and write in an organized manner to a specific audience. Specifically, you need to be able to write concisely for a senior executive or with sufficient detail for a peer.
- *Presenting persuasively.* This doesn't necessarily equate to your PowerPoint skills. It's related to how you communicate to others in a manner that captivates their imagination and inspires action. For additional context, think about how people who want to start a company might pitch their idea to an investor.

- *Influencing others.* Influencing is the ability to get others to do what you need them to do. This could be to enlist support, obtain resources, or energize a team. Leaders expect that business people, with or without direct reports, will always need to gain the support of others to share ideas, work on projects, and produce work products that represent the combined outcome of many people.

Group 5: Interpersonal Skills

- *Building positive relationships.* Relationships may be enhanced when you're seen as "available" and approachable. People want to see you as friendly and helpful. This is important because it sets the stage to your becoming more visible in the day-to-day interactions in your business environment. This is achieved by engaging in conversation with people, finding common interests, learning about their work, and understanding the issues they face. It also includes the ability to help others feel valued and important.
- *Developing customer relationships.* Conversing with, observing, and understanding customers are vital to the success of any business. As business people evolve in their careers, it is imperative to create durable, long-lasting relationships with customers! Frequent interactions allow you to understand how customers "do what they do" so that implicit needs can be uncovered. As you progress in your business career, you will likely be called upon to focus on uncovering and solving customer problems.
- *Developing external relationships.* Your organization may maintain business relationships with other firms, such as suppliers, distributors, or ecosystem partners. These relationships are built through a common understanding of all objectives for all stakeholders, as well as through all contractual obligations. This also means that when issues emerge, they can be dealt with to the satisfaction of all.
- *Including others.* People come from everywhere! Business people must develop competence in communicating within and interacting across cultural, ethnic, gender, and geographic

boundaries. One approach to tap into this brain power is to proactively seek information from others with different personalities, backgrounds, and styles, and including them on teams in problem solving and decision making.

- *Helping or coaching others.* Business people know that others may need help from time to time. Communication proficiency equips business people with the skill to uncover clues about where people need help. Oftentimes, those who need help don't realize it, or you may need to facilitate conversations between team members who have different perspectives in order to promote collaboration and cooperation.
- *Being a reliable team player.* Business people work on teams all the time and, ultimately, will lead teams. Whether a team member or leader, you should be able to understand the purpose of any team and the roles of people who are responsible for the achievement of the team's goals. To foster teamwork, you will need to provide assistance to others when needed and reinforce the contributions of your teammates.
- *Negotiating.* In the big picture, negotiating involves gaining the best position at the least cost where everyone "wins." Negotiating in an organization is more easily accomplished on a long-term basis when goals are agreed-upon, issues are understood, and everyone's interests are represented so that you can get to "yes" as required.

Group 6: Business Performance

- *Being results oriented.* Business people earn credibility when they are able to set and achieve challenging goals. They excel when they feel a sense of urgency to achieve more in less time—which is highly desirable in the eyes of senior leaders.
- *Evaluating business performance.* Financial skills are used to establish budgets, forecasts, market share assessments, and cash flow estimates. Nonfinancial performance indicators provide other important insights into the business. These financial and nonfinancial measures must be melded to evaluate the performance of the company versus established plans so that timely corrective actions can be taken.

- *Improving business processes.* Business people can contribute greatly to the achievement of company goals when they can evaluate the effectiveness of work activity across the organization. They can earn credibility when they evaluate key performance indicators associated with those processes and take action on vital process improvements.
- *Taking action.* Action-oriented people understand the need for speed and agility in shifting markets and are ready to take on new challenges every day. Those who work hard and are full of energy are assets prized by company leaders.
- *Assuming accountability.* In the production of business results, the person who must ultimately deliver on a commitment (or hold others to the commitment) is considered accountable. This should not be confused with the term *responsible*, which means that a person is the doer of work.

Group 7: Yourself

- *Earning credibility.* One of the most important characteristics that all managers must demonstrate every day is credibility. Your leaders and peers (and subordinates, if you have them) must perceive you as responsible and reliable based on your commitment to the business, doing your fair share, and being responsible for your own mistakes.
- *Acting with integrity, ethics, and trust.* Acting with integrity means that you have a sense of ethics and values. Being trustworthy means that you behave reliably, fairly, and honestly, inspiring others to trust you.
- *Being confident.* Confidence in your ability to contribute to the successful operation of the business is vital. The greater your own achievements, the more self-assured you are. When you are more self-assured, you are more likely to take on new challenges with a can-do attitude. However, overconfidence can be seen negatively, which means an occasional dose of humility may be needed.
- *Exercising managerial courage.* This refers to the ability to stand up for your convictions, values, and beliefs. Managerial courage is observed when a business person faces a difficult issue and says what needs to be said.

Later in the book, I provide greater context for you, with specific "how-to" steps to raise your game in each of these areas.

THE BUSINESS ACUMEN ASSESSMENT

Now that the characteristics have been identified and described, it's time for you to reflect on these and to carry out your self-assessment. There is tremendous value in doing this assessment, which includes:

1. Having a baseline measurement of your level of knowledge and experience with respect to each characteristic.
2. Being cognizant of the areas on which you can focus to improve your understanding as you encounter various topics.
3. Knowing that I'll provide you with ways to "check in" at various points throughout the book to ensure that you're on track to continue your learning.

Now, as you consider each group and the descriptions of all the characteristics in each group, think of how you might rate yourself using an easy rating scale. Refer to Figure 1.2 for rating guidelines. A sample

Figure 1.2 Assessment Rating Scale

RATING	DEFINITION	POINTS
Limited	This means you haven't had a many opportunities to focus on this skill or apply it in your work.	**1**
Intermittent	You have had some opportunities to use the skill intermittently and are developing more familiarity with its use.	**2**
Frequent	You frequently utilize this skill, yet encounter some challenging situations where you may need some guidance from your manager.	**3**
Consistent	You effectively and consistently utilize this skill, and are able to coach others.	**4**

Figure 1.3 Sample Self-Assessment

GROUP	CHARACTERISTIC DESCRIPTION	LIMITED	INTER-MITTENT	FREQUENT	CONSISTENT	SCORE
					GROUP TOTAL:	

self-assessment form that can be used to rate yourself for each group of characteristics is shown in Figure 1.3.

The complete Business Acumen Assessment is located in Appendix A. In the assessment, I've distilled the key items into a number of phrases that you can use to easily rate yourself. Whether you take the assessment now or when you've completed the book, you may surmise that there could be many more statements associated with each characteristic. That's good, and it should motivate you to study more deeply in areas that are of interest to you or where you should focus your development. For now, this should be sufficient to allow you to come up with a useful approximation of where you're situated.

As an adjunct to this book, I've created an online version of the Business Acumen Assessment. What's terrific about this online assessment is that once you're done, you'll immediately receive a report with your scores, as well as a comparison to all the people in the world who have taken the assessment. You'll also be provided with some helpful hints to help you identify the best areas on which to focus your professional development efforts. This assessment is also a great tool to share with your manager when defining your goals. To access the assessment online, go to http://survey.sequentlearning.com/s3/business-acumen.

If you complete the self-assessment now, use the table in Figure 1.4 and transfer your total for each group into the column labeled "Total Score" and add them up. This grand total is the baseline measurement

Figure 1.4 Self-Assessment Summary

GROUP	TOTAL SCORE
General Business	
Business and Market Environment	
Mindset and Orientation	
Communication	
Interpersonal Skills	
Business Performance	
Yourself	

from which you can begin your professional development action planning. As you read through the book, take note of what's discussed, work on the suggested exercises, and refer to the action planning template at the end of each chapter as well as your professional development strategy from Chapter 12. These will help you to more easily associate various characteristics with the content of those chapters. My overall goal is to provide you with the wherewithal to improve your business acumen and become a better manager.

SYNTHESIZING THE INFORMATION FROM THE SELF-ASSESSMENT

Once you complete the self-assessment, you may wish to dive right in and start working on any number of items. This is only natural, as it's a personal process and most of us want to improve. Such a self-assessment is also important because it provides you with the ability to link the different dimensions of your own professional and career puzzle.

Contemplation allows you to think more carefully about your own strengths and weaknesses. Therefore, I suggest adopting a technique that strategic planners use to capture and synthesize characteristics of their business. This technique is known as SWOT analysis. SWOT is an acronym that represents four main areas on which a business can be evaluated: strengths, weaknesses, opportunities, and threats. You can use your self-assessment to capture and synthesize important aspects of your own situation so that you can create strategies for your professional development. Figure 1.5 shows a personal SWOT analysis that you can use as a template.

As you might surmise, it's a good idea to appraise your strengths and weaknesses and to consider emerging threats before working on your opportunities across the entire spectrum of business acumen characteristics. *As you evolve, you can consider a number of opportunities collectively that will help you form a more purposeful professional development strategy* that can be discussed with your boss or others, helping you to clearly delineate your goals for any given time frame.

Figure 1.5 A SWOT Analysis Based on Your Assessment

STRENGTHS	OPPORTUNITIES
• In which areas do you perform well? • What evidence do you have? • What would others say about your strengths?	• Based on what's included in the other quadrants, what are some of the characteristics that you can work on to continue to improve your effectiveness?
WEAKNESSES	**THREATS**
• In which areas has your performance not delivered the best outcome? • What evidence do you have? • What would others say about your weaknesses?	• Are there other areas where your bosses can go to get done what you may not be providing (e.g., replacing you, outsourcing, etc.)? • What would others say about threats you should be concerned with?

THE VALUE OF A SECOND OPINION

In these types of assessments, you might find there is some bias in your self-assessment; this is normal. With this in mind, it might be a good idea to validate your responses. You may need a second opinion—or several second opinions. The only true test is to find out how others have observed you or have seen the evidence of your actions and behaviors. That's why I include "What would others say . . .?" in the SWOT matrix in Figure 1.5.

You may wish to begin with a friendly peer to review your findings. She could offer you feedback in terms of how she sees you versus how you view yourself. Open up about where you feel some of your weaknesses are and see what she says.

When you feel more confident, you can arrange a conversation with your boss to describe what you're doing and why. She might also be able to share with you some of the things that are important to her managers. You can also speak with peers of your boss if it is politically acceptable to do so. By reaching out to others in this way, you demonstrate that you are both vulnerable (a great way to build trust and political capital) and interested in self-improvement. Sharing information with your peers may also help you in creating a support network. For those whom you do trust, and who trust you, you may find that sharing this information will also provide some unique insights about others whom you might work with in future roles. Regardless of who you speak with, you'll come away with some invaluable perspectives that can be utilized for your own self-improvement program.

LEARNING NEVER STOPS

The term *learning curve* is used to describe the life cycle of learning and the rate of progression in a given discipline. However, a learning curve for any specialty never stops, and it's important to understand that there's always more to learn and do to improve your business acumen and your managerial competency. Regardless of the term you apply, during your professional career, you'll undertake new challenges and learn new skills as you encounter various experiences or take on new roles. You may move from a large company to a small company. You may take on an international work assignment. Whatever you do and whatever situation you encounter as a student of management, you're always going to come across opportunities to engage in new areas, reenergize, and improve your managerial competencies along the way.

To help you along, at the end of each chapter that follows I offer you two ways to raise the bar:

1. A list of suggestions for improving your managerial competency
2. A summarization of key areas of business acumen, along with an action planning template

In Chapter 12, you'll also find a template to create your own purposeful professional development strategy that you can use to plan your professional growth.

SUMMARY

Successful managers continually draw insights from the business environment. They process information based on the situations they encounter and update their goals and strategies accordingly. They are sharp, self-aware, and practical. However, the one thing that separates great managers from others is that they know they are a work-in-progress and commit themselves to continuous improvement. In the end, these managers position their companies for success. This is the process that will work for you as you gain further knowledge and experience in your business career, and as you chart your path to managerial excellence and leadership.

This chapter is crucial because it describes the key ingredients of business acumen and allows you to evaluate where you are in the path to achieving greater levels of acumen through self-reflection and meaningful assessment. The definitions and the Business Acumen Assessment are designed to help you figure out the areas on which you need to focus so that you can do what successful business people do—that is, achieve stellar results.

In the beginning of this chapter, I suggested that you can leverage this book's content to assemble your professional development strategy. To target your efforts, refer back to the Business Acumen Assessment from time to time and see if there are other areas that may be germane to any of those clusters or categories. You may wish to fine-tune your scores, or even take more immediate action by discussing a new goal with your manager. Alternatively, you can take the initiative to concentrate on an area that may not have been apparent to you. I am certain that you'll have the ability to focus on your business career in a way that you may not have imagined.

INCREASING YOUR MANAGEMENT COMPETENCY

1. Keep good records. Just as artists keep a portfolio of their work, you should do the same with your own work. This is especially important as you change roles in a company or get a new job in another company. Further, even if you stay in a given role but get a new boss, the burden of proof of your efforts is on you, so this portfolio of work will come in handy.
2. As you read the chapters in this book, try to key in on the professional development areas on which you might focus. You may also be able to augment the list of professional characteristics.
3. Start reading other books and articles on topics related to the main characteristics to fine-tune your understanding and to keep up with current thinking.
4. Reach out to your peers to ask for their feedback on what you do well and where you could improve. This will keep you focused on developing in the best areas.
5. Periodically, check in with your boss to make sure the work you're doing is consistent with your performance goals. Alternatively, as you establish your own professional goals, you can periodically reassess yourself so that you can account for your growth and development.
6. Challenge yourself to notice how other people in your work environment operate. Try to observe people who behave in a way that you think is interesting and creative. Get to know them so that you can find out what they do and why. (This is also a great characteristic when you need to observe customers.)

FINDING YOUR WAY AROUND THE ORGANIZATION

After you read this chapter, you should be able to:

- Evaluate how a business makes money.
- Understand how a company is organized and why.
- Navigate your way more easily around your company.
- Create positive working relationships across the organization.
- Determine what's needed to build political capital.

Business is a cobweb of human relationships.

—HENRY ROSS PEROT

In the Introduction, I mentioned that leaders want business people to see the "big picture" of the business. If a CEO says to an employee that intimate customer relationships are more important than products with great features, he's reinforcing the need to see the big picture. As humans, we see our world through our own lenses, but those are not always focused on the most important things. It's the same way in a business. In order for you to see the bigger picture of the business, you need to know what those business elements are and how they fit together. To start, the following questions must be asked, and answered:

- What's the purpose of the business?
- What's the strategy and why?

- How is the company organized?
- Who works in the company, and what do they do?
- Who are the customers of the company?
- What products are sold, and why do customers choose these products over those of competitors?
- How much money does the company make?

Knowing how a company does what it does is one thing. However, what you'll find is that companies change all the time—or, they go through a "re-org." When they do, you may have to find out what's not on the new "org charts" or what's going on behind the actual announcement. In my own career, I would talk to others to get the scoop on what was really happening. For example, if there was a major product line failure, or the company wasn't achieving its goals in a given area, the leaders would move people around and adjust the focus of the company. What I wanted to do was make sure I was observing these changes through the right lens so I could properly adapt to the shifting environment. Seeking this information from my network of internal contacts ultimately helped me to embrace the change and find out what I needed to do to continue to help the company work toward its goals.

My advice to you is to always be aware of what's going on so you don't lose sight of the big picture. That's why this chapter is important. I'll share techniques with you to always gain the right perspective by covering these topics:

1. Evaluating how a business makes money
2. Understanding how businesses are organized
3. Navigating through the business
4. Creating political capital and building relationships

EVALUATING HOW A BUSINESS MAKES MONEY

There are a variety of methods that can be used to evaluate a business. The term *business model* is used to generally describe how a firm is organized to make money. *Business people, regardless of their role in a company, should always know how their company is structured to deliver value to its chosen customers, and how it produces a profit at the end of the day.*

As you educate yourself about your company, you will likely learn how it started and evolved. As you study businesses in general, you'll encounter stories about entrepreneurs and how they disrupted the business landscape. As an example, Jeff Bezos at Amazon challenged the relevance of the brick-and-mortar bookseller business model in the age of the Internet. He set out to create a new business model and, over the years, continued to refine it. Elon Musk's Tesla Motors challenged the traditional automobile industry business model by avoiding a dealer network and selling its all-electric vehicles directly to customers in its own showrooms and online. Also consider Travis Kalanick's smartphone-based car service, Uber, and how he took on the regulated taxi industry around the world.

A book entitled *Business Model Generation: A Handbook for Visionaries, Game Changers, and Challengers* by Alexander Osterwalder and Yves Pigneur provides "a concept that allows you to describe and think through the business model of your organization, your competitors or any other enterprise." I recommend that you take a look at this resource and have listed it in the Bibliography.

To expedite your discovery, I will be covering the following *key business dimensions* in this and subsequent chapters so that you can learn about your company's business and understand how:

1. Businesses are organized (this chapter)
2. People work together to produce results
3. Financial tools are used to plan and track revenue and profit
4. Processes are utilized to get work done
5. Customer and market focus allows for the creation of competitive products
6. Strategy is vital in setting direction
7. Products are the lifeblood of the company
8. Marketing is a centerpiece of success
9. Performance evaluation keeps things on track

UNDERSTANDING HOW BUSINESSES ARE ORGANIZED

As I indicated earlier, whenever I wanted to keep abreast of changes in the business, I'd review whatever organization charts were available. One thing that became abundantly clear to me was that these charts were vertically oriented. In other words, the communication and information flow went up and down, but not necessarily across (that is, between people in different departments).

In these structures, leaders of a functional department usually operate by a set of goals (or agendas) that are not often shared with people in other departments. While there may be universal agreement among the senior leaders on the goals and strategy of the business, once the department leaders get back to their offices, there is a tendency to create vertical silos. When this happens there's insufficient information sharing and poor collaboration. Your job is to understand these challenges and to extend your study of your business beyond the charts to the people. I'll explain further.

No matter what business I worked in, I tried to relate the items on the organization chart with the questions I mentioned at the beginning of the chapter. When I would coach my newer managers, I'd draw portions of the organization chart on a whiteboard with arrows between the boxes that contained the names, titles, and roles of various people. This was to help them visualize the interrelationships and to alert them to the need to understand how information flowed between people. I also wanted to be able to coach them in the art of influence building and collaborating, which requires a person to build solid relationships across the organization. I refer to this tool as an "organizational connection chart"; others may refer to it as an influence diagram. I'll explain the connection chart momentarily.

However, to get started, I'll first show you how a firm might look when it starts up and takes its initial steps. Then, I'll share with you how businesses may organize or evolve when they focus on specialty functions, products, or geographies. Your understanding of organizations and how they evolve will be clarified when I explain:

1. The start-up structure
2. The functional structure

3. The product structure
4. The geographic structure
5. The matrix structure

The *start-up structure* is familiar to anyone who has been there right at the beginning—or who knows about firms that have done this. Whether you think about Daimler at the end of the nineteenth century or Facebook in the early 2000s, each began in a similar fashion. These firms started with one person or a small group of people who had a vision to create a product or solution they believed would help people, improve lifestyles, or challenge a system.

Figure 2.1 portrays the beginning phases of a business. Regardless of how many people are involved with a start-up, the business usually follows the heartbeat of one person: the founder. The business activities, such as sales, marketing, development, and finance, are usually a function of the workload of the business itself and are not bound by any particular time frame. They are merely carried out by the person best suited to that role at that time.

Figure 2.1 Beginning Phases of a Business

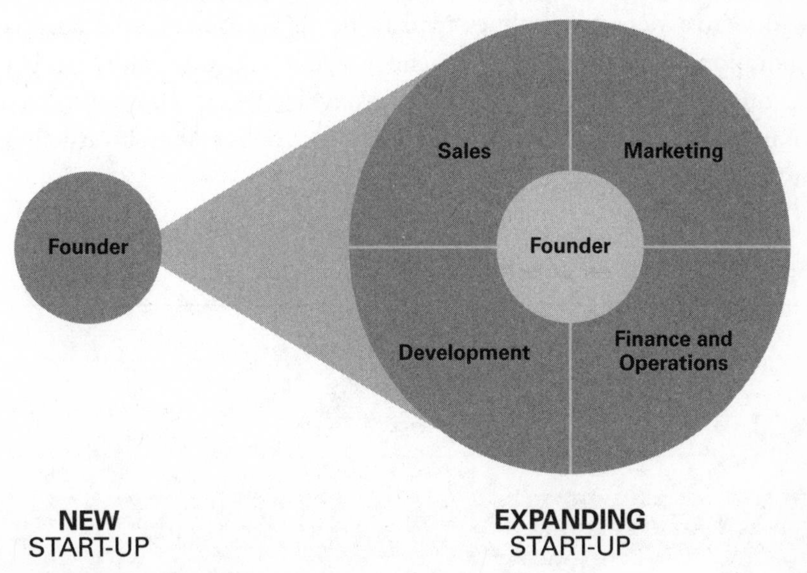

As a business grows or matures, it's not feasible for the founder to drive everyone; the organization must evolve to a different structure. *The organization must be designed to fit the strategic purpose* set forth by the original founders or by newer leaders or investors who may be hired to bring the firm to "the next level." In this maturation, the pace of functional evolution varies. For example, development and perhaps manufacturing become specialized sooner. Finance moves from "keeping the books" to funding, budgeting, and performance management. Marketing moves from outward communications to a more strategic role. Ultimately, leaders of an evolving business must make sure it has the right people with the right skills and experience to do the work required.

As businesses evolve, a *functional structure* becomes the norm because leaders find value in having vertical specialty groups, such as marketing, finance, operations, research and development, or customer service. This type of structure is generally effective when the organization's product lines are somewhat narrow or if they serve defined market areas. It's also a fairly effective design for smaller to midsize firms because they can more easily adapt to changing market conditions. A diagram of a functional structure is shown in Figure 2.2.

Software companies, financial firms, and the like may find happiness as a functionally aligned shop. A variation is to have a functional organization operate in a "matrixed" mode, built on the idea that people who work across department lines tend to be very productive because collaboration across the functions is encouraged. I'll explain more on this in a moment. As functional organizations evolve where they're producing more products or expanding their market coverage, they invariably get more complex.

Figure 2.2 Functional Structure

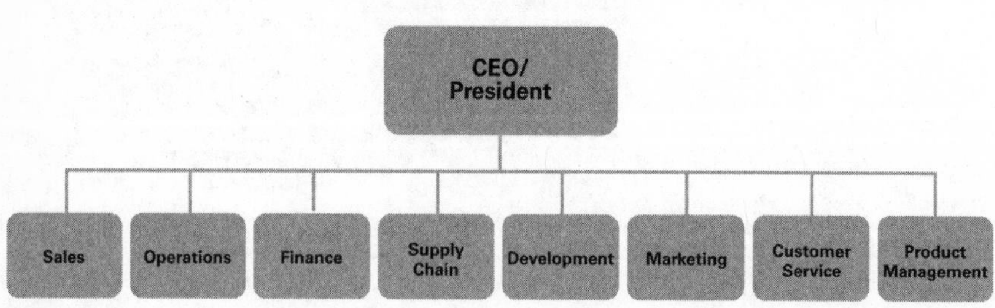

Successful functional structures require an effective leader. I worked with a company that had about 150 people with an effective president at the helm. The company had a fairly narrow line of specialty medical products, and the functional structure worked quite well. This was due to the fact that the president and the leaders of the functions set the strategy and aligned their resources so that the business could operate smoothly. This reinforces the point that a CEO, president, or business unit leader must create an environment that minimizes power struggles and encourages department leaders to see the bigger picture. As you learn your way around the world of business, you will see the good and the bad. Remember that when people are working toward common business goals instead of their functional goals, success is easier to attain.

A *product-oriented structure* is used by midsize to larger companies that divide their firms into product groups or product lines, with business or specialty functions that support each product line's business. As shown in Figure 2.3, this structure is usually the next step in organizational evolution from a functional structure because it divides the company into product lines with functional departments reporting to a product group leader or general manager. With this structure, products or product lines are often referred to as *profit centers*. In essence, they're like smaller functional businesses within the bigger enterprise. When the overall business strategy is focused on products, people may concentrate on creating innovations or devising products that have unique solutions for customer problems.

Figure 2.3 Product-Oriented Structure

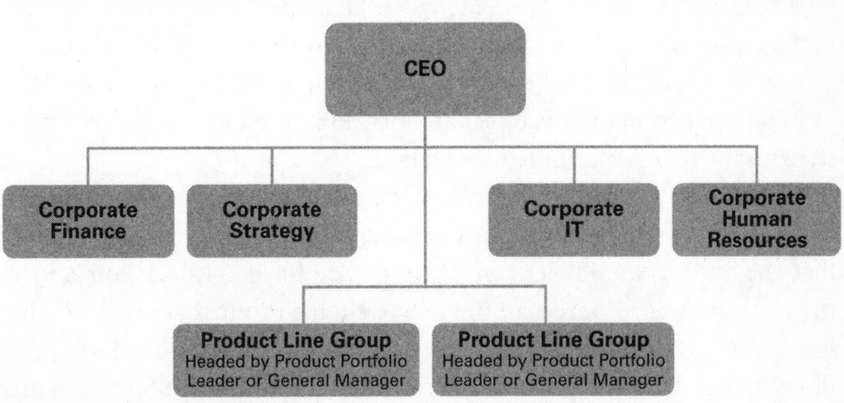

Firms that organize this way include automobile companies, insurance companies, food companies, industrial equipment firms, and others with the same type of product lines. Consumer goods and food companies may organize into brand groups or category groups that have similar supporting structures. An example of an organization with a product-oriented structure is Nike, Inc. This company is divided into four main groups: footwear, apparel, equipment, and accessory products (source: Nike, Inc., Form 10K). Leaders of product-oriented organizations also concentrate on making sure that that they employ managers with the right level of market or domain understanding. These people are often chosen to lead cross-functional product teams that are made up of the best functional experts to create the optimal strategies for the product lines and to manage those product lines holistically across their life cycles.

These organizations may also be more inclined to try to improve product quality, create more appealing designs, invest in specific technologies, and gain other efficiencies that will affect the product lines' contribution to the organization.

Companies that operate as a conglomerate or complex multidivisional firm should be able to effectively support a product-oriented structure. Based on my experience working in product companies, I believe this is one of the best organizational structures for larger, complex firms. However, I learned that in this type of organization, executives in other product divisions did not always share their strategies and plans with one another. Therefore, it was not unusual to find similar products from the same company in the market at the same time, which served to confuse customers. *Some companies have harnessed this challenge by forming platform committees, portfolio review boards, or cross-product councils that seek to rationalize product investments from a portfolio perspective.* This helps to reduce duplication, share lessons learned, and create common product components or capabilities. Figure 2.4 portrays this type of structure with a portfolio review board.

Although this additional oversight adds a layer of complexity or overhead, it serves a unifying purpose. Ultimately, companies realize that they are more efficient in making wise business decisions and in the allocation of resources to the most suitable product areas. The other imperative required to ensure successful operation is a unified sales and distribution strategy. Specifically, a good account management structure

Figure 2.4 Product-Oriented Structure with Portfolio Review Board

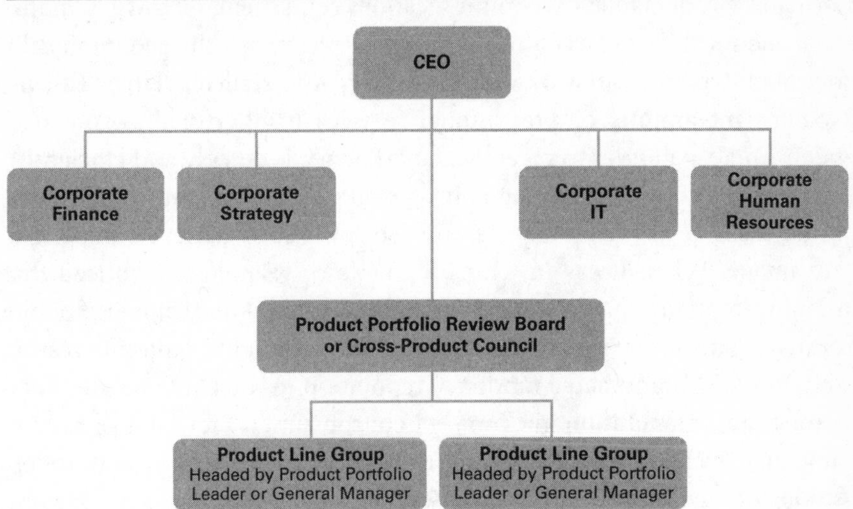

can help avoid channel conflicts (e.g., multiple salespeople and overlapping products) and duplication of effort. The more complex the product-oriented company, the greater the chance of conflict because of demand for support from the business functions. This is often solved when an executive or general manager owns the profit and loss statement (P&L) for the product line and serves as an executive-level cross-functional product team leader. In some modern companies, this role is taken on by a chief product officer.

Many product-oriented firms, including Amazon, Corning, and Harley-Davidson, organize their product and innovation areas into delegated cross-functional teams. These teams establish the strategy for their product lines and execute against those plans. The main point is that these teams are offered the autonomy required to manage the business affairs of the product and are held accountable for their business results.

A *geographically based structure* is used by a company that decides to focus on a given region. This type of firm concentrates its strategy on close customer relationships or a unique market in desired areas. Many global firms find that their local operations may hasten market access (as in restricted markets) or reduce operating costs.

In many of the firms I've studied, especially those that provide infrastructure products such as communications equipment, oil and gas, industrial chemicals, and large-scale computing platforms, the geographically oriented structure can work well. Service providers, such as large IT firms, systems integrators, or professional services firms, can draw on local talent and capabilities to meet local market needs quickly and efficiently.

When a company is situated in a given geographic area, it may adapt more easily to the local culture, thus enabling it to achieve competitive advantage. When I was in China a couple of years ago, I noticed that there were many Buicks on the road. Buick is an American automobile brand produced by General Motors (GM). I found it quite interesting that this GM brand had a moderate reputation in the United States but a strong brand reputation in China, where consumers viewed it as a desirable luxury car. GM had entered the market decades earlier and understood the needs of a market that was becoming more affluent. Having produced in China for such a long time, the company was well integrated into the culture, which helped the Buick brand to flourish.

Geographic firms may suffer from some of the same problems faced by large, complex product-oriented organizations that must share resources that are in remote locations. For example, if product or brand managers and product developers are in a region different from that of the "home office" organization, there could be problems in terms of product manager overload (too many requests from too many regions) or resource limitations that may hinder product development. In order to minimize duplication of efforts, capitalize on cross-geographic learning, and help balance the workloads of people in all functions, geographically dispersed firms utilize a portfolio council or equivalent corporate area to rationalize product platforms, reduce duplication, and minimize conflicts. A visual of a geographically oriented firm is shown in Figure 2.5.

The matrix. One of the terms used to refer to a business that integrates the functional structure with a geographic or product structure is the *matrix organization*. Business leaders realize that hierarchical structures may stand in the way of getting things done, and that informal business relationships between people across the organization are imperative to the achievement of business goals. Leaders realize that it's important to harness individual capabilities while motivating the organization to work collaboratively in an ever-changing environment. This is where the

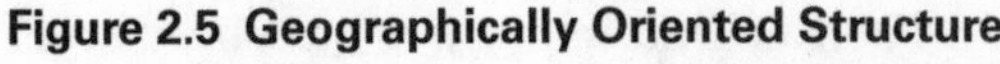

Figure 2.5 Geographically Oriented Structure

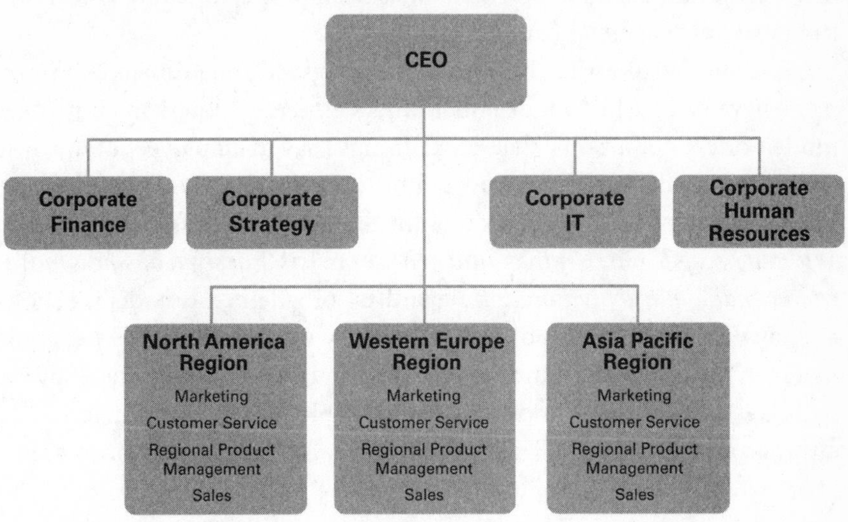

matrix structure comes into play. A matrix structure allows leaders of a business to focus on two organizational dimensions.

I've worked with several companies that use the matrix structure. One industrial firm I studied had global product managers who reported to a vice president of product management. However, the company sold products all over the world, and therefore, the global product managers had other "bosses" to whom they were responsible—the general managers for each geographic area, as well as their product VPs. Those general managers were responsible for regional revenue and profit, and the product managers were responsible for the global revenue and profit for their products. As you might imagine, the balance of power could move in the direction of the product's centralized business activity, but then be pulled in the direction of local market needs. Because of this degree of complexity, I am not a great supporter of the matrix. It requires an extraordinary amount of oversight and a lot of arbitration. In the preceding example, the regional general managers wielded too much power directed to local markets, causing duplication of effort because they couldn't get the product organization to do what was needed for the local markets when needed. I saw one instance in which a local general manager purchased competitor products to complete a deal. That said, there have been some instances when the matrix structure has been properly deployed with the right executive oversight and balance.

As I alluded to earlier, businesses are imagined and reimagined. Some firms have established models that others emulate. Others institute new models or create variants. One of the things I say to employees of my own firm is this: Although this is how our business is structured now, don't be surprised when it evolves in six months. If we have to pivot, we will do so. *Without an agile mindset that anticipates or reacts quickly, a business model can be made quickly redundant.* Regardless of whether a model is set out as shown in the diagrams or in a brand-new way, you'll greatly benefit if you integrate an understanding of the key business dimensions I shared with you earlier. Those important building blocks will encourage you to always consider the organization's vision, goals, strategy, and structure.

EXERCISE

- Find out what type of organizational structure is used in your company.
- As you talk to people to learn about the structure, try to uncover how people feel about the structure in terms of communication and overall effectiveness.

NAVIGATING THROUGH THE BUSINESS

Once you know how your organization is set up, you have to start to figure out who does what with whom and when. The key roles in a business can be likened to the actors in a Broadway production. All actors play a role and work from a script. They know what to say or how to act at a specific time. In business terms, people who play a given role must predictably deliver the outcome of their work—usually for someone else to use. The production of the work is the *responsibility* of the person.

While this situation is unlikely, what if an actor doesn't know his or her lines, is confused about the cues, or delivers the wrong lines? Undesirable outcomes result. As another bad scenario, think about how poorly the show would fare if it were not properly cast, if it lacked an astute director, or if it didn't have a well-trained production support staff working together to bring the show to life. Now think about this in terms of a business organization: What happens if people don't do their jobs properly or produce what's expected when needed? The result could be a poor-quality product, a system that doesn't work, or something else that causes inefficiency or rework.

When newer managers learn how an organization is structured and who is assigned work in a given business function, they have the basic tools to construct the *organizational connection chart* I mentioned earlier. Wherever you might be situated in the business, you will immensely benefit if you can build an organizational map that depicts roles, responsibilities, and how work moves between people in different roles. As briefly mentioned earlier, this is also a great tool to map out relationships within a desired sphere of influence. You can create an organizational connection chart when you gather information according to the following sequence:

First: Obtain the information about your own department, including:

a. Name of department or function
b. Name and title of the person who directs that department
c. Main department to which this manager reports
d. Purpose and/or outputs provided by this department
e. Names and titles of employees
f. Roles played by those employees
g. Data or inputs (work product from others) required for those employees to do their jobs
h. Actual work activities done by those employees
i. Output or work product produced by those employees
j. Where this role fits in relation to the CEO's office (You'll always want to map the path to the CEO to understand where you and others are situated.)

Figure 2.6 provides a template to use to secure this information.

Second: Obtain the information about another department, including:

a. Name of department or function
b. Name and title of the person who directs that department
c. Main department to which this manager reports

Figure 2.6 First Step in the Creation of an Organizational Connection Chart

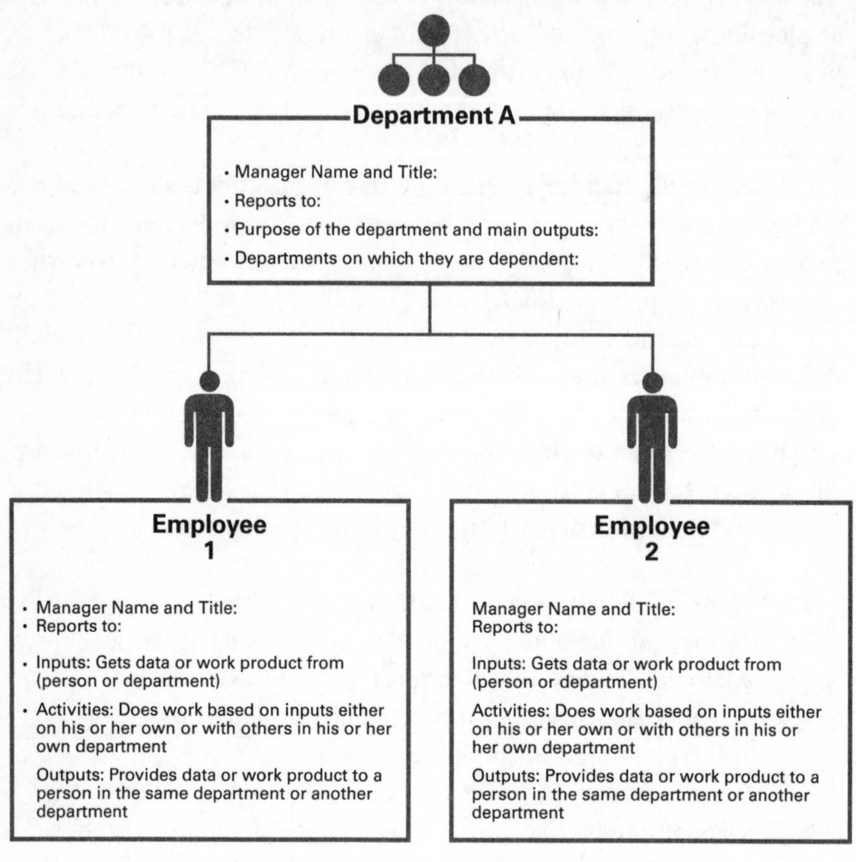

d. Purpose and/or outputs provided by this department
e. Cross-organizational dependencies
f. Names and titles of employees in the other department (or departments)
g. Roles played by those employees
h. Data or inputs (work product from others) required for those employees to do their jobs
i. Actual work activities done by those employees
j. Output or work product produced by those employees
k. Where the role fits in relation to the CEO's office

Refer to Figure 2.7 as a template for taking the second step to create an organizational connection chart.

Figure 2.7 Second Step in the Creation of an Organizational Connection Chart

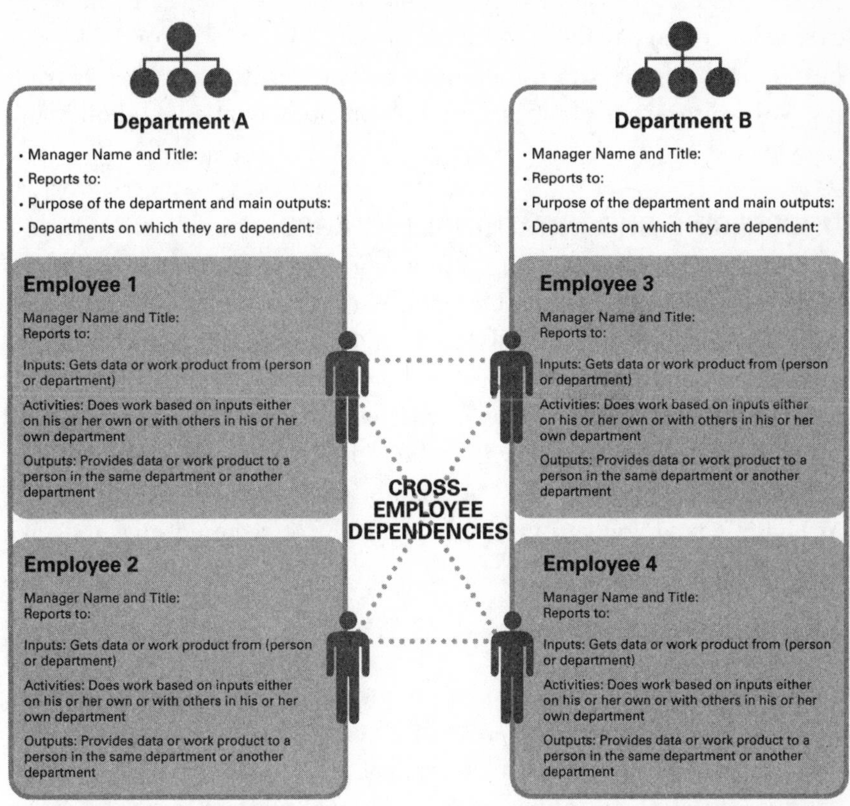

Now that you have the visual to map out the connections, you can continue your discovery process. It's time to make some appointments to speak with people in different departments. You can start with a person who works at your equivalent job level. Later, set your sights one level up, and speak with the department manager. Some etiquette and diplomacy is required to accomplish this work.

When I was new to any organization and building my organizational connection charts, I'd reach out to a manager (usually one level up) and explain that I was new and was hoping the manager would spend 15 minutes with me to explain what he did and how I might help. This approach not only gets the ball moving but helps you earn political capital as well. Depending on your role and how you're positioned, you may need to do a quick check-in with your boss to get the OK to reach out to others.

As an additional point, the work involved in creating a larger connection chart, as in Figure 2.7, may require some extra time. Your boss, I'm sure, will like your relationship building in your own department, but he may want you to pay more attention to your own work before venturing outside. My advice is to do as much as you can without this interfering with your responsibilities, and use your judgment as you build your network.

UNCOVERING ORGANIZATIONAL LINKAGES

As you are creating your organizational connection charts, you will inevitably realize that there are a host of other linkages to every connection you make. People in one department will invariably interact with others, depending on what's to be done or what process is being followed. As you learn more about who does what with whom and when, you will see that one department may be a "supplier" of information to another department or the "customer" of yet another. I've visualized this for you in Figure 2.8 so you can be more cognizant of required give-and-take relationships.

EXERCISE

- Use Figure 2.8 as a template to capture the essence of all of the connections that exist in your company. Can you apply the connection chart methodology to help you with this?
- Identify some of the challenges you encountered as you undertook this work and how those challenges might be overcome.

Figure 2.8 Departments in a Company That Are Customers and Suppliers to Each Other

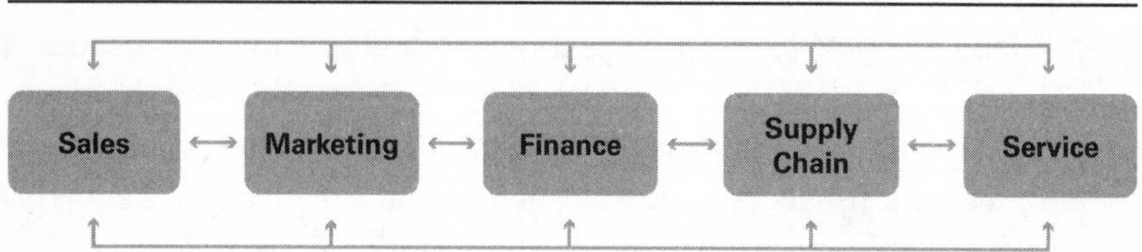

Knowing that there's an internal customer-supplier model at work, I would like to extend this further. Your company sells its products and services to customers, and you should, at some point, know who those customers are, what they buy, and how they interact with the company. If you don't have this information at your fingertips, a quick visit to your marketing department, a conversation with your manager, and some website exploration will provide some context. Further, your company probably procures parts, components, or services from other firms. A chat with one or more managers in your procurement department or the supply chain area might help you to understand this further. While it's not crucial, *business people should ultimately understand all customer and supplier relationships to have a more complete picture of how the company operates.* To enhance your perspective on this topic, I've created a visual, shown as Figure 2.9.

The organizational structures I reviewed earlier in the chapter are referred to as *closed systems* by many academics because they focus on internal operations. A number of them have studied and written about organizations as *open systems*. These organizations are said to be influenced by external factors such as customers, suppliers, politics, economics, social trends, and others. Consider then, that Figure 2.9 is a simple way to view an organization from a systemic, holistic perspective—almost as an ecosystem. In other words, when you see things from both a vertical and a horizontal standpoint, you will have a better chance of seeing how to set the stage for more collaborative and productive work.

Figure 2.9 Holistic Perspective on Internal and External Customer-Supplier Relationships

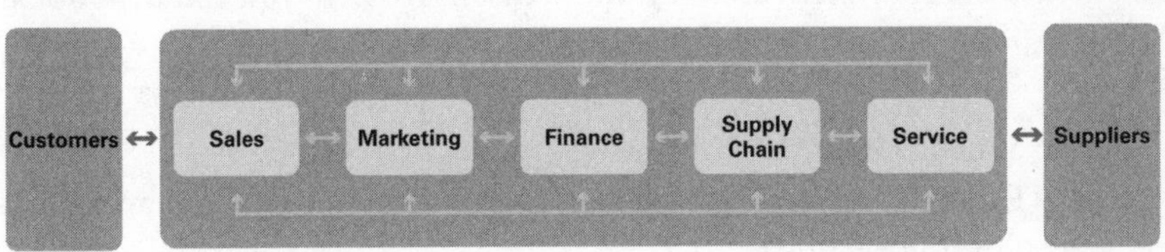

CREATING POLITICAL CAPITAL AND BUILDING RELATIONSHIPS

On paper, organizations seem relatively easy to understand. In real life, however, organizations are dynamic, living systems that sometimes do unexpected things. Like geologists who place sensors in the ground to detect shifts in the earth's crust, so must business people have various sensors placed across the landscape of the organization. This is done through the establishment of relationships with individuals in different departments to tap into those pulses or signals. *Over time, managers who get good at this tend to develop something of a sixth sense or instinctive understanding of goings-on in the company.* Some refer to this as *organizational instinct.* It's said that a CEO is that type of person. However, CEOs and other leaders want their managers to also possess the astuteness to build these connections, listen to the signals, and take care of things.

In the world of business, the term *capital* usually refers to a tangible or financial asset—something of value. A business that's starting up tries to raise capital from others in order to invest in the business. A business person can also raise capital—not as a tangible or financial asset, but as a political asset.

To extend this to the discussion on organizational navigation, it is imperative for you as a manager to create value, or become an asset. The capital asset of *you* can evince tangible results (e.g., you improved a process or launched a successful product). *You can also create intangible capital assets in the goodwill you foster through the relationships you build with key influencers across the organization.*

As you embark on this part of your journey, I want to impart a word of caution. Most leaders know the difference between relationship building to further the interests of the business and improve your expertise versus just plain politicking without purpose. They can smell it a mile away. So be careful as you tread through the hallways. It's harder to earn true political capital and easier to blow it if not carefully nurtured.

There are four main areas I want to discuss to help you create political capital and build positive relationships:

1. Synchronizing with your own manager
2. Establishing ties with managers and peers in other departments
3. Finding Mentors
4. Becoming visible
5. Dealing with conflict

SYNCHRONIZING WITH YOUR MANAGER

Needless to say, you need to build strong ties with your manager. Your manager and your manager's manager are, or should be, your biggest allies. Although you may be able to quickly learn how the organization works, you cannot achieve optimal organizational agility without the support of these people. They can help you navigate faster, pave the way for introductions, and gain needed visibility.

However, you will need to understand some of your managers' preferences by learning how they wish to interact or receive information. For example, some may have "office hours," while others may be comfortable when you stop by for a casual conversation. To more easily align with your manager, here are some easy-to-follow steps that you can take to build those connections:

- Find out about your manager's history in the organization and how he progressed in his career. You can do this over an informal lunch or coffee in the morning.
- Find out about the history of the organization and how it has evolved from your manager's perspective. Try to gain an understanding of the prevailing atmosphere in the organization, especially if it has gone through a lot of changes.
- Visit often. Casual interactions with shared snippets of information, or spontaneous situational sharing can deepen a relationship with your boss, if he's open to it. Since bosses are always busy, and they don't always remember to reach out, you may need to bear some of this responsibility. However, remember, casual doesn't always mean what was done last weekend. Always have your "homework" done, just in case he asks.
- Clarify your goals, and check in as often as needed. Understanding what your boss expects of you will always be of vital importance. From this, you can provide quick updates on the phone, in person, or via e-mail or a text to communicate what you're up to.
- Ensure that your goals are contributing to your manager's success. When you're helping your manager, you are helping yourself.
- Demonstrate your capability and commitment. Look for small victories all the time. When you understand what your manager

values the most, you can gear your work activities to fulfill those expectations.

- Earn testimonials. Your manager knows a lot of people, and they talk to each other. If you're doing work that matters to your manager and you're involving people from other areas, your name will be brought up. When others share with your manager positive feedback about who you are and what you do, you will earn important credibility points. One way to do this is to work on a project with one or more people who work in different functions. Make sure to provide readouts and updates to the managers of the people in the other areas. These check-ins will provide you with great visibility and will secure those "honorable mentions" when the managers speak with each other. *It matters what they say when you're not in the room.*
- Minimize needed interventions. If your manager sees you as a person who brings in problems and challenges or if you complain excessively, you will be seen in an unfavorable light. Try to be proactive by examining the challenges you face and solving those problems independently.

When people discuss issues inside an organization, they often refer to misalignment. They feel that they cannot move in lockstep with another because they don't see the objectives in the same way or they miscommunicate. When it comes to harmonious actions in your department and across departments, your strongest allies are your manager and, often, his or her manager. Therefore, when you get your manager on your side through ongoing positive interactions, and you reinforce vital linkages to strategic goals, work plans, and visible deliverables, you contribute to your political capital account!

EXERCISE

Ensure that you have an explicit set of goals and responsibilities from your manager. What is the impact you are expected to have, and what are the time frames involved? What are you empowered to undertake to make things happen? What kinds of things does your boss want to be consulted on?

ESTABLISHING TIES WITH MANAGERS OF OTHER DEPARTMENTS

While you'll do a lot of your work with peers from other areas, it goes without saying that these people have managers. Therefore, it's a good idea to establish relationships with the managers who lead other functions. This "up-and-across" approach will help set the stage for more fluid communication across departmental lines and allow you to be viewed more favorably by others. These relationships are very important because sometimes you'll need their help to catalyze action in one of their employees, or people in another area. Offering to help them or providing them with useful information can be one way to spark a conversation. Nurturing these relationships will contribute to the establishment of *knowledge-sharing networks*, which are like informal communities of practice. *Sharing information and helping others can help you to earn influence when action is required from others who don't work for you.* In other words, it's a way to influence others.

To get started, consider requesting a brief meeting with a simple agenda that won't tax the manager's schedule. For example, if you do some outside research into the category of work being done by a specific department, and request a dialog with the manager about that topic, you'll spark a more meaningful conversation than if you just want to get to know that manager and what he did over the weekend. As an example, I was once a business manager in an IT area. There was a manager who was responsible for data storage equipment, and I needed to complete a business analysis and forecast for the deployment of that gear. I was fairly new in my role and wanted to figure out a way to not just show up and ask for information but to establish a dialog. I did research into some new storage technologies and leveraged what I studied as a vehicle to reach out to that person and to start a conversation. When I introduced myself and asked him a question related to the topic, his eyes lit up and he invited me into his office for a chat. I didn't pursue my agenda for a couple of days after, but when I asked for the subsequent meeting, he agreed to meet with much enthusiasm.

For a more formal approach to start conversations with managers of other functions, there are some areas you might want to cover:

1. Offer support. Ask him what you can do in your job to help him, or to help people in his department. This is perhaps one of the most important aspects of any business person's job.

2. Try to learn about the work done in his department, the people who work there, and the processes they follow. Ask him to sketch out those processes so you can better visualize them and so you can learn about the "to-and-from" between that department and yours—and others!
3. Ask him about himself—where he came from, what he did before, where he went to school, and so on. You can ask some (not overly) personal questions to get to know his family, sports interests, etc.

Depending on how you pose open-ended questions, this manager may also ask you questions that will build a healthy dialog. These are designed to help you look for common interests and other dimensions on which you could build a work relationship. As your rapport evolves, I suggest you try to learn about the information flows between people in his department and your department. Are there any that can be improved upon? Also, in subsequent interactions, you might be able to leverage this knowledge of goings-on in the organization. When you show interest, you show you're committed. When you build rapport, you build trust. When you offer to help, you create an invitation to bond.

EXERCISE

To start, create an organization chart to identify who's who in relation to your department. Then, pick one or two managers whom you don't know to devise an action plan to establish a productive working relationship.

FINDING MENTORS

If there's one thing that I've learned about being successful in business, it's that you can't do it all by yourself. To make the leap from a business person with promise to a truly successful one, you need to find mentors. On the other side of the coin, to seek a mentor, you have to be able to put yourself in the position of protégé. Therefore, positive mentor-protégé relationships are like partnerships, and there's a role and responsibility for each person.

Over the course of my corporate career, I benefitted from the wisdom and experience of a number of mentors. Some were formal arrangements made between my managers and other leaders who were assigned to work with me on specific areas such as earning influence, working with people, or learning a unique dimension of the business. It was also recommended that I locate other mentors to deepen my perspectives from those who possessed expertise in specific areas, or if I encountered a challenging situation. As an example, when I was assigned to a team to evaluate a product portfolio during an acquisition, because I had not done that analysis before, I sought the guidance of a leader who I knew had this experience. The lessons I learned from her helped me to contribute positively to the due diligence exercise and solidified my membership on that team.

A number of years ago, I attended a seminar, and the facilitator asked, "What are the four most important words you should master in your corporate life?" The answer was "I need your help." I've never forgotten this. Think of a time in your life when you asked for help from a friend, teacher, parent, peer, manager, or religious leader. Consider how the lessons you learned helped you to solve a problem—and more, how that breakthrough may have opened the door for you to embrace new challenges. What you seek and what you learn will vary over time, so mastery of the mentorship process is vital.

Mentors don't get paid to help you. They do it because they care and want to make a difference. Therefore, if you want to be an effective protégé, here are a few suggestions to consider:

1. You may have to adapt your behavior to learning new ideas and doing things differently.
2. You should be committed to increasing your management competency and focus on achieving positive results.
3. You will ultimately need to harness the perspectives of people with different backgrounds and experience.
4. You must be able to accept and process feedback, and take action as needed.

A senior leader in a major commercial real estate firm stated, "A mentor is an essential relationship for the newer corporate executive because it helps fill the knowledge gap. In the commercial real estate business, a new broker cannot possibly know all the landlords, or the nuances of a particular market area. An experienced mentor can help the less-experienced broker by teaching him about the history of the area and how, for example, the business cycle affects property values." In sum, a good mentor can accelerate your learning curve exponentially because he or she not only helps you fill gaps in your knowledge but also can teach you the ins and outs of a particular corporation.

To locate a mentor, you can speak with your manager, find others at professional events, or locate experts on LinkedIn. And when you are in a position to share the skills you have learned, give something back by becoming a mentor yourself. I continue to mentor others through the speeches I deliver, the books I write, and even by being a mentor to founding entrepreneurs through The Founder Institute (www.fi.co).

BECOMING VISIBLE

One of the things that distinguish great managers from others is what they achieve. When others start seeing you as a positive contributor due to the actions you take and the positive results you deliver, you've become visible. Some business people are content producing their work product in isolation. They may work from home, forgo traveling, and put their phone on mute during important conference calls. Others seek some of the limelight. They're present, connected, and helpful and are trusted to get things done.

In an earlier part of my career, I wasn't sure how to go about being visible, even though my boss's boss advised me to do so. At that point, I was working as a financial analyst. My manager asked me to work on a business case for a new manufacturing facility. When I look back, it was pretty overwhelming. I plotted a strategy that included a visit to the current plant to meet the people and learn how things worked. I also had many meetings with people in research and development, operations, marketing, and supply chain. I learned much about plant design and work flow through a factory—and a lot about automated production lines. I also learned much from the managers in each department. I spent a significant amount of time in one-on-one sessions and in small group meetings as I assembled the case for the new plant. Over the course of the few months I worked on this, the functional managers coached me by having me rehearse my presentation with them! Little did I realize they were all taking me under their wings, not only because they wanted me to be successful, but because they wanted to ensure that their interests were properly represented.

From the interactions I undertook and the findings I documented, everyone in the organization was connected to the project and to each other, and I had earned credibility that was visible to others from my actions. In the final presentation, there were no surprises, because as I was doing my work, the managers were all talking with each other. I received a number of pats on the back as well as newfound respect from my manager. Although I had been told to improve my visibility, I wasn't told how. I figured it out based on my problem-solving ability and through the relationships I had cultivated prior to having the project assigned. From then on, I understood what it meant to become visible, and I hope you will have an opportunity to work on this as well.

What happens if you work remotely? How can you be off-site but not out of mind? How can you actively participate and contribute more? It's no longer sufficient to just do our job as you might think of it when you're working at home. You might need to work harder at producing results. I can tell you, it doesn't mean cc'ing everyone on the planet for every e-mail you generate. I can say that you might want to offer to work on or lead an important project where there is significant evidence of your work to your boss and others. Alternatively, you could produce summaries of important conference calls in which you participated and provided input (not opinions, but recognizable contributions) so that the right people are up-to-date on the company's achievements.

DEALING WITH CONFLICT

Throughout this chapter, I've provided guidance to you so that you can more easily find your way around a company and, at the same time, put stakes in the ground to establish your place. Regardless of where you work, conflict is inevitable. Most people avoid conflict because it has a negative connotation. They feel that it will harm a relationship, or it's just too emotionally upsetting. But what's implied is that they are fearful of engaging. Avoidance leads to short-term relief, but it rarely gets to the heart of the matter because the conflicting feeling is still simmering inside. When conflict is avoided, people don't want to work together, may blame each other, mistrust one another, won't listen attentively, or act with indifference and just do other things. All are unacceptable and unprofessional.

Conflict does not have to be as bad as it's portrayed. In fact, it can be embraced, and managers who do so will find that their work relationships may be enhanced. If you find yourself in a conflicted situation, you have to try to understand what's really going on. It doesn't mean you have to gird for battle or for an argument. You have to find out what's at the heart of how you're feeling and what your goals are, and you should try to initiate a conversation with the other person to figure out what he's trying to get done.

Let's say you're assigned to a project that requires the help of a person in another department and you find out your boss assigned a different task to a colleague—but it involved using the same resource in the other department. If you're caught off guard about this, you might get angry at your colleague or your boss for putting you in a bind. On one hand, you could send a nasty e-mail to either of those people and complain about how this is getting in your way. You might think that they're conspiring against you and want you to fail. Or, you could simply approach your coworker and put the "I need your help to figure out what to do with this" card on the table to understand his perspective and work on potential solutions. This will work better if you've established a working relationship with your colleague and have built some trust with him.

Plato once said, "Courage is knowing what not to fear." You can minimize your fear of conflict by having clarity about what's going on as you search for common ground with others. In business, this could include staying focused on the goals of the business and encouraging conflicted people to express what's going on within the context of those goals. As you grow, you'll see conflict as an opportunity to make sense of a tangle by seeing both sides and adopting a more objective perspective. Your effectiveness will be enhanced when you deal with conflict positively and collaboratively.

SUMMARY

One of the characteristics that separate good managers from others is a thirst for organizational knowledge—how they "get" its people, processes, and purpose. The charts and templates in this chapter are designed to help you get your bearings and to adopt an uncanny ability to "get around" and get things done. This is how you develop the organizational instinct required to be successful and is one of the items in the Business Acumen Assessment. This is generally the easy stuff to talk about.

However, in many organizations, it's not always as cut-and-dried as your knowledge of the organization charts or your relationship with your boss. Some managers have agendas that they want to carry out, and it may seem that they're not moving in lockstep with the strategy. Or your independence and initiative may be quashed by a micromanager boss. Or people might say, "That's not the way we do things here." Regardless of what you encounter, if you can keep an eye on what's best for the organization, you can properly align your actions with the situations you encounter more easily. While you will sometimes feel the need to compromise, you can store the experience in the back of your mind and remember what "better" looks like or feels like as you move into other roles.

With this, it should be apparent that the organizational discovery process is not a one-and-done exercise. This dimension of your mindset must be fine-tuned as frequently as needed so you can do the best job possible to anticipate what might happen. This keeps you ahead of the curve and provides you with the tools to lay out what's next on your agenda. It allows you to transcend the "getting to know you" communication by getting to the business at hand with the people you know. Because you've created paths of communication, you've preemptively eliminated blockades and political walls. This helps you as well as the people you work with to focus on the exigencies of the business.

INCREASING YOUR MANAGEMENT COMPETENCY

1. Use the questions at the start of this chapter to construct the business model of your current employer. You can also refer to the *Business Model Canvas* book I mentioned earlier to as a way to start.
2. Obtain a current organization chart, either from your manager or from someone in the human resources or organizational development function. Although that chart may not be completely up-to-date, you can use it as a

blueprint for navigating the organization and in establishing relationships with key individuals.

3. Find out from your manager or from others which organizational structure is used in your company and why. Ask about the overarching strategic goals and how the organizational structure is designed to help achieve those goals.
4. Review your job description with your manager. Make sure you understand your role, responsibilities, and key deliverables. Ensure that you know which departments you're expected to work with. Clarify what decisions you're responsible to make and what decisions require your manager's approval.
5. Locate a coach to help you understand the informal structures of the firm. Find out about some of the cultural norms in the firm to build consensus and get things done.
6. If there's a business that you're particularly interested in studying (as in competitive analysis), go to its website and try to create an organization chart based on information you find. Look at leadership teams, product lines, mission, vision, and a host of other information. If you're inclined to study a publicly traded company, download the investor reports from the investor relations section of the company's website.
7. Take action to put your organizational connection chart together. If you're in a complex firm, start slowly at first in your own department. Then, work with your peers or managers to learn how information moves between departments and why.

Action Planning

In this chapter, the following characteristics were either explicitly or implicitly revealed. You may wish to identify where these were mentioned to reinforce your understanding of how these might be applied in your own work. You can also utilize the following template as a way to associate what was discussed in this chapter with your scores from your Business Acumen Assessment. From this, you can create an action plan for yourself or work with your manager to come up with specific goals and plans.

- Managing
- Being a self-starter
- Developing organizational instinct
- Creating political capital
- Exercising political judgment
- Building positive relationships
- Including others
- Earning credibility

ACTION ITEM + GOAL	STEPS TO BE TAKEN	OUTCOME PRODUCED	WHAT YOU LEARNED	WHAT YOU WILL SHARE

YOU CAN'T DO IT ALL YOURSELF

After you read this chapter, you should be able to:

- Clarify the purpose and benefits of cross-functional work teams and the foundational principles of team success.
- Understand team operations, cadences, and communication to become an effective contributor.
- Harness the efforts of people in other functions and to promote cooperation to achieve established goals.

No man is an island, entire of itself; every man is a piece of the continent.

—JOHN DONNE

A professional football team is a business. If you drew an organization chart of a football franchise, you'd have a general manager, the coach of the team, and coaches for different specialties (functions). In the game of football, it is the teams that play against each other that make the sport so much fun. However, in the scheme of things, these teams are successful because each player fulfills his role, follows his assignments, and acts in harmony with a common goal. With sports teams, it's all about winning.

In a company, teams are used to get work done, and fostering teamwork is critically important.

Leaders want to empower people both to work on teams and ultimately to lead teams. They also want the teams to be self-directed and to achieve their appointed goals. Of course, when people with different skills are brought together to work on a team, everyone benefits. Despite this simplicity, as you may surmise, it doesn't always work smoothly.

In this chapter, I discuss the essential elements of team formation and how you can improve your chances to harness the power of the team to foster business success. To that end, I explain the following:

1. Why teams are important
2. Characteristics of successful teams
3. Team operations and playing your role
4. The benefits of leadership and collaboration
5. Extending the team to a community of practice

TEAMS YOU WILL ENCOUNTER

Just as organizations have different structures, so do teams. A group of people who work in one department, for one manager, will work on a *functional team*. For example, a company controller in charge of the accounting department may have a small team of accountants work to "close the books" every month.

A *Skunk Works*® team, devised by Lockheed Martin Corporation, is assembled by leaders to work on a project in an exceptional manner—to develop something rapidly with the slightest number of restrictions. Verbiage that appears on the Lockheed Martin website (http://www.lockheedmartin.com/us/aeronautics/skunkworks.html) provides this statement: "For more than 70 years, the Skunk Works has existed to create revolutionary aircraft and technologies that push the boundaries of what is possible."

A third kind of team is the *cross-functional team*, made up of people from different departments who work toward common goals. Cross-functional teams can come together to plan and complete work on a designated project. An alternative approach used in some companies involves a cross-functional product team, where people work on many projects associated with a product over an extended period of time.

THE ROLE OF TEAMS AND WHY THEY'RE IMPORTANT

People who work in the news media and deliver news all day long utilize *cross-functional teams* to produce many stories throughout the day. Each story is a short-duration project that illustrates how a team operates in a fast-paced world to produce the "news products" that meet the needs of their audience. These teams achieve success when they follow this process:

- Obtain information from many sources, such as reporters on the street or in news trucks, citizens who take pictures of crime scenes, and law enforcement officers.
- Synthesize the information and break it into digestible pieces because they understand how their audience consumes news. These news organizations know their audience and can tailor the messages to be consistent with user preferences.
- Collaborate with others to fine-tune what's produced. Journalists may come under the umbrella of a department led by a senior editor who solicits opinions, processes information, and aligns with larger organizational objectives.
- Make it available to whomever wants to consume it, wherever they are, on whatever device they choose.

When I discussed organization charts in Chapter 2, I indicated that the structure of each functional department in a company is set up so that information generally moves up and down. However, I suggested that information also needs to flow across the business to optimize communication. Cross-functional teams embody the "up, down, and across" approach needed for this structure to achieve success. Therefore, *one of the main benefits of cross-functional teams is their role as a hub of activity, including information processing and dissemination.*

This idea is portrayed in Figure 3.1. The diagram shows a team with four members and a team leader at the center. Each participant brings facts or figures to the team, as evidenced by the arrows that point to that participant. The documents or reports (as inputs) are what's brought to the table so that the team can process the information and produce an output (further information or other work product) to be used by others, as required.

If we understand the role of the team as a hub of communication, processor of inputs, and producer of outputs, then what contributes to its success? This has been studied extensively, and one author who has

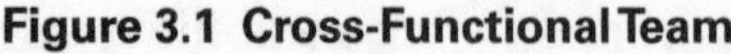

Figure 3.1 Cross-Functional Team

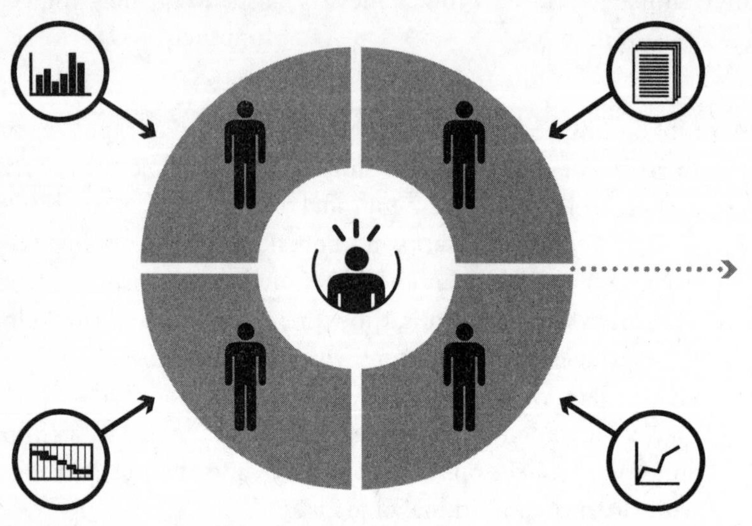

contributed a lot to the discussion is Patrick Lencioni, whose books include *The Five Dysfunctions of a Team* and *Overcoming the Five Dysfunctions of a Team: A Field Guide*. These books, and many other books about organizational behavior, motivation, and collaboration, identify certain basic building blocks of successful teams. These eight *foundational team principles* include the following:

1. All team members commit (or "buy in") to the team's purpose and goals.
2. People who are delegated to work on the team can devote their attention to what's to be produced by that team.
3. Team members have sufficient knowledge, skill, and experience to fulfill their responsibilities.
4. Participants have a chance to build personal relationships with one another, allowing them to build the trust needed to rely on each other.
5. Team members are able to communicate with each other and with additional supporters or stakeholders if they encounter

obstacles or are challenged in fulfilling their responsibilities. In other words, they know how to raise their hands when they have a problem and to ask for help from their management when they "hit a wall." In these situations, communication is established through effective writing and speaking.

6. Team members earn the respect of others through the things they do, the impact they have on others, and the production of a quality work product.
7. Team members recognize that they are part of a bigger picture, especially in larger organizations, and work to help that larger body fulfill its strategic intent.
8. Team members know that their output must be on time, with the right quality, and within the parameters set by management (financial, etc.).

These guidelines are simple to read and understand. However, they may be a bit more difficult to put into practice. Lencioni does a superb job of describing the dysfunctions of work teams. To get a glimpse of why teams fail, just take the opposite of each of the items listed.

When people are delegated by their managers to work on these teams and the relationships haven't been formed yet, then it's the first order of business for people to get to know one another. You can leverage what was mentioned in the previous chapter for that. However, one of the things I've found helpful in creating teams that are geared for success is sharing my passion for the opportunities ahead. Like a sports team coach, I try to build a competitive sense of urgency, and when I demonstrate my commitment and determination, I model what I want others to do, too. I'll speak about these as this chapter unfolds.

EXERCISE

- What project teams have you worked on?
- What factors contributed to the teams' success?
- What contributed to any failures, or what made projects difficult to complete?

TEAM OPERATIONS

A number of years ago, I observed an experiment at a university. The goal was to find out whether an orchestra could play a piece of music without a conductor! There were about 60 people in the orchestra divided among four major sections: strings, woodwind, brass, and percussion. They were not laid out as a typical orchestra might be. They were organized into quadrants of a circle—like a pie divided into four slices. In the middle was a small open area where four chairs were arranged to face one other. The section representatives sat in the four chairs, with the people from each section and their instruments behind them.

Everyone had the sheet music in front of them on a stand, and the musicians were instructed to start to play the music at a specific time. And so they did. It sounded awful! They kept playing for a few minutes until the person at the front of one of the sections stood up and said, "Stop!" Although he screamed his instruction, it took the others a minute or so to listen. "It sounds horrible," he said.

"What should we do?" the other three section representatives said, almost in unison. He described what he wanted, and they started again. This second session went on for a few minutes until another person stopped the music. At that point, a fight nearly broke out! The four section representatives started arguing with each other about how the piece should be played. Then, various people in the sections started to talk amongst themselves. Others left the room, and some just seemed indifferent. Without further elaboration, you can probably predict where this went: nowhere. Anyone would be aghast if they observed this in a performance of Beethoven's Fifth Symphony by the New York Philharmonic!

If you can envision what a well-rehearsed orchestra sounds like, you can envision how a well-functioning team might behave, especially with regard to the list of eight principles I shared with you earlier. For a team to be successful, *everyone needs to understand how to play his or her role on a team and a leader is needed to facilitate the work of the team.*

The first step in the process is to understand the purpose of the team. The term *charter* is widely used to describe the purpose of a team. When managers form a team, or even if you want to form your own work team, you need to be able to explain the *goals, roles, expected activities, and outputs.* Most teams have constraints placed on them by their managers, which usually include time frames and budgets. Prospective members should be able to agree with each other and be able to understand the eight principles. Perhaps it's a stretch, but a team charter has similar characteristics to a constitution for a country because it addresses values, purpose, and rules (or laws). In preparing to write this book, I interviewed a number of business leaders who work in large organizations about the process used to charter work teams. Interestingly, they all said essentially the same thing about how they set up these teams. They communicate with peers to agree on the goals and appoint people they feel are capable and available. Once the team is formed, they assign time frames and require frequent updates.

I also asked if they believed that those delegated to work on the team knew how to establish the foundations to work with each other, communicate, and so on. I learned that most leaders assume that the participants should already know what to do. This is usually the case when people have worked together before and have gone through the process a number of times. However, I probed a bit more deeply into aspects of team performance such as the quality and timeliness of outputs. Their responses indicated otherwise.

Here are some helpful suggestions that will contribute to your awareness and know-how so you can become a positive team contributor and an effective manager:

1. Make sure you *know what your role will be and what you'll be responsible for*. Then, fulfill your commitments to the team so that you'll be seen as a reliable contributor. Often, a team charter (or similar document) will be used to state the team's goals.
2. Use *attentive listening* techniques by paying close attention to what's being discussed and gaining the proper perspective. Then, ask the right questions when required, or in summarizing and verifying what was said during a team meeting or an interaction with someone on your team. Good listeners tend to be seen as approachable, available, and friendly.
3. *Pitch in and help* when the team faces challenges and obstacles. You will build credibility and trust and earn a positive reputation when you help your teammates to solve problems or overcome hurdles.

4. *Work to earn trust by following through and communicating clearly.* Earning the trust of others is easy to discuss and advise people about, but it's a fair challenge to achieve. Each of us has our own value system when it comes to trusting and being trusted. Sometimes, the things we say or the way we act doesn't mesh well with others who have their own value system. A number of years ago, one of the people who worked in a department I managed seemed distant and aloof. Our one-on-one meetings didn't always go well, and I was feeling impatient, but I couldn't figure this person out. One day, I asked her to have lunch with me. I thought this would be a neutral area (not my office or hers) to have a chat. At lunch, I casually asked if she was angry with me or upset. I used a couple of examples where I felt she was being short with me. One thing led to another, and in that conversation, she opened up a little about herself and her upbringing. This actually evoked an emotional response from me because I learned we shared some common issues from our upbringing. Needless to say, she helped me see that my somewhat overpowering personality made her less willing to say what was on her mind, which made me perceive her as withdrawn and, thus, difficult to trust, and she had a similar perception of me. It was eye-opening to realize that if we had not found a way to communicate and to trust one another, we might not have come to terms. Instead, we opened up new possibilities to learn from each other. Consider such situations from your past where issues of trust emerged. You may find some clues about what it takes to be a trustworthy teammate, or what you might be able to communicate to others that will help them to earn your trust. This could certainly be an area for self-study and continuous consideration.

HOW TO LEAD OTHERS AND INSPIRE A COLLABORATIVE ENVIRONMENT

If you have worked on a team, you may come to value the guidance of a good team leader. Alternatively, you may be appointed to lead a team. We all have a range of experiences with team leaders—some good and some not so good. Earlier in my career, I found that some of the teams I worked on seemed rudderless. I found that if I started to take some initiative to engage others instead of complaining about what wasn't happening, I could actually get people to pay attention. When they paid attention and I could set a course of action toward a goal, they tended to go along. My conclusion was this: most people need a leader. The conductorless orchestra mentioned earlier is a true case in point of this need.

Leadership is an inescapable component of business and an indispensable asset for aspiring managers. Unfortunately, the qualities of genuine leadership are diluted by the overuse of the word and its many, many definitions found in business literature, the media, and human culture. Not all of us are "born leaders," but you can learn from the style of others to achieve your own success. Considering the various concepts of leadership can help you achieve this.

There are those who make a distinction between the meaning of the word *leadership* as "an act of influence or inspiration" and the meaning of the word *management* as "an act of authority or direction." There are those who associate leadership with force of personality and charisma and, alternatively, those who agree with Ralph Waldo Emerson's lament on leadership and identity—"Who you are speaks so loudly I cannot hear what you say." The words *leader* and *leadership* are often defined by the context and nuance of the situation in which they are used.

For any business person, leadership comes in many different shapes and sizes, covering an astounding spectrum. The reality is that when it comes to being a leader, some people have an innate gift, some are able to learn bits and pieces, and some just do not get it. Some people can be leaders in one part of their lives (as in a religious organization) and followers in another area (as in a project team at work).

Leadership is an acquired skill. It's not a delegated power, an innate ability, or some black art that can be achieved through trial-and-error checklists. In short, a job assignment doesn't imply leadership. Some innate or "born" leaders (those thought of as charismatic) may inspire and influence, but unless they really understand how they're getting those results, they may falter or collapse at precisely the wrong moment. The person who knows that most elements of leadership are learnable—and who takes the time to learn them—will be able to thoughtfully address situations that many so-called natural leaders cannot handle.

If you would like to take positive steps toward being seen as a leader, you must begin to act like a leader. Visible evidence is better than words. Using the orchestra example from earlier, if you want to conduct an orchestra and have people follow along, you have to learn and study music to become a master, have the passion in your heart and soul, and have confidence to envision the beauty in the piece. You can't just pick up the baton.

In developing your leadership skills, you can set your sights on adopting the characteristics and behaviors that are commonly used by exceptional leaders:

- In the overall scheme of things, stand up for what's right, even if it's not popular. This demonstrates your commitment to ethical standards of business and becomes a model for others.
- Adopt a market focus. In Chapter 7, I'll show you what's needed to achieve this "outside the company perspective." However, leaders have an uncanny knack for understanding customer needs and behaviors, the actions of competitors, and their overall impact on competitive positioning and strategic advantage.
- When challenging situations arise, stay calm. Take the situational barometer to process what's going on, even if your insides are jumping around. This skill requires that you detect body language, tone of voice, and other clues as to what's going on.
- When a problem appears, break it down into understandable pieces. Seek the advice of others or build a small team of advisors to dissect a situation and come up with possible solutions. The leader reserves the right to make the final decision—not always explicitly, but through her actions.
- Be accountable and meet your commitments, because when you do, you'll be perceived as responsible and trustworthy. Also if you assume a leadership role where you are fully accountable, you must ensure that others for whom you are responsible are fulfilling their commitments.
- Include others in strategizing, planning, and decision making. People who are connected because they have a say in direction will more easily contribute to the success of the business.

Another dimension of leadership I want to mention to you is centered on the requirement in many firms for people to demonstrate leadership behaviors even if they're not directly managing employees. In other words, individual contributors must lead, too, and *contribution* is the watchword. As examples, a cartoon animator in an entertainment company contributes to the production, and a salesperson with an uncanny knack for connecting with customers contributes significantly to business success. While you may not have "position authority," you certainly have the wherewithal to influence others through the relationships you establish, the decisions you make, and the business logic you bring to the table. As the book unfolds, you'll see how your use of finance, data, and processes can be leveraged to your advantage as an influential business person.

Good leaders learn to understand the dynamics behind various business situations, ask a lot of questions, and bring people together to solve problems. Whenever the team is faced with a challenge for which there are various potential solutions, a manager with superior facilitation skills will be able to steer the team in the right direction.

EXERCISE

- What are your overall strengths and weaknesses in the area of leadership?
- What area would you like to develop, and what will you do to achieve this?

As you work on teams and fine-tune your own leadership skills, you'll find that one of your roles is to inspire conversations—either within a team environment, within your functional area, or cross-functionally. Collaborators are those who engage people both within and outside of the company to work toward common goals of the firm. As you may surmise, a collaborative mindset will almost certainly contribute to your ability to effectively influence others. It will also add to your ability to develop organizational instinct as you become more aware of your firm's culture and how you can appeal to the interests of others, again with an eye toward the achievement of important goals.

You probably collaborate every day through various social channels and through the use of different technologies. These methods will continue to evolve. To improve your collaborative capability, you will need to be able to connect people and ideas, both internally and externally. In Malcolm Gladwell's book *The Tipping Point*, he used the term *connector* to refer to people who maintain numerous links to people in various places. For you to excel in your role as a manager, and to improve your leadership skills, you'll need to take on the role of cross-functional facilitator—a person who inspires collaboration among others. In my own career, I attended numerous conferences, joined associations, and became a voracious scanner of business news. I would frequently assemble a summary of what I learned and who I met and share it with key stakeholders. Alternatively, when I assigned others to attend events or speak at conferences, I'd ask them to read-out what they learned and to share any insights they gained. Also, when I meet people who I feel have valuable experience or a unique perspective, I'll invite them to speak to my team to share their points of view. All leaders know that helping others is important, and this approach works quite well.

As you consider your role as a leader, as both an individual contributor and as you expand your span of control, you will need to pay close attention to the "society" of your company—its culture. Areas that are most important to focus on include:

1. Understanding what drives or motivates people and your overall sensitivity to the needs of others.
2. Listening attentively so that you can be attuned to the moods or preferences of other people.
3. Capitalizing on the informal social networks of a company and adapting your behavior based on implicit or undocumented norms.
4. Engaging people in conversations and appealing to them based on their needs or interests.
5. Soliciting input and supporting team members.
6. Encouraging others to cooperate in the achievement of important objectives, especially when they work in different departments.

In the final analysis, leaders of today are expected to be collaborative and inclusive. This cannot be achieved through force of level or power. Effective leaders exhibit a passion and belief and are able to capture the hearts and minds of others, and they cultivate this capability over time as they encounter new situations and gain interesting perspectives. They realize that they don't have a monopoly on creativity and therefore bounce ideas off of others. Furthermore, they care deeply about the goals and strategy of the firm and how to best achieve those. And when the victory is won, it is shared and celebrated. Without a doubt, if you can learn to harness the energy of others, you will excel beyond your wildest imagination.

HOW COMMUNITIES OF PRACTICE CONTRIBUTE TO THE PERFORMANCE OF TEAMS

Peter Drucker, the esteemed author and management consultant, suggested that people who want to perfect their skills in a given profession need to engage with others who encounter similar challenges and situations. Communities fill a need because they help interested individuals accomplish personal and professional goals through the sharing of experiences and the exchange of ideas. Such communities can also serve as an effective means of improving a business.

Communities of practice are nothing new. They've been around since ancient times. In the Middle Ages, for example, there were guilds, whereby each trade craft occupied its own sector or section of a city. This provided a built-in community of people with similar interests and strong connections to each other. Today, industry associations and online communities offer tremendous opportunities for professionals to meet and share best practices. Whether in medieval times or today, people who work in the same profession like to gather to discuss happenings, share information, and catch up on the latest news. This reinforces the feeling of affiliation and community.

In our global business community, technology has made it possible for people to work anywhere. While this may prevent people from working together in person, it doesn't keep people from communicating and sharing. Video, online meetings, and the like are powerful technologies that contribute to the formation of knowledge-based communities.

Formal communities of practice exist in many parts of an organization. You might have a community on diversity management, a community on environmental policy, a community of scientists, or a community of innovators. Some communities are formed on a short-term basis to solve a problem. Some groups stay connected over the long term because of common interests, such as research and development, engineering, or marketing. For the most part, communities are voluntary efforts; some can sustain themselves, and others are unable to.

Without a doubt, communities of practice for business people can be created in your own company if you have the time, the wherewithal, and a willing audience to participate. However, there are a host of other platforms that you can use. Meet-up groups and other user-generated conferences or networking events provide a way for people with specific interests to get together and share experiences in person. Online social communities, such as LinkedIn groups, provide discussion forums, and those who write blog posts make space for comments and discussions. In all of these settings, you can both learn from others and hone your craft.

In many firms, longer-lived communities tend to work on real problems that are defined by senior executives. A pharmaceutical company may have a community that focuses on drug safety. A financial institution may have a community that focuses on cyber security. Regardless of the kind of community of practice you may wish to set up, or one that is established by management, there are several dimensions worthy of your consideration, including:

- *A charter.* Just like any business work team, a community of practice requires a statement of purpose so that the right people will be drawn in with a desire to participate or contribute.
- *A leader.* For a formal community, a leader is usually needed to organize or facilitate events or other programs.
- *Destinations.* Forums for sharing knowledge and experiences are the main idea behind a community of practice. If a community cannot meet or talk at appointed times, there is no community. Organizing events and activities with themes or topics will attract community members and help you build momentum.
- *Teams.* To have a physical community, there's work to be done, and you need people who can help with organizing, event

planning, arranging speakers, and other items. An online community may just require a moderator or facilitator to start discussions and keep them moving along.

SUMMARY

Today, people are doing business not only across town but also around the world—and things happen at lightning speed. Because business isn't done in a neat and tidy way, you need to figure out the best way to conduct business and optimize teams. It's not always easy, and regardless of the size of the business in which you work, it's important to recognize that people are working in various locations and environments.

As I wind up this discussion on teams, I want to reinforce three dimensions that I've expressly mentioned or alluded to throughout this chapter. These apply to any team, regardless of location, and are visualized in Figure 3.2. To help make them clear, I associate them with the human body. Just as the human body is made up of complex systems that work together for optimal performance, these three factors must be present in any high-performance team.

Figure 3.2 Three Dimensions of High-Performance Teams

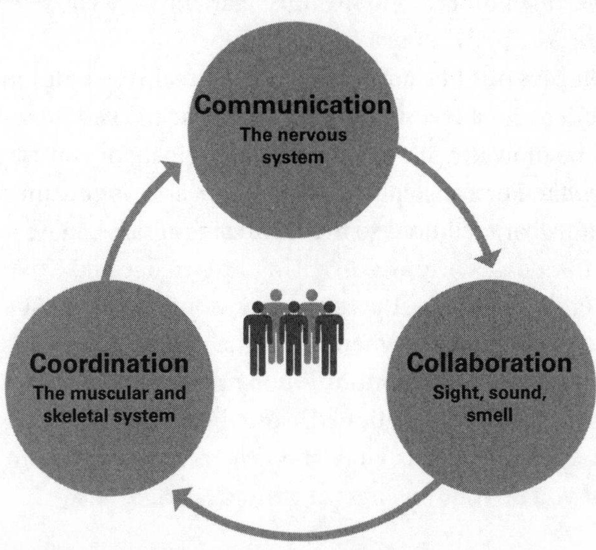

1. *Communication* is the nervous system. A team cannot operate without the right level of information moving back and forth at the right time. Communication may require work tools, such as virtual meeting systems, video, online meeting rooms, and centralized data storage, to ensure that documents and other information are easily accessible. The key is to ensure that information is shared and people are connected. Team participants must make sure they do their part to share information in a timely fashion.
2. *Collaboration* brings together all the senses using sight, sound, and smell so that the body can operate as a whole. There's a check and balance that needs to be orchestrated. The mind of the business person serves to facilitate and collaborate, ensuring that the right things are done at the right time. Eyes and ears are everywhere, including those of the team members who may be located anywhere. People who work in different departments must be focused, which requires ways to capture and share information. If you have to work on documents together, ensure that your part, either as author, editor, or otherwise, is undertaken in a timely manner. Ensure that there's a way to keep track of updates and edits so that duplicative efforts are avoided and things don't fall through the cracks.
3. *Coordination* relates to the muscular and skeletal systems. A business "body" at rest cannot compete; therefore, all the team members must be active and engaged to keep things moving. If you're in a leadership role, the virtual team needs an extra effort to reinforce the shared sense of purpose and the inspiration of all. If you're in a participant role, you owe it to your team members to do what's required so that the team's efforts can be realized.

In the end, it's all about getting work done in the most expeditious manner. Teams work best when the right people are focused on clear goals that are tied to the bottom line, and they fulfill those goals in a timely manner. As I've mentioned, your behavior and performance as participant and/or leader is vital to the success of your team. Anything less will put you or your business at a disadvantage.

INCREASING YOUR MANAGEMENT COMPETENCY

1. When you work on a team as a participant, *elicit feedback* from team members or the leader to ensure that you're doing what's expected and your contributions add value to the achievement of the team's goals.
2. To be a capable team member, you will always need to earn the trust of others. Trust is established first at the personal level. Moreover, you can try lending a helping hand in cultivating relationships between team members so they feel more comfortable with each other.
3. One way to learn about team effectiveness is to *observe* the team members as if you were an anthropologist. When you watch people working in a team environment, such as a team meeting, you can detect positive attributes, including collaboration and creative problem solving. You may also see signs that indicate disagreement, lack of trust, and so on. What you learn will provide you with insights about the culture of your organization and the effectiveness of teams.
4. There are psychological profile tools that are used by organizational development specialists. Tools such as the Myers-Briggs Type Indicator (MBTI) or other assessments may afford greater insight into why people behave the way they do.
5. Ask a leader if it's possible for you to observe a number of working team meetings. By doing so, you will better understand team operations, the benefits of collaboration, and how conflict is managed.
6. Find out about the *processes or work tools* used by the teams on which you work. These may contribute to your understanding about team operations and associated performance indicators that allow for teams to operate efficiently.

Action Planning

In this chapter, the following characteristics were either explicitly or implicitly revealed. You may wish to identify where these were mentioned to reinforce your understanding of how they might be applied in your own work. You can also utilize the following template as a way to associate what was discussed in this chapter with your scores from your Business Acumen Assessment. From this, you can create an action plan for yourself or work with your manager to come up with specific goals and plans.

- Managing
- Developing organizational instinct
- Listening attentively
- Influencing others
- Helping and coaching others
- Being a reliable team player
- Building positive relationships
- Acting with integrity, ethics, and trust
- Including others
- Assuming accountability
- Earning credibility

ACTION ITEM + GOAL	STEPS TO BE TAKEN	OUTCOME PRODUCED	WHAT YOU LEARNED	WHAT YOU WILL SHARE

MONEY IS NOT A FOREIGN LANGUAGE

After you read this chapter, you should be able to:

- Explain how money flows into and out of the company.
- Understand the purpose of each financial statement.
- Describe the concept of discounted cash flow.
- Define the financial planning techniques used for budgeting and forecasting.

Not everything that can be counted counts, and not everything that counts can be counted.

—ALBERT EINSTEIN

In my workshops, I often ask the question, "Who pays the bills in your family?" Inevitably, about 30 percent of the people raise their hand. Then I ask, "How many people like dealing with financial issues?" Not many people raise their hand. Regardless of whether you found yourself raising your hand as you read those questions, your success as a business person is dependent on your ability to get your mind into the numbers game.

In this chapter, I provide you with a basic overview of business finance so that you can get your bearings and establish a game plan for your own education and development. This is only a primer, though, as you can't learn it all in an hour.

I became interested in money and finance in my entrepreneurial escapades when I was a kid. While others were playing sports, I was figuring out how to make some money because money gave me choices. Later, while I was studying finance in graduate school, I learned the complexities of business and finance. After that, I worked as a financial analyst, as a product manager, and as an owner of a company. I hope you will continue your study of financial topics after you've completed this book and as long as you are a business person.

To get you on the best path, here's what I discuss in this chapter:

1. An introduction to financial fundamentals
2. A review of the basic financial statements used in business
3. The importance of cash flow management
4. How financial planning is integrated into the work you do

FINANCIAL FUNDAMENTALS

The term *finance* signifies the movement of money into and out of the business, and *accounting* refers to the record keeping and summarizing of financial transactions. The field of finance extends into many parts of the world of business. Universities have broad and deep curricula on it, supported by vast libraries of books, journals, and periodicals. Do not underestimate these; they are important resources! However, this immense body of knowledge on finance can frighten anyone who aspires to be a more effective business person.

My goal is to encourage you to take the needed steps to learn what's required to do your job, and then to inspire you to pursue other areas in the field of finance that are of interest to you. If you're an experienced financial person, you can use what's in this chapter to ensure that others you coach have the tools they need. If you want to be a better business person and haven't mastered finance, we have to start with the basics.

To simplify the foundation of money flow into and out of a business, consider the three dimensions depicted in Figure 4.1.

1. Money comes into the business from the sale of products and services.
2. Money is spent by the business to pay people, to support processes, and to encourage the further sale of products and services.
3. Money is accumulated by the business to reward employees or shareholders, or to be saved for future investments. If day-to-day cash inflows are less than outflows, money saved (as "retained earnings") is redeployed to operate the business.

Figure 4.1 How Money Flows in a Business

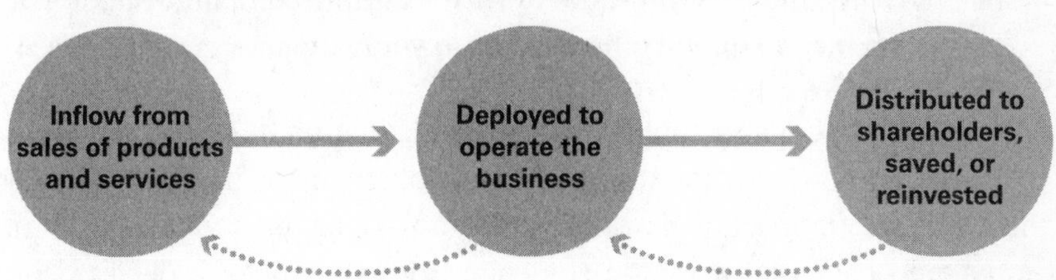

To support this simple process, and to be an effective business person, you must be able to understand and assess how revenue is derived, where money is spent, and how additional funds are recycled in the business. In a moment, we'll start our journey with *financial statements*. However, what I'll discuss focuses on accepted principles and practices that are used in all companies. Yet, you may work in a smaller firm or a private company that doesn't afford you the visibility you might expect. My advice is that you learn the basics from this chapter and be alert to opportunities to learn more about the numbers as you grow in any organization in which you work.

FINANCIAL STATEMENTS

Business people should be able to understand financial information as presented in three basic financial statements. When business and financial people speak about gross margin, depreciation, working capital, and cash flow, they must comprehend the meaning of these terms and feel comfortable discussing a wealth of financial matters. Because the language of business is derived from the accounting field, being familiar with this vital business vocabulary will increase your effectiveness as a business person and help you earn respect from others in your organization.

Financial statements are the most important and universal documents utilized by businesses. They are the instruments used to manage the business, make decisions, and communicate results to various interested parties. Business people use these statements to:

- Create and communicate budgets
- Analyze business results

- Make decisions when results don't align with projections
- Disclose information about the firm's performance to stakeholders, team members, and other leaders in your company

Understanding and applying financial techniques does not automatically bestow knowledge about the mechanics of corporate financial management and accounting. If you work in a medium- or large-sized organization, you should have easy access to someone from your finance department. This expertise is required to ensure compliance with budgeting or reporting standards. Financial people also provide guidance on important documents, such as business cases, product plans, or strategic plans.

In the following sections, I describe the characteristics and usage of each financial statement—specifically, the income statement, balance sheet, and cash flow.

THE INCOME STATEMENT

The income statement is also referred to as the profit and loss statement, or just the P&L. Because the P&L tracks business performance over a given time period (e.g., a month, quarter, or year), it is referred to as a *periodic* statement. The P&L helps to determine whether the business earned a *profit* or *loss* over the specified time period. The basic format of the P&L is shown in Figure 4.2.

As you can see in the diagram, I've divided the P&L into two halves:

- The *top half* of the P&L considers *revenue* and the specific costs to create that revenue.
- The *bottom half* includes the *expenses* incurred by the functional departments as they support the business or carry out their daily activities.

The top half of the P&L first accounts for the revenue brought in from the sale of products or services to customers. Revenue is calculated by multiplying the unit selling price by the number of units sold:

$$\text{Revenue} = \text{Unit Selling Price} \times \text{Units Sold}$$

If your company produces tangible goods, then it incurs a variety of costs related to producing them. (Note: service-based businesses or software companies may not have material costs; however, you should always check with your finance department to determine if there are any costs

Figure 4.2 Basic Profit and Loss Statement

		BUDGET	
SALES (REVENUE)			TOP HALF OF THE P&L
Number of units		20,000	
Price per unit	$	29	
Total Sales	**$**	**580,000**	
COST OF GOODS SOLD			
Materials	$	25,000	
Labor	$	37,000	
Overhead	$	12,000	
Total COGS	**$**	**74,000**	
GROSS MARGIN	**$**	**506,000**	
GROSS MARGIN %		**87%**	
EXPENSES TO RUN THE BUSINESS			BOTTOM HALF OF THE P&L
Sales	$	57,000	
Marketing	$	48,000	
Research & Development	$	41,000	
Operations	$	72,000	
General & Administration	$	34,000	
Total Expenses	**$**	**252,000**	
EBITDA	**$**	**254,000**	
EBITDA %		**43.8%**	
Depreciation & Amortization	**$**	**21,000**	
Taxes	**$**	**34,950**	
NET PROFIT	**$**	**198,050**	

in this category.) These production-specific costs, in total, are referred to as *cost of goods sold* (COGS). They include the *direct* costs incurred to produce the product and any overhead costs allocated in the production of the product. COGS is generally composed of the cost of raw materials, the associated labor to assemble the product, and various direct and allocated overhead costs (e.g., rent and electricity for the facility used in the production or assembly of those products):

$$\text{Material} + \text{Labor} + \text{Overhead} = \text{Cost of Goods Sold (COGS)}$$

Gross margin refers to the money earned directly from the sale of the product. It is derived by subtracting the COGS from the revenue. Gross margin represents a very significant initial measurement of business profitability. It must be large enough to cover the expenses incurred by other departments that support the business as well as deliver a net profit at the end of the financial period. Gross margin in absolute dollars, and as a percentage of revenue, is also an important measurement when comparing the performance of one product line to that of another, or in comparing your company's results to its competitors':

$$\text{Revenue} - \text{COGS} = \text{Gross Margin}$$

$$\frac{\text{Gross Margin}}{\text{Revenue}} = \text{Gross Margin \%}$$

The bottom half of the P&L lists the different functional expenses. These expenses are categorized by departments, including sales, marketing, research and development (R&D), and other expenses. After business expenses are accounted for, the next level of profitability must be calculated. That is called the *earnings before interest, taxes, depreciation, and amortization*, or EBITDA. In some companies, this might be referred to as "income from operations." This allows for the separation of interest and taxes from the actual operating P&L for the product:

$$\text{Gross Margin} - \text{Operating Expenses} = \text{EBITDA}$$

There are some additional expenses that are often charged in a P&L: interest and taxes. Interest is included to cover any costs incurred as a result of the company borrowing money to finance its operations. Taxes are levies by federal, state, provincial, and local governments on profits earned by a company.

Oftentimes, many of these categories are beyond the control of business managers. However, it is common in large companies for positive gross margin or even EBITDA to "evaporate" because of other allocations or charges, such as interest, taxes, depreciation, and amortization.

The true profit of a business's *bottom line*, or its net profit, can be calculated by subtracting all expenses, interest, and taxes from EBITDA:

(EBITDA) – (Interest, Taxes, Depreciation, and Amortization) = Net Income

$$\frac{\text{Net Income}}{\text{Revenue}} = \text{Net Income \%}$$

Net income (or net profit) is the whole reason that your company is in business. If the bottom line isn't greater than the interest one might make from a bank account, why run the risk of operating a business at all?

Your business may use tangible *assets*, such as machinery, equipment, facilities, or computer systems. It may also leverage its patents, trademarks, and other intellectual property as intangible assets. (Note: assets are listed on the balance sheet, which will be mentioned later.) A portion of a physical or tangible asset's value is taken each year as an expense on the P&L as depreciation. When the value of an intangible asset is spread out over its stated useful life, its portion is prorated and taken on the P&L as amortization. *Depreciation and amortization are how companies indicate the use and declining value of assets.* Because the company lays out money for the equipment or facilities in advance, it lists those assets on the balance sheet. The company already paid the "cash" for the equipment when it was purchased. Therefore, your product is "charged" each year for a portion of the normal wear and tear caused by usage of the equipment (depreciation) or the remaining life of a patent or trademark (amortization).

Depreciation and amortization are not really current cash expenses because the company didn't spend any money (except when the original asset was purchased). However, the company does have to account for the portion of the asset's value in a given year. Depreciation and amortization have to be captured and accounted for somewhere. Therefore, they are recognized in a line item of the P&L as if they were a cash expense.

Although I've walked you through the mechanics of the income statement, you'll notice that I've put the heading of "budget" at the top of the column with the financial information. Later, I'll talk to you about budgeting.

EXERCISE

- Obtain a copy of an income statement from your finance department. Ask if someone will go over the details with you and explain how it's analyzed.
- If your company is private and financial information is not available, do some research on a publicly traded company that sells a product you own, or one you like, by going to the "investor relations" page on their website. Download a recent Form 10K and study the P&L and read through the explanations as published.

THE BALANCE SHEET

The balance sheet is a financial statement that represents a "snapshot" of the *assets* and *liabilities* of a company at a specific point in time. It depicts the overall *net worth* or *equity* of the company at that particular point in time. It is different from the P&L, which shows results for a financial period.

The balance sheet depicts the assets owned by the business and how those assets are financed with money from creditors or the capital of its owners or shareholders, or both. The balance sheet shows how the business is in balance. Like any living organism, the balance sheet *must* be in a state of balance, or homeostasis, if it is to function properly. The balance sheet employs a basic arithmetic formula or equation:

Assets – Liabilities = Owner's Equity

Assets are the items of value that a firm controls, all of which are measured or *valued* in terms of money. Assets are utilized by a company's management to create value. For example, a manufacturing plant is an asset that enables the company to build products. Consider the forms and sources of assets: assets are more than just cash in the bank; they can also be money that's owed to the company by customers, called *accounts receivable.*

Current assets are those that can be easily converted to cash within one year. They include cash in the bank, marketable securities, accounts receivable, and inventory. *Quick assets* (as they are sometimes termed) are the subset of current assets that are essentially already in *liquid* form, such as cash and marketable securities.

Fixed assets are those that are more difficult to quickly convert to cash: buildings, manufacturing equipment, and land. Collectively, these are also referred to as property, plant, and equipment (PP&E).

Intangible assets are a financial representation of nonphysical items that, nonetheless, have some monetary value. These include patents, brands, intellectual property (acquired knowledge), and goodwill. (Goodwill may include a brand name or a proprietary technology.) Intangible assets are considered difficult to measure and value, but companies, as well as accounting governance bodies, are focusing more and more on finding ways to account for them.

Liabilities generally represent the means by which assets are financed. When your company incurs a liability, it is obligated to pay for it at some point—either in the near term or over the long term. Think of a personal automobile loan or a home mortgage; this is a liability. Thus, liabilities represent a future cash outflow. Liabilities are divided into two categories: current liabilities and long-term liabilities or debt.

Current liabilities are those obligations (debts) that must be paid off within one year. These include payments for operating expenses, supplies, and materials as accounts payable. Current liabilities may also include short-term loans, the interest on those loans, the current portion of loans required to be paid within one year, and taxes owed.

Long-term liabilities (often called long-term debt) are obligations that mature beyond a year. Many companies incur long-term debt (or issue bonds) in order to finance capital expansion or to finance other business activities. This is where the term *leverage* often comes into play. When a company is *heavily leveraged*, it is said to have a lot of debt—money it owes to others.

Net working capital refers to one of the derivative financial principles. If you subtract current liabilities from current assets, you get net working capital. It represents the share of the owner's equity that's actually tied up in day-to-day operations and could be extracted within one year if the company ceased operations and paid all outstanding bills. Thus, it's called "working" in the sense this capital is "doing work" rather than "available to do work." *Working capital* is a particularly sensitive subject for many financial people because its application and use has to be carefully balanced. If there is too little working capital available, the company won't be able to meet its monthly financial obligations, such as payroll and rent. However, if the balance sheet shows too much, it can indicate certain problems, such as excess or slow-selling inventory, slow payments by customers, or even uncollectible accounts. Any one of those situations needs to be immediately analyzed and rectified.

Owner's equity is the collection of assets that actually belong to the owners or shareholders. Also known as *net worth*, it is the difference between assets and liabilities and, therefore, a representation of the true "book value" of the ownership of the company. Consider the ownership of a home as a simple comparison. The value of the home could be $750,000, but if you have a $200,000 mortgage, the amount of your true ownership, or equity, in the home is actually only $550,000. The forms and sources of owner's equity include contributed capital (money invested in the company by its owners, private investors, or shareholders) and retained earnings (the company's accumulated net income over its time in business). A sample balance sheet is provided for you in Figure 4.3. Notice that it shows two snapshots: one from December 31 of the prior year and one from December 31 of the current year.

Figure 4.3 Balance Sheet

ASSETS	Dec 31 of PRIOR YEAR	Dec 31 of CURRENT YEAR	INCREASE/ (DECREASE)
Current Assets			
Cash	$381,000	$432,000	$51,000
Marketable Securities	$248,000	$364,000	$116,000
Accounts Receivable	$731,000	$836,420	$105,420
Inventory	$826,000	$747,000	($79,000)
Total Current Assets	**$2,186,000**	**$2,379,420**	**$193,420**
Property, Plant, & Equipment	**$2,147,600**	**$1,973,600**	**($174,000)**
TOTAL ASSETS	**$4,333,600**	**$4,353,020**	**$19,420**
LIABILITIES & OWNERS EQUITY	**Dec 31 of PRIOR YEAR**	**Dec 31 of CURRENT YEAR**	**INCREASE/ (DECREASE)**
Current Liabilities			
Accounts Payable	$381,000	$361,000	$20,000
Short-Term Loans	$248,000	$244,000	$4,000
Taxes Payable	$731,000	$727,600	$3,400
Total Current Liabilities	**$1,360,000**	**$1,332,600**	**$27,400**
Long-Term Debt	**$625,000**	**$548,000**	**$77,000**
TOTAL LIABILITIES	**$1,985,000**	**$1,880,600**	**$104,400**
OWNERS EQUITY	**$2,348,600**	**$2,472,420**	**$123,820**
TOTAL LIABILITIES + OWNERS EQUITY	**$4,333,600**	**$4,353,020**	**$19,420**

As briefly described earlier, financial leverage refers to the situation in which you use borrowed money to purchase an asset (to create value), and then repay the money with an overall net gain that exceeds the return you would get on your own capital.

For example, let's say you could buy a product for $100 and resell it for $125—but you only have $100 of working capital. Without leverage, you can buy one unit of the product, sell it, and keep $25 profit, for a gain of 25 percent. After four such sales, you could afford two more products to sell, and so on, each time making only 25 percent return on your investment. On the other hand, you could borrow $300; add it to your $100 in order to buy four products; sell them for $500; return the $300 loan; and reap 100 percent profit on your original investment of $100. Even if you had to pay 10 percent interest (i.e., $30.00), you'd still net 70 percent profit from your original $100.

Business people may not be concerned about how the chief financial officer (CFO) or controller finances equipment or other assets. However, when analyzing their competitor business, people may find it is important to know whether they are overleveraged. Whereas overleveraged organizations (i.e., those with too much debt on the balance sheet) may be limited in whether they can invest in new products or new marketing programs, companies that are not heavily leveraged (i.e., don't have a lot of debt) and that have cash on their balance sheets have the advantage of being more financially agile, which counts in competitive situations.

Business people might refer to the balance sheet for details in the event that a capital investment is required (like a new machine) to produce a new product. If you find yourself in this situation, you will need to justify the expenditure to your management, which will have to provide the money to buy the machinery and account for the future depreciation. Another scenario might require you to evaluate the inventory position of the company. If there's too much inventory, it ties up working capital and delays sales. If you tie the two scenarios together—a need for a new machine but no money to buy it because the company's cash is tied up in inventory—there's a bigger problem to solve: where to get the money for the machine? Will the company have to go to the bank for a loan? Does it have sufficient credit to do so? Business people who see such big-picture issues will have a greater context to evaluate the issues and find solutions.

Now, refer to the sample balance sheet in Figure 4.3. Notice that the snapshots are taken at two points in time and that the third column is headed "Increase/(Decrease)." If you were evaluating a company, you might want to know things like, "Where did the additional cash come from?" and "Why did accounts payable increase?" To better understand what happened, financial people use a technique called *sources and uses analysis.* This analysis of funds determines if the company is relying on debt (leverage) to operate the business, or if excess cash is generated from ongoing operations. In summary, sources and uses analysis helps managers to understand the financial direction of the organization and what it must do to encourage sales or to manage its expenditures.

EXERCISE

- Obtain a copy of a balance sheet from your finance department. Ask if someone will go over the details with you and explain how it's analyzed.
- Visit the website of a company with which you're familiar, click on the page for "investors" and review the balance sheet as contained in the regulatory findings. In the United States, it can be found under Form 10K.

CASH FLOW

Every month, the company receives money from sales of products and services (revenues) and disburses money in order to operate the business (expenses). This is also captured in the diagram shown as Figure 4.1. To understand this better, consider your own experience. You may receive money from a salary or other sources, and you disburse money for your living expenses. In a nutshell, that describes cash flow.

Cash flow management (also referred to as liquidity management) is largely the responsibility of the CFO or treasurer of the company. However, a fundamental understanding of cash flow is important for any business person because all financial plans and/or forecasts involve the translation of prior cash usage and future sales projections into financial information. This information is synchronized with the calendar so that the appropriate plans can be made coincident with the expected arrival of money from sales and the outflow of money to support operations. The CFO reviews the budgets of all departments within the company to

Figure 4.4 Cash Flow Analysis Template

	INFLOW FROM SALES [A]	OUTFLOW FROM PAID BILLS [B]	NET CASH FLOW [A] − [B] = [C]	CASH ON HAND AT START OF MONTH [D]	CASH ON HAND AT END OF MONTH [C] + [D] = [E]
MONTH 1					
MONTH 2					
MONTH 3					

determine how much money is needed to finance business operations. If shortfalls are predicted, the CFO needs to work out where to get money to pay the bills. If there is an excess of cash flow, then the CFO has to have a plan in place to invest the money so it doesn't sit idle. This concept should be fairly familiar to you because you use this method to manage the cash flow of your own household. In Figure 4.4, I provide a simple template you can use to better understand the essence of cash flow management.

In the world of business, you'll find that leaders tend to be risk averse. However, when presented with compelling opportunities, they will want to invest for the future. The challenge is that cash in the future is harder to predict and, therefore, can present a risky proposition for CFOs and other leaders. This brings us to the accounting concept known as *present value.* According to this concept, a dollar (or unit of currency) today is worth more than a dollar tomorrow. Sometimes inflation plays a role. Sometimes it's because borrowing costs erode the value of the money. Ultimately, cash flows are important because of the concept of the present value of future expected cash inflows. In other words, *the farther into the future the cash is expected to arrive, the less value it has to the company in today's terms.*

You'll find that there are always going to be requests for funds for various projects. These will originate from different departments. Some may be budgeted, and others may not. Either way, the executives who make decisions will want to know how much is needed, for what purpose, and when they will see an acceptable *return on investment* (ROI).

Not all investments are equal, either in the amount needed or the *payback period* (the period of time required before the amounts realized cover the cost of the investment). Many firms account for this by rating and ranking investments based on time horizon, strategic importance, and other parameters. One of the tools used to evaluate an investment is referred to as *discounted cash flow.*

UNDERSTANDING DISCOUNTED CASH FLOW

As I indicated, many departments request investment funds from management. This is consistent with what the CFO, working with the executive leadership team, does. CFOs generally take a portion of the company's profits, after providing for normal working capital requirements, and invest those funds. One way to do this is to reinvest in the business. This may be in products, facilities, operational improvements, and so on. If one department wishes to make an investment, it must "borrow" money from the CFO (or investors). Just like if you borrow money to buy a car, any monies borrowed from the CFO must be paid back with interest (providing a rate of return that is better than what might be received if the money is just deposited in a bank). In the corporate world, this interest is referred to as the *discount rate.*The discount rate is based on what is called the cost of capital. Companies supply their checkbooks with money from a variety of sources (as in taking out a loan or issuing stock), and each source has a different cost. The discount rate is also considered a function of the company's risk of loss—for example, if the requesting department doesn't pay the money back when expected. The discount rate may be increased for investments perceived as riskier. Suffice it to say that the CFO charges you a discount rate that accounts for the fact that money expected to arrive farther into the future is discounted back to the present. Hence, we have the financial expression *discounted cash flow*. Here's a simple example of how this works:

Suppose the R&D group needs $150,000 to develop a new technology for a product. The finance representative feels that the business case (the investment justification document) has a low risk for failure and that a discount rate of 12 percent will be sufficient to cover the cost of capital and the relevant risk of the investment. Figure 4.5 shows how the cash flows are actually discounted.

Figure 4.5 Discounted Cash Flow Calculation

	CURRENT YEAR	YEAR 1	YEAR 2	YEAR 3	TOTAL
Money Invested	(150,000)				
Anticipated Cash Inflow		55,000	93,000	235,000	383,000
Discounted Amount		48,400	72,019	160,146	280,565
Cumulative Discounted Cash Flow		48,400	120,419	280,565	

- In the *current year*, the team gets $150,000 from the CFO. This is shown as a negative number because it represents an outflow of funds.
- In *year 1*, the net cash inflow from product sales is $55,000. However, because it's one year into the future, the $55,000 needs to be "discounted" back to the present. In our example, it would be calculated as $55,000 × .88 = $48,400, with .88 allowing for the discounting of the cash flow by 12 percent.
- In *year 2*, the product provides $93,000 of positive cash flow to the company. This money must be discounted twice (that's compounding the discount rate), which means it's discounted by 12 percent two times, calculated as $93,000 × (.88 × .88 = .7744) = $72,019.
- In *year 3*, the company receives positive cash inflow of $235,000. This money must be discounted three times, and the discounted cash flow is calculated as follows: $235,000 × (.88 × .88 × .88 = .6815) = $160,146.
- Then, each individual future cash flow amount is discounted "back to the present" and then added up. Adding up the future discounted cash flows is called the *cumulative discounted cash flow* (CDCF).

Most financial analysts will take the CDCF and subtract the original investment to arrive at the net present value (NPV) for the investment. A positive NPV means that the investment will generate a return to the business. The CFO and the leadership team of the company will likely compare different NPVs based on timing (cash flows received sooner are generally viewed more favorably), risk, and the absolute amount of the initial investment. *Net present value* or *discounted cash flow* are expressions you will probably hear many times during your career and while you are involved in the world of business.

FINANCIAL PLANNING

Whether you're planning your family's budget, figuring out how much to spend for your next vacation, or deciding what's required to operate your department at work, financial planning is involved. Financial planning means figuring out the funding required for operation and how those funds should be deployed. In many cases, financial planning considers from where money should be secured if there isn't enough in the bank to provide for operations or unique business investments. If there's no formal process, the company may find itself out of money—and out of business.

Throughout my corporate life, I recall some people who would manipulate figures on a spreadsheet to "make the numbers work" during the budget cycle. Certainly, the power of automated tools makes it easy to revise "estimates," but without a clear picture of reality, the company is exposed to undue risks and a possible cash crisis.

For example, imagine that you want to start a business. You get things going in January. You diligently figure out how much it will cost you for rent, utilities, and other necessities. Then, you figure out how much to spend on sales and marketing because you assume these efforts will drive traffic to your website. By your analysis, you believe that orders will be coming in during April, and the cash will be flowing in. You're totally positive that you saved up enough to get you through June without any revenue. All is well until April rolls around and there's little web traffic and no orders. In May, you get a few orders, but only enough to pay one-half of one month's expenses. By June, your bank account is tapped, and you have to ask your brother for a loan—but he's got no money. By July, you're out of business.

Diligent financial planning requires an astute understanding of many facets of business. Your ability to manipulate numbers on a spreadsheet cannot guarantee the success of your business. Very large companies have extensive resources and can usually survive some of the mistakes made in financial plans. However, smaller firms are in greater danger of a *liquidity crisis* (i.e., the inability to meet cash obligations) if backup resources are not available. Even with a solid accounts receivable backlog, there's no guarantee your customers will pay you when you think they will.

PREPARING BUDGETS

Business people from all around the company need to participate in the budgeting process. Typically, budgets cover the next fiscal or calendar year. They are spending road maps that link business goals to the spending required from the operating departments. They are also revenue road maps that depict inflows from sales of products and services.

Budgets are used for near-term planning, coordinating functional department activities, communicating to management and other team members, and tracking progress. When all the spending estimates for all the functions are "rolled up" into the total budget, they can be carefully evaluated by management to make sure that the spending plans are both affordable and achievable—based on the financial resources available to the company. Budgets need to be linked not only to the strategy but also to the cash flow requirements used by the CFO to make sure there is enough money to run the company.

In large companies, budgets are often submitted for the following fiscal year during the fourth quarter of the prior year. If it's June of the current fiscal year, and revenue is slower and expenses are higher, you'll usually have to pare back. Often, these companies will do a "rebudget" exercise based on a revised set of assumptions. Budgets in smaller firms are subject to scrutiny on a more frequent basis. In my business, I evaluate cash flow on a daily basis and assess the budget each month. This allows me to accelerate an investment if conditions are favorable, or delay some programs if I see that the numbers aren't just right.

The budget is a great communication tool. It uses the language of money to describe to management or other stakeholders the action plans of all departments in the business—and how the business operates as a unified whole. Further, when a team is working on a project and the team isn't operating within the established budgetary guidelines, a team leader can use the financial data to inform management of issues and possible causes.

Budgeting is a fairly simple mechanical exercise. You can see this clearly in the spreadsheet template in Figure 4.6. The challenge for any business person is to understand what's behind the numbers. Before you look at the template, follow along with me as I explain how I worked on budgets earlier in my career.

When I was a financial analyst, my job was to evaluate past cash inflows and compare them with actual cash outflows. Because I was always monitoring the sales mix, COGS, and department expenditures and analyzing those against the budgets, I understood the difference between normal activity and anomalous activity. I also used a cash flow

Figure 4.6 Budgeting Template

	JAN	FEB	MAR	APR	MAY	JUN	JUL	AUG	SEP	OCT	NOV	DEC	TOTAL
SALES (REVENUE)													
Number of units													
Price per unit													
Total Sales													
COST OF GOODS SOLD													
Materials per unit													
Labor per unit													
Overhead per unit													
Total COGS per unit													
GROSS MARGIN													
GROSS MARGIN %													
EXPENSES TO RUN THE BUSINESS													
Sales													
Marketing													
Research & Development													
Operations													
General & Administration													
Total Expenses													
EBITDA													
EBITDA %													
Depreciation & Amortization													
Taxes													
NET PROFIT													

analysis template like the one shown in Figure 4.4 to verify the inflows and outflows of cash in the company. This should be your first step in preparing a budget. If you're just starting out, you won't have any prior period information, so you'll use a "zero-base" budgeting technique.

The next step I took was to talk with the product managers, marketers, and salespeople to understand their proposed product forecasts, market penetration assumptions, and potential competitive activity. The overall "sales mix" included the number and type of products, the predicted product prices, and the resultant overall revenue. One company I worked in produced many of its products in a factory, so I had to work with the cost accounting department to determine the standard costs for all the products—which went into the COGS category. Other products were procured from external vendors and included in larger solutions; those costs were included in a category separate from that of the manufactured products and business services offered by the firm. Externally sourced products that were passed through the company and marked up were placed into a revenue category called distributed products.

Next, I met with the leaders of all the operating departments. I had good working relationships with them and understood how their departments worked. We discussed items such as headcount, salaries, and other expenses they were to incur. We also discussed the specifics of their plans and programs. Some of these were part of their standard operating model. Others were to be driven with special project teams that would explore ways to support revenue growth or operating efficiencies. From these, we created a number of versions that we called profiles. These profiles were connected with various assumption sets. This helped us position budgets with both conservative and aggressive profiles. These profiles also helped me to analyze actual spending patterns as the fiscal year unfolded.

In the end, I consolidated all of the different budgets—product sales mix, COGS, sourced products, and operating expenses from the departments—into a total company budget.

EXERCISE

- Find out about the budgeting cycle in your company. What are the steps followed to prepare the annual budget? How frequently is the budget updated throughout the year?
- Review a department budget with your manager and find out about inputs and assumptions used for that budget.

Now that you have a basic sense of financial statements, financial planning, and budgeting, I can provide you with some additional information to help you improve your knowledge and understanding of finance. I do this by introducing you to the following topics:

1. Using business cases for investments in products, facilities, or operational improvements
2. Assembling forecasts
3. Testing planning assumptions (sensitivity analysis)
4. Deriving product cost models
5. Establishing pricing models

CREATING BUSINESS CASES FOR IMPORTANT INVESTMENTS

The business case is the primary document used in an organization to justify investments in new products, facilities, equipment, market expansion programs, operational systems, and other items to improve or change the business. The term *investment* is revealing. It means that someone in a functional department is requesting money from management, and he or she intends to prove that the investment will deliver a positive return to the business. There are usually many others in the company who are competing for money; thus, realistic, believable business cases usually garner greater levels of support from management. It's incumbent on anyone who's producing a business case to create the best, most realistic business cases possible because these documents help to establish the credibility and business acumen of those who are to support these investments in the eyes of management. In Chapter 9, I'll offer more detail on this vital business document.

ASSEMBLING FORECASTS

A forecast is an estimate based on assumptions about possible future situations. Business people may be responsible for summarizing or creating forecasts of market share, sales volumes, and production capacity. Each of these forecasts is based on a host of variables that are ultimately linked back to the strategy for the business. Forecasts are built on assumptions formulated by people who work in various departments. Their goal is to determine "future state" scenarios that are eventually translated into unit volume forecasts and sales forecasts.

Forecasts are also created to determine the market share for products of the business. Market share postulations and assumptions are built on a solid foundation of industry and competitive research as well as needs-based market segmentation models—things you'll learn about in Chapter 7. For example, assumptions for sales volumes are evaluated in conjunction with the sales department, because sales needs to be able to commit to delivering those volumes and, of course, needs to be appropriately compensated for selling the product.

Assumptions are also linked to demand forecasts for tangible goods so that the factory's production schedules can be created. In addition, forecast assumptions are linked to the work of the marketing department, as marketing programs must be appropriately timed to stimulate interest in the product and drive sales activity. If the sales forecast is too low, there won't be enough products available, and customers will find another way to satisfy their demand. If sales volumes are too low, inventory positions will build, wasting company money. Of course, each and every assumption about the future in any forecast is expressed in financial terms.

TESTING PLANNING ASSUMPTIONS USING SENSITIVITY ANALYSIS

Once you begin to consider investment decisions, forecasts in budgets, and business cases, you will find yourself asking, "What if . . .?" "What if the cost of materials goes up in six months?" "What if we increase the price by 10 percent?" Eventually, you will want to create various assumption sets to see what *might* happen. Testing assumptions means changing a variable (a unit volume, a product cost element, or a unit price) to assess how sensitive any given variable will be with respect to future profitability. This process is called *sensitivity analysis.*

When carrying out a sensitivity analysis, you should not change multiple variables at the same time. Instead, change one variable to see the overall impact on gross margin or net income. For example, if you believe that the most likely market situation will yield a unit volume of 1,000 units at $250 per unit for one year with revenue of $250,000, what happens if the volume is 20 percent less and the price is the same? Then, revenue would be $200,000. Would that be enough to sustain the business and deliver the targeted product profitability and market share?

As you carefully consider these variables, don't get drawn into the ease of changing a figure in a cell on the spreadsheet and seeing if what comes out looks good. You'll want to make sure that you're really considering actual scenarios that are realistic and relevant to the case under study.

DERIVING PRODUCT COST MODELS

As suggested earlier, all tangible products have costs associated with their production. Businesses that make or buy goods to sell deduct the COGS from their revenue in computing gross margin. This information applies if the business is a manufacturer, wholesaler, retailer, or engaged in any business activity involving the buying or selling of goods to ultimately produce revenue. This does not generally apply to businesses that provide intangible services unless there's an externally sourced component that must work with software produced by your company.

Business people should have some ideas about the cost models used to plan and manage products. The three methods discussed here include standard costing, target costing, and activity-based costing.

Standard costing of a product is based on the company's cost of direct material, direct labor, and overhead. During planning or budgeting, many companies don't assign an actual cost of material, labor, and overhead to a product. Rather, they establish a standard cost, usually at the beginning of a new fiscal year. This is done by estimating the costs based on what's already known, or based on products that have already been produced (especially if there is inventory that has a cost associated with it). You can think of the standard cost as the "cost used for planning purposes." Typically, the standard cost is set at the outset of the fiscal year; as new costs are realized for producing the product (in different volumes), these actual costs will be compared to the standard costs. If there is a difference between the actual costs incurred and the standard costs, they can be analyzed and attributed to variations or fluctuations in volume, material costs, or overhead. As products evolve across their life cycle, business people (or those designated as product mangers) will always be interested in reducing production costs. Therefore, they require relevant reference points from which to carry out these cost analyses.

Target costing is a method for specifying the proposed product costs so that a targeted gross margin can be realized. These costs are linked directly to the product's features and capabilities. Key players such as product people, engineers, procurement specialists, and cost accountants carefully assemble these targets. The benefit is that management can closely monitor cost metrics and take immediate action as required. For additional context, if a gross margin goal of 75 percent is established and the market price of the product is $100, then the targeted cost cannot exceed $25.

Activity-based costing is a technique that logically allocates overhead to products based on actual usage of factory facilities or machinery. The best way to describe this is with an example where there are two products in one product line: product A and product B. Product A is ordered by customers in low numbers. However, for product A to be produced, it requires some additional engineering, testing, and many machine setups. Product B is ordered frequently by customers, and its production runs are longer and not interrupted by setups or other activities. If your company applied standard costing, it would probably allocate the overhead based on the number of hours of machine time. This means that product A would have little overhead because it uses less machine time, and product B would have a lot of overhead because it uses a lot of machine time. Activity-based costing considers not only machine time but also engineering, testing, and setup, which are activities used in conjunction with the production of the product. Therefore, utilizing activity-based costing, product A's overhead would be higher. Product B's overhead would likely be reduced because there is less overhead to be spread over a larger amount of product; product B would be charged only for machine time, not for those additional costs incurred by product A. In many organizations, activity-based costing is not always easy to implement and track. However, it is an option if these cost-recognition mechanisms are available in the corporate accounting systems. Activity-based costing can be a helpful approach when looking deeply at cost reduction or process improvement initiatives.

ESTABLISHING PRICING MODELS

Every product has to be priced, and pricing models abound. The most appropriate model is a value-based approach. Nonetheless, many companies use cost-plus pricing, which I do not advocate. Pricing is both art and science, but it should be built upon a solid foundation of well-researched and understood customer needs and competitive pressures. This basis ultimately determines how any product is positioned in the market. Pricing should also be determined based on the strategic goals set for the product. Introducing a new product at a lower price can "buy" market share. If your product is sold in the luxury consumer segment, its price is usually at a premium. Some companies price for short-term gains in revenue or profit; some try to sell as many units as possible.

Strategic pricing may require some assistance from a financial specialist due to some of the intricacies involved. A person who has a deep understanding of the market and company pricing policies can help, too. During the strategic planning process, or when forecasts are revised, an assessment is created that determines how well one or more products has sold, at what prices, under what conditions, and to which customer types. Although list prices may reflect what is believed to be the product's value proposition, actual pricing performance, as in special bids, discounts offered for purchases in specific quantities, and so on, may have brought about shifts in the average selling price for the product. These are usually visible in product-level P&L statements. Such pricing details need to be factored into future pricing strategies. For pricing planning, the product managers, financial specialists, and other business people should continually consider pricing within the context of financial planning and the desired future financial performance of the business. Revenue forecasts are dependent on the pricing model, and gross margin is ultimately calculated based on the units that are sold. The price, therefore, is one of the most important lynchpins in the P&L!

SUMMARY

As I've indicated, money is the language of business. If you know your company is doing well, it's producing a good profit that adds to the cash position. It goes without saying that the more cash the company has, the more options it has to invest in new products, pay off debt, or return dividends to shareholders. If the business doesn't do well, then the company is forced to pare back and save money. Which would you prefer?

As a person who runs a business, I cannot emphasize enough the importance of constant financial vigilance. Daily perspectives on cash inflow and outflow and continual analysis of spending against the budget are vital to help steer the company. To that end, astute business people should establish financial perspectives as frequently as needed to keep things on track.

Also note that every situation you encounter, or any decision that must be made, has a financial consequence. If you're caught off guard, your company is exposed to undue risk and competitive actions that can erode pricing power and cause your customers to shop elsewhere. If you're on guard, then you are poised to act strategically and to stay ahead of the curve. Again, which situation would you prefer?

Even though finance is a fairly technical area, I've attempted to provide a practical overview for you in this chapter. With this information, the stage is set for you to continue your work and explore the areas that will make you a well-rounded business person.

INCREASING YOUR MANAGEMENT COMPETENCY

1. If you have never had any formal financial training, you may wish to enroll in an Accounting 101 class and a Finance 101 class. This will give you basic tools to navigate the world of finance. I don't recommend the quick one- or two-day "finance for nonfinancial managers" type of classes.
2. Make an appointment with someone in your finance department. Ask if he or she can help you understand the format and structure of the firm's financial statements in order to become familiar with the financial language in your company.
3. Ask a financial manager to attend one of your work team meetings to explain the financial tools used by the organization. This will help ensure that you're all speaking the same financial language inside your company.
4. When you have the opportunity, or if you have budgetary responsibility, work with your financial representative to help analyze variances in the P&L. Determine the steps involved in analyzing the variance and answering the question, "What happened?" This will enable you to carry out an investigation

on your own or to work with your financial team member to discover the causes of such variances.

5. Work with your management during the annual budgeting and planning process. Ask managers to explain the process. If you're involved in the budgeting process, ensure that you are clearly identifying all of the assumptions used in the creation of your budgets.

Action Planning

In this chapter, the following characteristics were either explicitly or implicitly revealed. You may wish to identify where these were mentioned to reinforce your understanding of how they might be applied in your own work. You can also utilize the following template as a way to associate what was discussed in this chapter with your scores from your Business Acumen Assessment. From this, you can create an action plan for yourself or work with your manager to come up with specific goals and plans.

- Managing
- Evaluating business performance
- Systemic thinking
- Critical thinking
- Solving problems
- Being results oriented
- Earning credibility

ACTION ITEM + GOAL	STEPS TO BE TAKEN	OUTCOME PRODUCED	WHAT YOU LEARNED	WHAT YOU WILL SHARE

LEVERAGING PROCESSES TO GET THINGS DONE

After you read this chapter, you should be able to:

- Explain how processes are used in your company to achieve its business goals.
- Take a systemic perspective by analyzing how processes are connected as work moves across an organization.
- Examine processes with an eye toward reducing waste, improving efficiency, and saving time and money.

The first rule of any technology used in a business is that automation applied to an efficient operation will magnify the efficiency. The second is that automation applied to an inefficient operation will magnify the inefficiency.

—BILL GATES

Have you ever gone into a clothing store where you felt that both the service and the experience were amazing? Owners of great retail stores rely on creative merchandisers, effective sales staff, and a host of other people to make the "system" of the store work every day. Yet every day is different because of the variety of customers that walk through the doors, the selection of styles offered, or even the mood of the manager.

Like any store, your corporate environment is an interconnected system of processes that must come together to keep the business moving toward the fulfillment of its goals. On the path to the achievement of those goals, obstacles and challenges always emerge. Then, crisis-mode management steps in as many people are redirected to fix the problem. The unfortunate side of crisis-mode management is that lessons learned aren't always captured and errors are likely to be repeated. This is not an effective way to run a business.

Business people know that quality products, happy customers, and organizational efficiency are required to be successful. However, even with a general appreciation or an intuitive understanding of how work gets done, business performance will suffer when established processes are not properly followed. Whether it's because the process steps are not known or because the process is not fit for purpose, the result is still the same: a poorly produced product, an unsatisfactory customer experience, or reduced profit for the business.

With this in mind, this chapter offers you an introduction to processes so you can be grounded in the essentials.

INTRODUCTION TO PROCESSES

According to Businessdictionary.com, a *process* is defined as a "sequence of interdependent and linked procedures which, at every stage, consume one or more resources (employee time, energy, machines, money) to convert inputs (data, material, parts, etc.) into outputs. These outputs then serve as inputs for the next stage until a known goal or end result is reached" (http://www.businessdictionary.com/definition/process.html).

The first step is to understand which processes are used in your company and how they are applied. One way to quickly obtain this information is to find out who manages or "owns" the business processes in your company. In many firms, one or more people are assigned to keep the documentation and serve as the focal point to harness organizational learning. They also ensure that people comply with various rules that govern usage, enable measurements, and help with optimization to improve those processes. Loosely managed processes cannot be properly "institutionalized" or adopted for consistent use in the business. In companies that do a good job, you may find that these people work in departments with names that include Center of Excellence, Business Process

Management, Process Excellence, and other similar titles. There are also *standards organizations that operate to set guidelines for consistency in specific processes.* One such organization is the International Standards Organization (ISO). Information about the ISO can be found at www.iso.org. The American Productivity and Quality Center (APQC) is another organization that has developed a process classification framework. The APQC can be located at www.apqc.org. The APQC's model is very robust and worth evaluating. The framework is open source and available at no cost.

Because all organizations want to effectively use processes, and to improve them over time, a generic hierarchy of processes is present in all companies. I'll share this simple structure with you to show you how the hierarchy works.

1. *Major business process.* This is the highest-level process. It is usually guided by one function, but with complex interdependencies on other departments. A major business process serves as a focal point from which key business goals can be broken down into more meaningful work areas. Some of these you might find in a company could include the strategic planning process (as I'll discuss in Chapter 8) and the new product development process (covered in Chapter 9).
2. *Business process.* This process level provides a rational sequencing of steps that have basic *inputs, activities, and outputs.* These outputs, when completed, are integrated or consolidated at the major business process level. Let's say that your marketing department must produce a product brochure to support a product launch. The brochure team might include a project leader, a copywriter, a graphic designer, and a legal person who work on various parts of the brochure. The process output (the brochure) is provided to the marketing department leader and contributes to the product launch process.
3. *Subprocesses* are merely small portions of business processes that contribute to the goals of the process. For example, for the graphic designer to produce what's needed for the brochure, she has to go through several steps to integrate company design standards, photography, and other items to complete her

contribution to the brochure design. At the same time, a copy editor will have to work with various subject matter experts to create the narratives for the brochure. When the designer and the copy editor are done with their subprocess work, it is integrated into the process of brochure creation.

4. *Activities* include the work that's done within a process or subprocess, carried out by one or more people in one department. One activity associated with the brochure creation might be to take a photograph of the product.

Figure 5.1 illustrates a basic process hierarchy of these activities.

You'll invariably find that different processes move at different rates of speed. Fast processes coexist with slower processes, and the outputs from some processes become inputs of others. As an example, suppose your company is creating a software product. The product development process might be broken up into smaller development processes representing the coding of specific software modules. Some of those modules are complex and take longer than less complex modules. Ultimately,

Figure 5.1 Basic Process Hierarchy

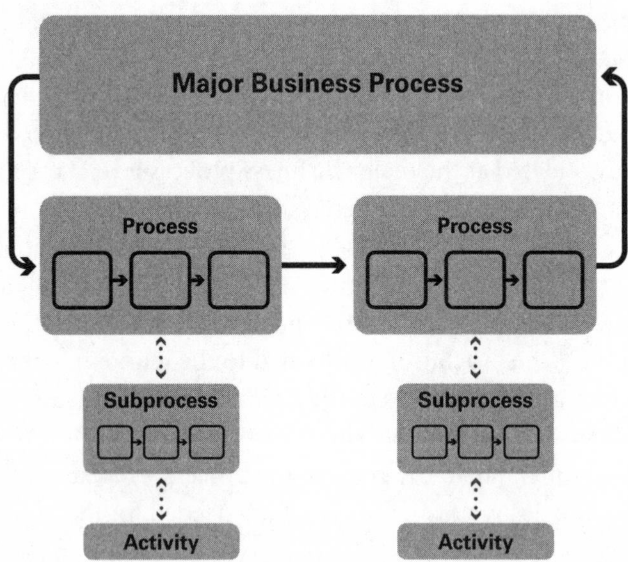

each module of code has to be handed off to the quality assurance (QA) department to be tested and integrated. If the QA people don't properly test and integrate the modules, the software won't work. An astute manager might check in with the development leader and QA manager to make sure things are moving along. If someone wasn't assigned to oversee and coordinate these different work streams, a bottleneck in the process would occur, and in the end, delay the release, reduce functionality, or adversely impact product quality.

When business managers have to consider many different processes and the impact on the operation of a company, they are said to be *thinking systemically*. Noted author Peter Senge wrote a book entitled *The Fifth Discipline: The Art and Practice of the Learning Organization* in which he utilizes the term *systemic thinking* to characterize what's needed to see how various people or processes interact and then to see the whole picture. On the first page of the first chapter of this book, he writes, "From a very early age, we are taught to break apart problems, to fragment the world. This apparently makes complex tasks and subjects more manageable, but we pay a hidden, enormous price. We can no longer see the consequences of our actions; we lose our intrinsic sense of connection to the larger whole."

In sum, *managers have a duty to care about how work is carried out and completed.* If the work of people in the company is not done properly, whatever inefficiency or quality problem results will invariably impact your customers' perception of your company. Processes matter.

EXERCISE

- Identify a major business process and draw the process hierarchy. List the key functional departments that are involved in this level of the process hierarchy. If you're unfamiliar with the process, then identify a manager with whom you can speak to gain an understanding of her perspective on how the process works.
- If you happen to be working on one or several activities on a project team, try to create the bottom-up perspective to see how all activities roll up to subprocesses, and so on.

LET'S HAVE DINNER!

Recall a time when you ate at a great restaurant and you left feeling that the food was outstanding and the service was wonderful. Maybe you'll tell your friends or write an online review. But how did the restaurant make that happen? What do they do in order to deliver such a great experience?

The restaurant is a "system" made up of many processes and activities performed by different people who have various responsibilities. You can associate the term *system* with *major business process* and call the process "running a successful restaurant." Therefore, if the restaurant is to be successful, it must fulfill its goals, which could include a memorable dining experience, a unique menu with great-tasting food, and remarkable service.

For the restaurant to operate properly, there are four main functions that follow a unique process. For example, the *kitchen management process* starts out early in the morning with the chef. She arrives early, plans the menu, visits the market to order food, and then instructs the cooks in the kitchen to create all the samples for the waitstaff to taste. The *service management process*, led by the headwaiter, participates in the menu sampling so that the waitstaff can enthusiastically explain menu choices. During the day, the *environmental management process* led by the restaurant captain ensures that tables are properly set up, centerpieces arranged, and lighting and music create the desired atmosphere. In the meantime, the *maintenance management process*, led by the maintenance manager, makes sure the restaurant is clean, plates and cookware are prepared, and the bar is sufficiently stocked. Finally, the restaurant manager who runs the business makes sure it all comes together in time to open the doors for another day.

It takes a lot to run a restaurant, and as the restaurant operates during the day, glitches happen. Managers know this because they set performance standards so they can track their progress. Invariably, there are gaps between what was planned and the results achieved. As examples, the chef may make the wrong dish, or the waiter may bring the wrong order. Perhaps the music is too loud or the flowers on the table cause several people to have an allergic reaction. As you can imagine, there is a lot that can happen.

For a restaurant, or for any business to operate efficiently, its processes must be properly managed. In this case, management provides for proper *control* of all operations and processes. There are two types of measurements that can be used to evaluate the performance of any business: *quantitative* measures and *qualitative* measures. Quantitative measures of performance are all about the numbers, and for a restaurant, it could be the number of customers, how much they spend, how long they stay, how many pounds of chicken were used, or how much money was made in a day. It could also focus on the cost of food, the percentage of main courses not expedited on time, and so on. Qualitative measures can be about feelings: what customers experience when they are in the restaurant, what they may say on a comment card, and whether they'll tell their friends.

As every business carries out its work using these interconnected processes, and measurements are applied to those processes, the business can be fine-tuned. In a corporate environment, daily measurements may not be available or may be imperceptible. However, a restaurant is a great example of the need for speed in evaluating measurements and making adjustments. To make my point, there are three types of control levers that can be applied to the business in order to fine-tune its operation:

1. *Feedforward mechanism.* Based on feedback from the end of a prior workday or at the start of a new day, what can or should be done? A feedforward mechanism is important so that problems can be prevented before they happen. As an example, when the waitstaff tastes the food before customers arrive, they are better prepared to describe items on the menu to customers who might need a little persuasion. Did you ever ask, "Do you recommend the steak or the fish?" You know when waiters haven't tasted them, they'll say, "The fish is popular," but that doesn't help you. When they say "I just had the steak for lunch, and it melted in my mouth," you'll know what you're likely to order! In a corporate context, if you were a manufacturer and you added a pre-inspection of your raw materials before the manufacturing process started, you might head off quality problems later on. Feedforward sets the stage for great feedback, so consider it your best early warning system because you can't change the past, but you can guide the future.
2. *Concurrent management.* What can be done in real time to make changes or adjustments during the day to make sure

things are going well? If the manager notices that there are people waiting for a table but no one's cleaning the two vacant tables in the corner, she can take immediate action so that the waiting customers don't walk out the door. If the cycle time (the period from the moment an order is taken until it's delivered) is too long, how can that be sped up? The manager can see if it's the waitstaff or kitchen staff causing the bottleneck. In some companies, the technique "managing by walking around" is a tried and true way to see how things are going. In a restaurant, the manager visits guests and pays attention to the ambience in order to keep things running smoothly.

3. *Feedback mechanism.* This information shows how effectively processes were carried out and whether performance goals were met. Measurement of actual results provides valuable input to feedforward to the next cycle. In a restaurant, it could be a review of the comment cards or qualitative feedback gathered by the manager. If the mix of menu items was unbalanced (you sold out the chicken and there's too much leftover fish), what can be done to better predict the next day's requirements? How much money was made? Do we need to sell more of the higher-profit products?

As a diner in a restaurant, you know what a good experience feels like. You know when the food and service are exemplary, and of course, you're likely to recommend the restaurant to your friends or post an online review. I provided this example to you to ensure that you consider the complexity of the processes in your own company from many perspectives—from the internal point of view and from that of the customers. In the final analysis, the customers vote with their wallet. Even if you believe your company has great products, if the processes won't support those products and the customers don't buy, the business will not be successful.

EXERCISE

- For a business process in your company, identify two quantitative measures and two qualitative measures.
- Create a list that captures feedforward, concurrent, and feedback mechanisms for that business process.

PROCESS INTEGRATION

Systemic perspectives can be more easily expanded when you evaluate several interconnected business processes. In a business-to-business company, one such major process that you can learn from is known as "quote-to-cash." This process has become critical to the success of complex firms that operate globally with customers and suppliers everywhere. This is because there are many more facets to these companies with a greater chance for more things to "slip through the cracks." When these slippages occur, they can lead to inefficiency, delayed shipments, reduced cash flow, and excessive costs to the company—which reduces profit.

This process takes into account the steps required to receive quotation requests and the stages that an order goes through, from the time the order is received until the time the company gets paid. Just by its name, you can surmise it's very important to get this process right because of its impact on cash flow. To set the context for this major process, keep in mind that any business is more likely to be successful when it's properly organized to carry out the following activities:

1. Marketing and advertising that targets new customers or inspires current customers to choose the company's products or services when the need arises, or direct selling by people in the business to find out about customer needs and to ensure that customers know of the value and benefits of products offered for sale.
2. Customer service or other function to handle inbound requests and to interface directly with sales as the need arises.
3. Salespeople who are geared to generate quotes along with the requisite approvals, close deals, and obtain orders.
4. Operating the company to manage orders, handle logistics, and ensure that shipments are efficiently handled.
5. Accounting for the order, collecting the money, and reporting the results.

Now, let's take this further. If you worked in a business role in a product distribution company, you would need to know:

- Where do orders originate?
- What happens with them once they're received?

- What people from which departments are involved?
- What's needed to pack and ship the order?
- When does the company get paid?
- How long does the entire process take?

Now, refer to the diagram in Figure 5.2. This is a visualization of the quote-to-cash process in a format known as a *process map*. In this process map, you can see that each department is situated in its own row. Some people refer to these rows as *swim lanes*, as you might see in an Olympic swimming pool. In this example, it's fairly simple to see how one thing connects to another. This is generally the easy part. The bigger challenge lies in understanding what actually happens in each department and where potential problems may arise.

Let's take a look at the first swim lane: marketing. The company may have a number of marketing campaigns designed to stimulate demand or create sales leads. The assumption here is that the e-mail or other outbound campaigns were carried out, resulting in a sufficient number of telephone calls made by customers to request a quotation. A process analyst would benefit from a number of quantitative measures to understand how many e-mails were sent, how many were opened, how many will be acted upon, and overall, which e-mails were most effective. Marketing and sales managers would want to know how many inbound phone calls were received and how many new requests for quotation were secured. They would also be interested in the number of deals that were won in relation to the number of quotes issued. Management would need to know if there were sufficient orders coming in so the company could be properly staffed. If there weren't enough orders, the capacity of the organization would have to be reassessed. Or, if there were too many orders, the system would be overloaded. And this is just the tip of the iceberg. What if the sizes of the orders were too small? Or too large? What would happen if the accounting department didn't send invoices out on time but the CFO was counting on a certain cash inflow—and didn't get it? Then, the CFO would have to figure out where to borrow money to pay the bills for the company.

Thus, what appears to be a very simple process is really quite complicated. Business people must have the wherewithal to evaluate major processes like these, examine documentation, assess the movement of

Figure 5.2 Generic Quote-to-Cash Process

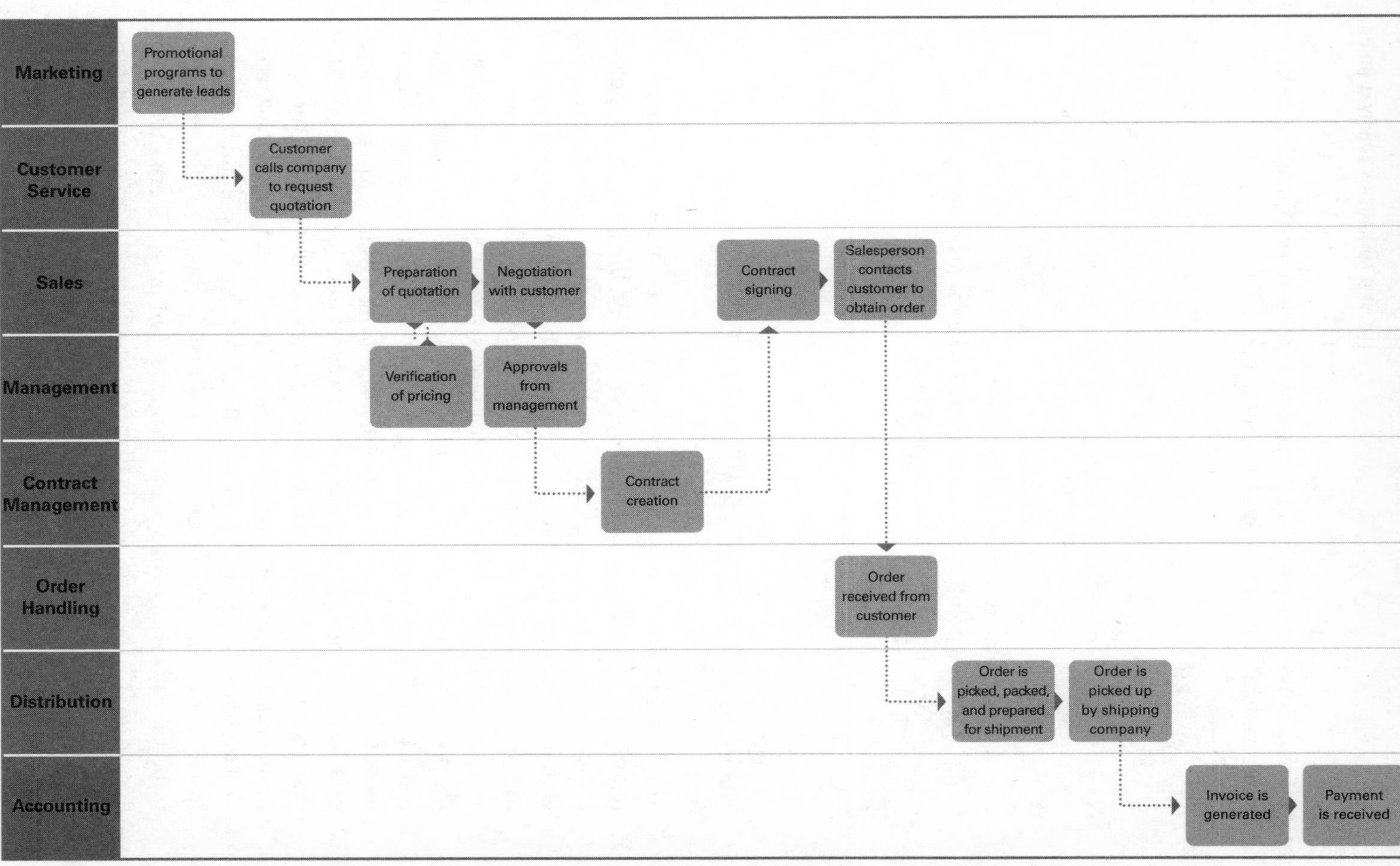

information at each point, and examine qualitative and quantitative measures to determine if the goals are being met.

EXERCISE

- Find out who's responsible in your company for the quote-to-cash process and review that process documentation. Ask about the aspects of the integrated process that cause bottlenecks and others that operate smoothly. Also find out who keeps the statistics on the performance metrics.
- Make a point to visit each of the people who are responsible for various aspects of the process.
- If you were to critique the process, what would you suggest to improve the process that might make it more efficient?

BUSINESS PROCESS ANALYSIS IN ACTION

Through working in or consulting with large, complex companies, I've learned that executives want managers to view the business through a critical lens. Furthermore, they want managers to examine processes with an eye toward reducing waste, improving efficiency, saving time and money, and improving the bottom line. Processes, like work templates, serve as guidelines. When you learn how a process works by following the prescribed steps, you're becoming familiar with the mechanics. That's just beginning. Because problems and situations arise, those who are most familiar with a process are able to consider ways to adapt the process. Think of process adaptations the way lawyers use precedents. Each case may require a fresh perspective or a new interpretation. The worst thing for a business person to do is ignore the situation and go back to the process documentation. That would reveal a lack of proper judgment and would undermine the person's credibility. One thing you'll never want to be caught saying when something goes wrong is "That's the way we always do it." The main idea is that you should be able to consider possibilities to enhance, improve, or revise a process to make work easier, faster, and more efficient.

During my corporate life in product management, several of my products focused on business process automation software. These products automated processes used to respond to customer complaints, handle repairs, deal with service requests or telephone sales, and so on. Because I was curious about how customers did what they did, I'd often visit their operations areas and call centers. I always learned a lot when the managers of these organizations explained what they did, drew flowcharts on boards, and even allowed me to sit next to people on phones or take rides on trucks with field technicians. This was important to me because it allowed me to connect the dots between what was on the process charts and the work that was actually done. In the world of business process analysis, the proposal for automation can be evaluated by analyzing how work is currently done versus how it could be done in the future. The analytical technique that looks at how a process is currently done is referred to as the *present method of operation* (PMO). It requires a thorough analysis of how information and documents currently move through an organization. Here's the rationale: *If you can follow the paper (or electronic documents), you can figure out who touches it, when, for how long, and why.*

I'll tell you a short story about one of my products. It was a complex system that covered the reporting of service problems by customers and the dispatching of field force technicians used by communications companies. The software operated in an environment where customers of the company would call in with a service problem. A customer service representative (CSR) would take the call, pull up the customer record, and try to remotely diagnose the problem. Then, if a problem was found, the CSR would engage the field force repair process so that a technician could be dispatched to the customer's home to fix the problem. In its time, it was a well-designed, effective system, and the processes, as well as the computer systems and associated system interfaces, were well documented and extremely robust. As I became more familiar with the product, and as I studied the utilities industry (communications, water, electric power, etc.), I began to realize that there were opportunities for the products I managed to be used outside the communications industry. As I continued my research, I considered technologies that are common today—including wireless data transmission, global positioning systems, vehicle routing, and many more.

Hopefully, you have a clear visual in your mind now about the functionality of the product. However, when looked at through the lens of a dispatch manager and the technicians in a dispatch center, you may see another picture. I'll now characterize what happens here:

1. CSRs transmit trouble tickets to the dispatch center.
2. Early in the morning, a dispatch manager reviews the tickets and manually puts them in a basket for a technician scheduled to be in a given geographic area. There are six tickets in the basket because the dispatch manager believes that the technician will take 45 minutes per job plus travel time and breaks.
3. One technician picks up his tickets at 8:00 in the morning and drives 20 minutes to his first job, arriving at 8:20 a.m. It's more complex than expected and takes two hours. He completes the job, returns to the truck, scans the pile of tickets, and heads to the next job. It takes him 30 minutes to get there because of traffic, plus he stops for coffee. He arrives at the next job at 11 a.m.
4. On the next job, he realizes that he doesn't have the right parts on the truck and he'll have to come back another day. He calls the CSR on his radio and reports this problem so that the part can be ordered. Meanwhile, the customer is angry because he had to stay home from work and still has a broken phone line. It's lunchtime. The technician breaks for 75 minutes. He then scans the pile of tickets and decides to head for the next job. He drives 30 minutes and arrives at the next job at 1:45 p.m. After a quick diagnosis, he starts the repair, which takes two hours. He calls the disposition in to the CSR and figures it's almost time to quit, so he drives back to the depot.
5. Of the six jobs the technician was assigned, he completed two, couldn't complete the repair on one, and returned three jobs to the bin of incomplete work.

I don't know about you, but many customers would find such an experience maddening. The interesting thing about this situation is that it's what really happened. This present method of operation (PMO) was "business as usual" and acceptable by everyone associated with this process—except for me. It was incomprehensible that customers take a day off from work to wait for a technician who's a no-show. I don't need to elaborate; you've all been there. This work flow is visualized for you in Figure 5.3.

Figure 5.3 Present Method of Operation

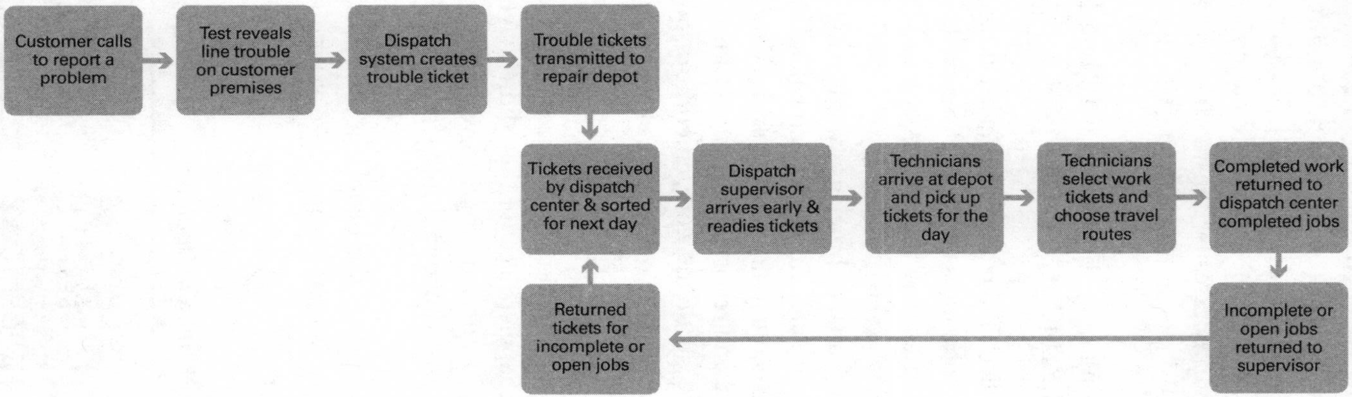

I always think about customers and how a customer interacts with or experiences a business or a product. It didn't occur to the previous product manager to consider new methods that might make things simpler and faster. Business people should always be thinking of enhancements to current processes by considering a possible future method of operation (FMO)—shown in simple steps in the simplified flow chart in Figure 5.4.

To make a long story short, here's what I ultimately focused on with the product as the FMO.

1. We installed GPS receivers in the trucks and gave the technicians portable computers that had wireless data access. The technicians, in many cases, took their trucks home to save commuting time to a dispatch center.
2. In the morning, technicians would go to their truck and turn on the computer. They would download the best job for them based on geographic location, skill set, tools and equipment on the truck, and reported traffic conditions. The technician would get to the job, do the work, enter the disposition in the computer, and download the next job considering the same parameters.

The result was a 50 percent improvement in productivity, happier technicians, and a reduction in the size of the workforce. Additionally, customers were happier because they didn't have to stay home all day; they were offered a three-hour window in which the technician would come to their house. Although the system wasn't perfect, it worked about 75 percent of the time.

The key here is that the people in the system had not been scrutinizing their process; they were just carrying out their basic duties.

Figure 5.4 Future Method of Operation

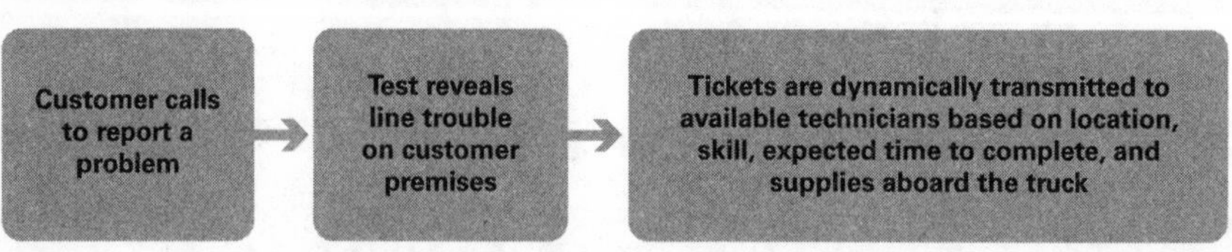

They weren't taught to look for efficiencies and to streamline work with new technologies. Needless to say, it should be part of every business person's job to keep an eye out for how things can be done more efficiently.

PROCESS IMPROVEMENT

Into the fabric of this book, I have woven some very important points. Among them is the need for businesses to have the right people who can understand customer needs and produce products to meet those needs better than the competitors. The other is for these companies to rapidly adapt to changing conditions.

Improving operating efficiency is no small task. In my research, I've learned that process improvement is fraught with challenges. When I spoke earlier about the importance of being a systemic thinker, it was because of the need for business people to be able to view business activities from various intersections of processes and people. As businesses evolve, leaders try new techniques to improve processes and work efficiency—and there are many. In my research for this book, I came upon numerous texts and articles that espoused as many methodologies. Having worked in the corporate world for many years, I've also been exposed to a number of process improvement programs. Unfortunately, process improvements don't always "stick" in an organization. Here are a few reasons why:

1. Single points of failure in a department or a part of a company are addressed separately. These ad hoc solutions or fixes to process problems aren't well documented or shared. This distributed approach to informal process fixes isn't viewed from a corporate perspective, and therefore, others don't benefit, and the process failures are likely to recur in other areas when least expected.
2. Process improvement programs look good on paper and in books, but in fact, they are difficult for employees to adopt if there isn't a way to transition from what they do to what they should do.

3. Process "owners" are not well integrated within the firm and are seen as a separate silo. Employees see them as being the flavor of the week and believe that if they're sufficiently ignored, they'll go away. In reality, though, these process owners don't do a good job of educating employees and "selling" the ideas, clarifying the goals, and helping those employees to figure out what steps must be taken.

EXERCISE

Find out what process improvement techniques have been undertaken in your company.

One of the lessons I've learned about process improvement is that it must be ongoing and continuous. W. Edwards Deming was an engineer and management consultant. He became a champion of the continuous improvement method symbolized by PDCA, or plan-do-check-act (www.deming.org). Regardless, much of his focus was centered on improved product design, quality, and testing.

The PDCA model is a good way to look at work activities in cycles. The basic elements of the PDCA model include:

- *Plan:* identification of specific issues, quality problems, or any other items that could be the object of study. If you have a product in the market and customers continually complain about it, you need to know what the complaints involve and why those complaints are being made.
- *Do:* development and testing of the potential solution (as in a prototype, updated process, etc.). A team of people may brainstorm about various ways to solve the problem. Sometimes they'll develop *prototypes* or *models*, find new product materials, experiment with new systems, or devise other ways to come up with solutions. *Do* does not mean implement; it means *try out*.
- *Check:* evaluation of outcomes and feedback to prior phases as needed. Some teams may get people inside the company or customers to try the solution or test the updated product.

Feedback is needed at this point in order to improve the chances that the solution will add value to the business.

- *Act:* implementation of the solution. However, implementing doesn't mean that you're done. If you're committed to continuous improvement, then you'll keep evaluating the system of things going on, processes utilized, and other items that results in more responsive steering of the business.

To extend PDCA further, in my product management work, I use a product management life cycle model to look at a product's business from a holistic perspective. Figure 5.5 shows how gathered market insights and strategies contribute to focused product planning and product introduction and the positive business contributions after the product is launched. Notice that there are feedforward, concurrent, and feedback mechanisms as well, represented by the arrows. However, it's true work as a PDCA oriented model really comes into play when outcomes ultimately influence possible new products or innovations. Further, PDCA thinking for products is vital because it can pinpoint areas that need improvement that could cover product investment decision making, development cycle time, launch efficiency, and customer satisfaction.

Recall that like any improvement initiative, PDCA must be linked to specific goals that the company is trying to achieve. For example, if some products are more mature and less profitable and the goal for the company is to focus on more revenue from recently introduced products, then efficiencies would be sought in areas related to those newer products, and not to the older ones.

Figure 5.5 The Product Management Life Cycle Model

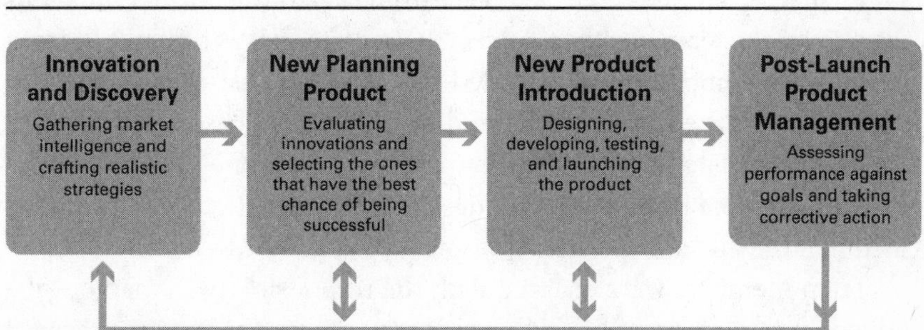

To extend PDCA and put it into a broader context, there is another method that is worthy of note. It's known as *kaizen* and was adopted in Japan after World War II based on both quality ideals from the United States and Japanese philosophies. A process improvement initiative is known as a kaizen event, and each event targets a designated process. These events are led by a delegated process improvement manager who trains the team members on the kaizen principles. Process team members are from the functions or areas that touch the given process. The team collectively studies the process and problem and then derives the goal for the process improvement, determines milestones, and manages the implementation of the improved process. Some team members may have unique expertise in the process and its use in the business and are designated as subject matter experts. As the team members explore the problem and come up with alternative solutions, they are in fact using PDCA methods. Here's a more detailed look at what happened in a firm I worked with several years ago.

A major human resources company created a single new customer service center to consolidate three smaller centers. The purpose was to reduce overhead, simplify workforce scheduling, and integrate the three customer service systems into one. The operation took approximately one year. While the implementation seemed to have progressed smoothly, it was learned that sales revenue had declined by 20 percent in areas that were typically from agent upsell programs. Executives in IT services, customer care, and finance decided to charter a kaizen team to investigate and solve this problem. They established a goal to improve revenue from upsell and cross-sell programs by 30 percent within six months.

The kaizen team was led by the IT services manager. Other team members were from marketing, operations, technology infrastructure, and finance. A service center manager from each of the former locations was also on the team. Lastly, a subject matter expert was brought in from the software company that provided the platform that consolidated all three systems. The kaizen leader and the executives described the situation and facilitated a workshop to make sure everyone knew what was to come, the time frames, and the desired outcomes. Leaders communicated that they would be available as needed.

Team members were charged with the responsibility to map out the individual process for inbound service requests for the past year as well to bring in a host of statistics. At the next meeting, the three former service center leads reviewed the inbound call process flow based on the procedures and systems that were in place. The software subject matter expert was familiar with those as well because he had been on the team that created the consolidated call flows. During the review, the call flow diagrams roughly included this information:

1. A customer would call in with a question.
2. The service representative would take the customer's name and look up the customer's record.
3. When the record appeared on the screen, it would show what services were currently in place, and the representative would address the issue on the call.
4. Two of the three centers had an automated routine that would "pop a sales script" on the screen that was triggered by the system's real-time analysis of the products being used by the customer and whether the call was a good call (with a customer that used the service, paid bills on time, and where the problem was easy to solve). The representatives would classify the customer and click on an indicator on their monitor that would pop the best script for that call situation so the representative could introduce the customer to the new product. Additionally, the representatives received a cash incentive for completing those incremental sales.
5. Other statistics were also examined such as hold times, time to resolve issues based on issue type, and postcall surveys of customer satisfaction.

What was ultimately learned during deep discussions and probing was that the new system did not have the agent scripting functionality in place. The team learned that the entire inbound call process was faster by about 20 seconds because the system would use the callers' phone numbers to look up their records in the database. Total call handling times had decreased as well by about a minute, due to the fact that the agents weren't selling new services because the scripts weren't popping up.

In the final analysis, the team realized quickly that the integration project had failed to consider the scripting module. No one could figure out who had made that decision, so it was a serious oversight. The final recommendation was to implement the scripting module. This took approximately two months, and within three months after that implementation, incremental sales increased by more than 50 percent.

Across the landscape of business process improvement, there are several common denominators that are predictors of success. First, the executive contributes greatly in the deployment of resources for a process improvement team. Second, the team members must have deep knowledge of the process and how people in their organization touch that process. As the team members learn about all the touch points, together, they gain the holistic, systemic perspective required to understand where inefficiencies occur. Third, the team should be empowered to uncover the ideas and opportunities that can be shaped into a final solution.

SUMMARY

Throughout your business career, whether you follow prescribed documentation or not, you will leverage processes to get work done. You'll also find that some processes have a lot of manual work, some are automated, and many are somewhere in between. Effective processes serve to help rather than hinder progress so that you can be productive and efficient.

To learn about processes so that you can be a more astute manager, you must turn on your process radar. This means you should know the main processes in your company, how work flows across departments, who the accountable people are, and how the work of these people is integrated so that business goals can be met. You'll learn much from who's who as you build your cross-functional network of contacts. Your systemic mindset will continue to form as you make mental connections between processes and people. Ultimately, you'll know which processes add the most value to the business, and which ones less. The most important benefit will be realized when you know which processes affect the quality of your products or the customer experience. When you master this knowledge, you'll have the wherewithal to prioritize your own work or to help others if they get bogged down. And when things go wrong, as they invariably will at times, you can focus your radar on the root cause of the problem using the control mechanisms mentioned earlier (feedforward, concurrent, and feedback) to keep things moving along in real time or near-real time. If those timely midcourse corrections fail to produce a more positive outcome, then a more structured process improvement protocol is called for.

INCREASING YOUR MANAGEMENT COMPETENCY

1. Find out if your company has a process management or process improvement group. If so, make arrangements to meet some of the people there to find out if there's a process library or equivalent collection of business processes.
2. As you meet new people in your company, ask them to sketch out some of the key processes that they utilize, both within their department and between their department and others. This will help you figure out who does what with whom, as discussed in Chapter 2.
3. If you're in a newer business and the processes haven't been carefully documented, think about how you can contribute. Take a look at how marketing, selling, finance, and other work activities are carried out. Create simple flow diagrams and short descriptions. Save these in a shared resource, and work on them over time. Then you can talk to others about things that work well and things that don't. From here, you can involve people in how to improve a given process. You'll continue to enhance your credibility and become more visible!
4. To better familiarize yourself with your company and how it works, *make the time* to visit call centers, operations centers, distribution facilities, and other parts of the company. You will become more conversant in company operations and add to your credibility.
5. If there is an innovation team in your company, see if you can observe a brainstorming session. These techniques are important when you're trying to figure out how to interpret and act on process data for potential process improvement programs.

6. Walk around your office. As you see what people are doing, perhaps you could introduce yourself and find out which processes they use. Sometimes, people in a given department put their performance charts on the wall. Those who created these charts could make a great resource.

Action Planning

In this chapter, the following characteristics were either explicitly or implicitly revealed. You may wish to identify where these were mentioned to reinforce your understanding of how they might be applied in your own work. You can also utilize the following template as a way to associate what was discussed in this chapter with your scores from your Business Acumen Assessment. From this, you can create an action plan for yourself or work with your manager to come up with specific goals and plans.

- Managing
- Defining processes
- Being a self-starter
- Adapting to changing situations
- Critical thinking
- Systemic thinking
- Solving problems
- Entrepreneurial thinking
- Listening attentively
- Observing actively
- Evaluating business performance
- Improving business processes

ACTION ITEM + GOAL	STEPS TO BE TAKEN	OUTCOME PRODUCED	WHAT YOU LEARNED	WHAT YOU WILL SHARE

USING DATA TO SOLVE PROBLEMS AND MAKE DECISIONS

After you read this chapter, you should be able to:

- Understand the business data in your company.
- Define data sources and the associated uses for that data.
- Link data usage with key business processes.
- Apply data to a structured problem-solving process.
- Describe how decisions are made.

All things are subject to interpretation.

—FRIEDRICH NIETZSCHE

We live in a world with an overwhelming amount of data. It's so pervasive that we don't think that much about it. Consider this: you're walking down the street as you pass a McDonald's. Your phone vibrates to offer you 20 percent off of a cheeseburger. You have an extra 10 minutes and you're hungry—why not? You're just about to drive into the Midtown Tunnel, heading out of New York City, when a sign warns you that it's 53 minutes to get to the Cross Island Parkway, which is only 12 miles away. That's a lot of stop-and-go traffic. You quickly open an app that has crowd-sourced traffic notifications so you can figure out if you should take the service road or head up to the RFK-Triborough Bridge to get through Queens. Every situation requires you to sift through what's important and make the right decision at the right time.

Businesses run on data. It's a premium fuel that gives everyone in the business the wherewithal to make plans, uncover and solve problems as they arise, steer the business, and keep things moving and growing. After all, no one wants a stagnant business.

OK. So we all know there's tons of data out there, but what can be done with it? We're all not imbued with an extra set of data analysis genes, yet the data spigot is open all the time. When this happens, we have a flood of data, and if we don't stay afloat, we'll drown in it. What you will want is a way to embrace what's important and to take action as warranted.

In this chapter, I explain why one of the most important anchors of any business is data. However, data in a vacuum is meaningless. Business people must know which data is needed from any number of processes in order to gauge progress and make corrections. Data, specifically good data, is vital for the following reasons:

- Data offers the ability to produce the evidence of progress toward goals.
- Data helps business people understand the source of business problems.
- Data supports optimal decision making.
- Data contributes to the creation of performance metrics that help to run the business and fine-tune operations.

Your ability to harness and manage data to solve problems and make decisions is critical to your success in business. As you play various roles in your business career, you'll always want to keep an eye out for data that's of sufficient quality. It should be complete, accurate, relevant, and timely. One senior executive made it clear when he said to me, "Data that's two weeks old in our business is obsolete. . . . If we don't have current, accurate data, we cannot stay ahead of the competition." Business people must also be adept at identifying the data needed to simplify complex situations, pursuing that data from appropriate resources, and using clever questions to draw out insights from others, especially if they're reluctant to share them.

Given my statements earlier about the abundance of data, when it comes to data inside a larger company, there are some challenges. Sometimes the needed data is inaccessible, insufficient, or just plain incorrect. Yet, in the realm of larger companies, data is often kept inside the walls of the functional departments, in multiple databases managed by the IT shop, and not always made available to others who might further contribute, or derive a benefit. When people seek out data because they have to work on a project of some kind, their perspectives tend to be limited to their ability to search, their available time, and their own paradigms. In fact, you may find instances in which people in various parts of the company do not know what data is available or where that data resides. When required, it is *essential* to understand:

- What data is needed and for what purpose
- Where data comes from
- How data is secured, by whom, and how it's aggregated to create information

Aristotle once said, "The whole is more than the sum of its parts." It's a vital reminder of what I've reinforced in preceding chapters, emphasizing the importance of seeing the bigger picture, not just a finite view of your own department or work area. To magnify this point, think about what you see when you observe a painting from afar versus up close. An up-close examination doesn't necessarily allow you to fully appreciate what the artist had in mind. *For data to convey the proper meaning, it has to be evaluated from the right vantage point.*

Even when the requisite data is available, you must consider your own mindset and preferences. If the bulk of your experience has been in a functional area such as engineering or operations, you're geared toward *vertical* evaluations of functional data. Instead, business people must be able to look at data both *horizontally and vertically* in an integrated, *holistic* manner to produce defensible insights and findings. This means that *data collection and analysis can and should be a collaborative undertaking,* leveraging a dynamic set of inputs and the perspectives of others, to more effectively isolate and solve problems.

TYPES OF DATA

In any company, data takes two main forms: financial and nonfinancial. Financial data relates to revenue, costs, and expenses as I conveyed in Chapter 4. These data elements are woven into various ratios or calculations that compare plans to actuals in order to uncover variances.

Financial data is organized according to standards set by accounting bodies, and its use is generally consistent across companies. The challenge with financial data alone is that it only provides mile markers with respect to near-term activity such as monthly revenue and profit.

Nonfinancial data is derived from the work of people in various functions and the processes that they utilize. This data can provide clues into activities and outcomes over time and can measure true progress in a given area, especially when associated with other data. Unfortunately, there are no standards that cover nonfinancial data, so its usage may be guided by leaders or people who work in different functions. To put this in context, if leaders want to improve their firms' market share (a nonfinancial indicator), they may want to invest more in R&D and marketing. Those increases in spending will result in lower profit in the near term, and hopefully, greater financial contributions later.

I'll be discussing the integration of financial and nonfinancial measures in more detail in Chapter 11. However, I do want to share with you some typical nonfinancial data used by companies. A company may record the number of:

- Orders per day
- Customer inquiries per month
- Customer complaints
- Product defects
- Website visitors
- SKUs used in a product
- New product ideas
- Late payments received
- Products owned by customers
- Purchase orders issued
- Kilowatts of electricity used in a factory
- Products listed in a product catalog

Imagine how much nonfinancial data exists in your company. If you put 10 people in a room and brainstormed for an hour, you could probably come up with a list of dozens, if not hundreds. Try it sometime, especially if you are serious about this topic. You'll find that every department has its own data. Some is recorded, and some is not. Some data elements are used frequently, and some are not. *With so many indicators, it's important to find the right ones that can be sensibly integrated to track progress, uncover problems, solve those problems, and take positive steps to improve the business.* How this data could be selected can be viewed in the following example.

At Starbucks, like any retailer, getting customers in and out of the store as efficiently as possible is of paramount importance. However, if leaders don't put this on their radar screen, then it won't be studied and a positive change to the business could be missed. Interestingly, a number of years ago, I went to visit my local Starbucks. I noticed a person with a clipboard and stopwatch observing the line of people in the store and recording notes. I had a feeling about what she was doing and decided to ask her directly. She was working for Starbucks and explained she was studying how much time people spent in line, how long it took to take an order, how much time a barista took to fill an order, and even how much time customers spent adding condiments to their beverage. Each click on-and-off of her stopwatch was recorded as a piece of data. In the big picture, she was studying customer cycle time—a major process! I surmised that leaders at Starbucks might have been getting complaints from people waiting in line. Whatever their motivation at the time, some nonfinancial indicators must have suggested to Starbucks' leaders that they needed to pay attention to this data and improve the customer experience. I learned later on that Starbucks changed its coffee machines from manual operation to automated (place the beans in the hopper and push a button) to improve cycle time and improve the overall customer experience. In this particular store that I frequented, it changed the customer traffic pattern, too. In reflecting on this experience, I have to believe that Starbucks studies each store to find out what products each customer buys, how long each product takes to prepare, and a host of other data. For you, the important takeaway is to understand that the selection of specific nonfinancial data elements associated with a given process can reveal important, actionable information.

EXERCISE

- Create a simple functional organization chart for your company, or the part of the company in which you work.
- For each department, find out which are the top five data elements used to operate that department, where that data resides, how often it is collected, and why it's used.
- What are the key issues that emerge when data is harbored in functional departments?

SOURCES AND USES OF DATA

As you may surmise, it's easy to speak about data; it's harder to secure it and use it. In a company, the CFO determines the working capital requirements by analyzing the sources and uses of funds. With data, sources and uses are dependent on what's to be evaluated. In many cases, data is associated with a process. As a first step in building your knowledge in this area, a *sources and uses of data map* can be created. This can be accomplished using the template shown in Figure 6.1.

Figure 6.1 Sources and Uses of Data Template

PROCESS	WHAT'S TO BE EVALUATED?	WHY?	WHAT DATA IS NEEDED?	WHERE IS THE DATA?	WHO OWNS THE DATA?

Now, I'll show you how to use this type of template. Suppose you work in the customer service department of a company, and your role is to track the number of complaints that come over the telephone or via the firm's website. Every month, you're required to produce a customer service effectiveness report to provide to the chief operating officer (COO) of the company. Right now, your goal is to educate a new person about the sources and uses of data. Refer to the sample shown in Figure 6.2 to see how this template can be used.

Notice how easily this tool can be used to carry out the training of another person. Imagine if a sources and uses of data map were in place across the entire business. Information might flow more easily across organizational boundaries with greater speed, contributing to overall organizational agility. This can be of extraordinary value when you're vigorously competing for business.

As you endeavor to enhance your ability to see the bigger picture about the business, use the following steps to connect some of the dots. I include some references to prior chapters that may shed additional light.

- To understand where data is kept, by whom, and why, you might use what I discussed in Chapter 2 as you construct organizational connection charts. This provides you with the

Figure 6.2 Sources and Uses of Data Example

PROCESS	WHAT'S TO BE EVALUATED?	WHY?	WHAT DATA IS NEEDED?	WHERE IS THE DATA?	WHO OWNS THE DATA?
Customer Complaint Handling Process	How many people call in by the hour and why they're calling	1. Evaluate customer call-in traffic patterns 2. Calculate proper staffing levels for the call center 3. Determine sufficiency of call-handling capacity to maintain service levels	Inbound call traffic data	Call routing data in the PABX (i.e., telephone switch)	The company communications manager in the IT department
			Incident report data	Customer complaints in the customer relationship management system database	The department head in charge of customer relationships

framework to carry out conversations with others as you better understand who does what with whom. As you become more experienced, you'll find that you may need to check multiple sources to ensure that you have the most complete set of data.

- To gain a deeper perspective on any process, refer to the process hierarchy in Chapter 5. If you're working with the data stakeholders (for example, the manager of a functional department), you should be able to determine which process requires which data set in order for the process outcomes to be achieved.
- Recall that everything boils down to money. In Chapter 4, I described how finances are used in a business. In the preceding example, if there were a lot of customer complaints from faulty products, and if people had a difficult time contacting the company, you would have some very unhappy customers and probably suffer from deteriorating finances.

DATA ANALYSIS

In one of my former roles as a financial analyst, one of my responsibilities was to analyze the profit and loss (P&L) for the company. I would compare the budgeted numbers to the actual performance and analyze the differences, or variances. When I performed this work, I learned how to look behind every number. In essence, I felt like I was examining the data behind the data. The insights I gained were instrumental to the conclusions and recommendations I made to my bosses.

I recently read an article in an auto enthusiast publication about self-driving cars. The story talked about how scientists installed hundreds of sensors in test vehicles. These sensors took in data about vehicle position, speed, obstacles, proximity to other vehicles, and a host of other signals to keep a car moving without crashing into anything. This led me to think about how those of us who drive cars have to process many signals, almost unconsciously, in order to keep the car in the correct lane, to slow down or speed up, and to safely get us to our destination—all within the time that it takes to blink an eyelid. Whether in a computer or your brain, a lot can happen in very short time intervals! Likewise, a business that operates in any market must be properly steered. To achieve this, it needs data about products that customers buy, prices paid, and revenue received. It also needs data about the operational performance of different departments designed to detect how efficiently the business is operating.

Data collection and analysis also plays a crucial role in strategic planning, a topic I'll explore in Chapter 8. Sometimes, insights and observations are collected through a technique referred to as *environmental scanning*. Business people who work in marketing, sales, service, or even finance can be quite adept at this from their internal and external observations and perspectives. Internal observations can also be reinforced by financial and nonfinancial data. Data about customers and competitors provides the external indicators. Therefore, data associated with profits earned from sales to a particular group of customers, against any number of competitors, is used as a set of factors that influence future strategies.

As your analytical capability evolves, you'll realize that the manner in which you assess data will be impacted by your paradigms and beliefs. These form what's known as a *mental model*. A mental model is simply an illustration inside your mind of one or more external realities. Mental models are concerned with our understanding or knowledge about the world around us. We don't come wired with one mental model; we have a woven mesh of them inside our heads. Knowing this, when it comes to analyzing a given situation, uncovering a true problem, and deciding how to address that problem, you will benefit from the opinions and ideas of others in different areas of the firm that help drive toward the best decision possible. This is also why it's so important to cultivate those relationships across the company.

Knowing how our minds are wired can help up to a point. Regardless of your title, you will benefit from an analytical process that contributes to your understanding of what's needed to steer the company. In business, the processes used and the data produced serve as mileposts to determine subsequent steps, just like your speedometer, fuel gauge, and visual observations help you keep the car on the road. Some processes may be straight through, and others may have twists and turns. Those who study decision making in universities and elsewhere use the term *heuristics* to describe the routines and subroutines that are followed to make decisions. To go through these routines, you must make sure you have the right data at the right time to keep the business moving in the right direction and to take corrective action when required.

In the sections that follow, I discuss two important uses of data: solving problems and making decisions. Notice the term *uses* of data, which represents an important part of the "sources and uses" model shown earlier.

USING DATA TO SOLVE PROBLEMS

Business people must both collect and analyze data so that they can uncover and solve problems. Those who do are valued by their bosses because of the curiosity they display and the insights they shape. As a business leader, I was always interested in the identification and validation of customer needs based on the problems they faced. However, oftentimes, customers couldn't express their need as a problem that required a solution. To reinforce this point, I once interviewed a market researcher who worked for a bank. She described a situation where customer representatives and bank branch people indicated that a number of customers were requesting a credit card with more control over spending limits. Although she believed she understood what they wanted, she conducted additional research and interviews to validate what she was hearing. She learned that the customers couldn't adequately explain why they wanted these limits. She discovered that the people who were making the request were in the Latin American market segment in the Los Angeles, California, area. Therefore, there were language problems that caused some confusion in how information was communicated from the customers to the bank. Thus, further research got to the data behind the data and ultimately revealed that customers in this population had an overall mistrust of banks and were concerned that their card numbers might be stolen or compromised, and the customers thought if they could make their credit limits lower, they would protect their families from financial ruin! What the marketing person ultimately learned was that these customers were concerned about the safety and security of their money. *In business, if you don't know what problem you're solving for a customer, it's hard to create something of value for that customer.*

How many times has someone come up to you and said, "I've got a problem." You have to ask a lot of questions to find out what happened to make sure that you see the same thing as the person who's reporting the problem. Now, think about what happens when you go to the doctor because of an ailment of some kind. The doctor asks you a lot of questions, runs some tests, and tries to narrow down the choices. Sometimes the doctor has to call in other specialists when the case becomes complex. Ultimately, the diagnostic process helps to identify the root cause of the problem so it can be treated. And so it goes in business.

In business, management often presents one person or a team of people with a situation that needs to be resolved. Sometimes it takes a lot of digging to find the right data. When you or your team get the data, it needs to be analyzed so that a host of alternatives can be surfaced and considered. Then, each of those alternatives needs to be analyzed so that a decision can ultimately be made. This is the same diagnostic process used by the physician.

I would like to provide you with a simple tool for diagnosing a problem and coming up with a recommendation that can be carried out. As shown in Figure 6.3, I use the acronym DECIDE to guide you through each dimension of the problem-solving process. Then, I present a brief case to walk you through the steps of the DECIDE process.

- *Define the problem.* In business, a host of challenges are presented to us every day. In order to set the stage to solve any

Figure 6.3 The DECIDE Problem-Solving Process

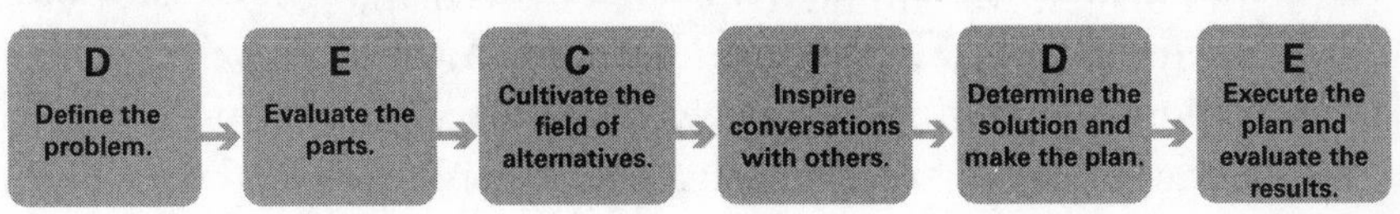

problem, it must be properly exposed and described. This is done through the creation of a *problem statement*. To compose the problem statement, you need to know what happened, to whom, when, where, and why.

- *Evaluate the parts.* It's always easier when you can take a complex problem and break it down into smaller pieces so that each can be examined more closely. The parts are made up of various data elements that verify that the problem is present and important.
- *Cultivate the field of alternatives.* Once problems are broken down into small pieces, you can start to consider what you might do. Whether you brainstorm on a whiteboard or with a couple of colleagues, you can come up with a number of alternatives or choices for further consideration.
- *Inspire conversations with others.* The cultivation of alternatives may present many options that need to be vetted. This is the time when your political capital can be invested through the solicitation of input from others. After all, in any organization, buy-in from the main stakeholders will help to fine-tune possible solutions and ensure that able resources are ready when needed.
- *Determine the solution and make the plan.* Ultimately, a decision will have to be made about what steps to take, who will be involved, and other considerations for implementation.
- *Execute the plan and evaluate the results.* Once you've chosen your path, all resources must be flawlessly deployed so that the plan can come alive. As the plan is carried out, results are evaluated to keep things on course.

Now, consider the following case analysis. I start with a brief situational profile and then take you through the steps of the DECIDE process.

CASE ANALYSIS: SMALL BANK VERSUS BIG BANKS

You are the general manager at a branch of a small, highly successful local bank. You have worked for the bank for many years and have developed great relationships with small business customers and the consumers in your community. As you were analyzing the bank's data and some local economic reports, here's what you found:

1. The number of consumer bank depositors is growing 3 percent per month.
2. The number of student checking accounts is up 12 percent over last year, but the average balance for those accounts is $250. That's not enough for any of those accounts to be profitable to the bank.
3. Five percent of business customers are writing checks with insufficient funds. While penalty fees are increasing, that's not where the bank wants to make its money.
4. Home mortgage applications are up 5 percent over the past year.
5. The Department of Commerce just issued a report that permits for new homes is up by 42 percent over the past year.
6. Your Net Promoter Score or NPS (a tool used to determine if customers will recommend your bank) has started to contract from a 9.5 to 7.2 (out of 10 points) over the past six months.

Your area is undergoing a lot of development. A state university opened a satellite campus in the area, and there are many new homes under construction. Many firms are leasing space in new office buildings, and shopping centers are popping up all around town. Business has been so great that two major banks are opening branches within eyesight of your branch. Both are set to open in two weeks. What should you do? Monitor the logic in the table shown in Figure 6.4.

In this case, the data that was analyzed by the general manager provided him with several indicators that the business could have been on shaky ground. As can be seen, the situation was more easily framed because it was supported by data, and that allowed for the DECIDE process to be undertaken. In the end, the bank made some solid decisions that positioned it for continued growth in a changing market.

Figure 6.4 DECIDE Model

<table>
<tr><td>D
Define the problem.</td><td>Oftentimes, small businesses are caught by surprise and without a contingency plan. They may feel constrained by their limited resources. In this case, the looming problem relates to a growing population and the opening of big banks. The general manager and a small team of employees discuss the situation and generate the following problem statement:

Our community bank has a great reputation and has grown steadily for many years. Now, our bank may lose market share because the big banks will steal the customers with teaser rates on credit cards and new programs for young college students.</td></tr>
<tr><td>E
Evaluate the parts.</td><td>There are many facets to this situation that may be surfaced and subject to deeper analysis. Some of the piece parts of the problem can be broken down as follows:
1. How customers feel about community banks versus big banks
2. How the products of smaller banks compare with those of the big banks
3. What the experience is like to do business with community banks versus big banks
4. How fees of community banks compare to those of larger banks
As you may surmise, this list could be quite extensive, and each area would require some research in order to qualify and quantify the impact.</td></tr>
<tr><td>C
Cultivate the field of alternatives.</td><td>Once the piece parts were researched and data was exposed, the manager and his team discussed the implications. They learned that their focus was on their fear of incursion into their market area. However, their research helped them to see that there were many benefits they offered to their customers. They decided to choose from one or two of these areas:
1. Capitalize on the personal service and stellar customer relationships. They felt they needed to invest some money into advertising and other programs to reinforce this.
2. Because they are in a growing area, and their small business loans are approved more quickly than those of big banks, they could focus on building their small business loan portfolio.
3. With the influx of students, they could sell more free deposit accounts to grow new longer-term relationships.</td></tr>
<tr><td>I
Inspire conversations with others.</td><td>The team prepared a presentation and workshop for the leadership team in the corporate headquarters. First, they provided a contextual backdrop for the situation and presented their findings. They emphasized the importance of the conversations and discussions about the pros and cons of each item. The leadership team members were pleased with the work that was done and shared some of the research they had conducted. At the conclusion of the meeting, the leadership team suggested that they meet the following week to agree on the final choice(s).</td></tr>
<tr><td>D
Determine the solution and make the plan.</td><td>At the follow-up meeting, the leadership team initiated a conversation to discuss revisions to the strategy. They first indicated that their excellent growth over the past several years was attributed to all the values they stood for: personal service and fast loan decisions. They knew that after the big celebrations of the big bank openings, they'd fall back on their traditional business models—lots of products, teaser programs, insufficient staffing in the branches, and so on. The team all agreed that they would do the following:
1. Invest in some remodeling of branches to include business work spaces. They believe that the business community would benefit from the ability to share success stories and help solve problems; after all, it's a community bank.
2. Increase advertising expenditures during the next month to remind their customer base, and new customers, of the benefits of simplicity and ease of doing business.</td></tr>
<tr><td>E
Execute the plan and evaluate the results.</td><td>Everyone was energized by the decisions that were made. The branch upgrades were completed in a few weeks, and the new work spaces were a huge success. Branch traffic actually increased as word got around. New deposits and new loan applications increased markedly. Also, when the school year began, the branch closest to the campus made arrangements to provide a university co-branded website to create a greater level of affiliation and closer ties. The bank was also invited to deliver workshops on financial planning for the students.</td></tr>
</table>

EXERCISE

Apply the DECIDE problem-solving model to a particular problem or challenge you may face at work. Once done, review the outcome to see how the process may have sped up your ability to solve the problem.

DECISION MAKING

One of the most important things that business people need to do, regardless of their job level in the company, is recognize there are always decisions to make because there are always problems to solve. As you can see from the case, the problem-solving sequence based on the DECIDE process had to consider alternatives so that a decision could be made.

Agility of thought and comprehension are of supreme value for all business people and those with whom they work. Experienced managers are thinkers who *decide* their way forward, always strategizing and restrategizing. They constantly ask, "What's right for the customers, the teams, and the business? What are the resources involved? What's the impact on the financial results?" Successful business people are continually reviewing situations in their minds and considering the available options second by second.

Optimal decisions can be made when you assimilate the varied cadences of the industry, evaluate the competition, consider the financial state of the business, and assess other data-driven performance indicators to properly frame a problem or situation. The greater the manager's familiarity with these indicators, the more rapidly they can be processed. This leads to greater rapidity in the decision-making process—and this speed is good for a business that needs to stay ahead of the competition.

In larger companies, many different people have to be included in the decision-making process. This involves dealing with various personality types. Some of these people need an endless barrage of data, which unduly extends the decision-making process. When decisions are delayed because of this drawn-out study, it's sometimes referred to as *analysis paralysis*. An unwanted outcome of extended analysis is a failure to act, opening you up to being beaten by a competitor. Others are seemingly comfortable with less data because of their "third eye" into other, more nebulous areas of the business environment. Sometimes, the less-is-more approach can lead to hasty decisions and ill-advised plans. The opposite of analysis paralysis is *rational ignorance* when you know you don't have enough data because the cost of securing the data might outweigh the benefit. Think of rational ignorance this way: if you want to find out what your boss wants for lunch, but he's in a bad mood, you'll get the tuna sandwich for him and hope you made the right choice rather than risk irritating him by asking.

Balancing the requirement for speed and the need for data is essential. As a matter of fact, this imperative is exerting increasing amounts of pressure on managers at all levels of the company. The multitude of variables in the equation for business people includes known strategies and tactics, cross-functional expertise, finances, competitor knowledge, competing initiatives, and your time, just to name a few. To reinforce a vital point: *accurate and timely data is your friend, and that data should be as correct and available as possible* so that the business decision maker is able to do what needs to be done.

An additional challenge in decision making today is in harnessing and analyzing huge troves of *unstructured data* moving through the company with increasing volume, speed, and complexity. For example, how can a company follow the interactions of customers on social networks, parse specific phrases, and equate those to other key performance indicators (KPIs) or financial information in the company to decide on what products to offer? What can be done with an ever-increasing influx of e-mails from customers to look for themes and trends? Further, there is a ton of data produced from people who are generally going about their business and connecting portable devices or even their cars to GPS receivers, or watching content on their digital gadgets. Software and other pattern-mapping tools will continue to add to the arsenal in data analysis, but ultimately, people have to be involved in making the call. In order to contribute to your knowledge on how decisions can be made beyond simple pros and cons, I'll offer you some options.

EXERCISE

One way to evaluate the complexity of required decisions in your own company is to identify the decisions that must be made, or those that are made. To do this, start to make a list of decisions that you're aware of that are being made by your executives, managers of other functions, and even your own department. How would you organize those? Which ones are strategic? Which ones involve meeting the needs of customers? Which ones are related to the improvement of a process? This may put you on the road to identifying more important priorities in your own work.

DECISION-MAKING TECHNIQUES

Perfect solutions are elusive. You can get closer to perfection through continued iteration and the combination of analytical techniques with some intuition. Ronald Howard wrote an article in the *Journal of Operations Research* (1980) entitled "An Assessment of Decision Analysis." One statement captured the reason for decision making. He wrote: "Decision making is what you do when you don't know what to do." Nonetheless, this process is made easier through adding some structure, allowing us to put alternatives into the proper perspective. In this way, we can drive the decision-making process to come up with the best conclusion.

However, if we get too caught up in the data itself, we might not be able to make the right decisions. For business people, the main questions to ask and decide upon would include:

1. How do we provide the best experience to our customers?
2. Who are the most important customers we should pursue?
3. Which products with which attributes will deliver the best value proposition?
4. What are the main problems or obstacles in our own company preventing us from achieving our financial goals?

Over the years, many of the managers I've coached and advised have stated that it's quite difficult for them to prioritize their work. The concept of prioritization falls into the same category as decision making. You'll always operate within an environment of constraints. In other words, you just can't do it all! Therefore, I present to you two methods for making fact-based, data-driven choices:

1. Combining options
2. The decision matrix

COMBINING OPTIONS

Although selecting between two options seems relatively simple, it's critical to consider the possibility that they aren't mutually exclusive. In other words, it is possible that both can be executed without working against each other in any noticeable way. In many cases when trying to come up with a decision, the choice of whether to execute *two or more options simultaneously* comes down to marginal cost and marginal value. When you're making a decision and you get hung up on two or three finalists that don't seem to stand out from each other, try to evaluate your options based on the following questions:

- Is there any reason why we can't do all of these?
- Can we find a way to afford them all?
- Do we have enough resources to execute them all?
- Do they interfere with each other?
- Is there marginal value in doing all of them?
- What is the marginal cost of simultaneously executing the second option? That is, what costs will the second option incur that the first option doesn't already cost us?
- What is the marginal value of simultaneously executing the second option? That is, what additional benefits will it bring that the first option alone won't achieve?

These marginal costs and benefits aren't always measurable in dollars, so be sure not to focus exclusively on budgetary impacts or benefits.

If we were to relate this technique to the bank case study described earlier, the team might have used this technique to select the options and costs so that they could connect those costs to the benefits that would accrue to the bank.

THE DECISION MATRIX

When you have a number of options, a more structured decision-making method is needed. Most of the time, this is where you'll find yourself. A decision matrix is a helpful tool to put options into perspective and to score each option based on a number of criteria. When you examine business challenges and opportunities from a holistic perspective, you have a better chance of making the right decision. There are two steps to follow in creating your initial matrix:

1. Identify the options.
2. Establish the criteria and rating scale.

For an easy example, refer to the case study highlighted earlier. First, I list a few items that the bank could spend money on; some were considered in the case, and others were left in the "suggestion box" at the bank. Then, I add some decision criteria against which each option can be evaluated. I use a rating scale from 1 to 10, with 10 indicating "most important." If you refer to Figure 6.5, you can see how these are arranged.

Now, knowing what you know, and if you could only choose two, regardless of financial outlay, it's simple to see that the advertising and branch upgrades should be considered above the others. Although I made it simple to see these differences between the lower scores and the higher scores, the difference between the first and second items is

Figure 6.5 Decision Matrix

CRITERIA / OPTION	STRATEGICALLY IMPORTANT TO OUR COMPANY	PROVIDES A BENEFIT TO OUR CUSTOMERS	DIFFERENTIATES US FROM COMPETITORS	DRIVES NEW BUSINESS	TOTAL
Advertising to reinforce image and brand	8	6	6	8	28
Investing in bank branch upgrades	8	9	7	7	31
Redesign of bank logo to enhance perception	2	2	5	3	12
Set up on-campus kiosk	3	8	2	7	20

less distinct. In the DECIDE process discussed earlier, this is where you'll want to focus on:

C—Cultivating the field of alternatives

I—Inspiring conversations with others

D—Determining the solution and making the plan

To continue this discussion, a more advanced way to use the decision matrix is to *assign a weight to each option*. The idea is to assign a greater or lesser weight to an individual criterion, or multiple criteria, depending on how important each is in the decision-making process. If you want to apply weights, then each of the criteria must be assigned some weight so that in each cell, *score* × *weight* = *weighted score*. Then, you total all the weighted scores in the rightmost column. In the end, you may not choose the option with the greatest score. The benefit, then, is to allow you to more clearly understand a given option based on its significance to the business and then debate the merits with others until a decision is reached.

You may now surmise that decision making is complex, but can be made simpler by breaking things down into smaller pieces and bringing cross-functional players to the table. When you have good relationships with others in the organization, these conversations become easier to inspire, and you can decide what to do with greater ease and efficiency in a more collaborative manner. In the end, those who can process signals and make quick decisions will keep their businesses in tip-top shape so they're as agile as they need to be in intensely competitive markets.

SUMMARY

To solve problems and make optimal decisions, business people must digest ever-increasing amounts of data. Your ability to understand and process data enables you to anticipate what might happen and consider the consequences of various actions. Business people who are adept at anticipating problems and developing contingency plans are highly valued by business leaders.

The challenge in business today is that the pace of data collection and the sheer volume of data can be overwhelming. Businesses are analyzing web traffic, click streams, and sales by the minute. Retailers and distributors transact business at lightning speed. B2B firms exchange electronic data to replenish inventories without human intervention. Many firms are even pairing their own business data with data from open sources. Also, massive amounts of data, both financial and nonfinancial, are being compiled and presented in interesting graphical formats, enabling business people to better assimilate the meaning. Other firms are drowning in data. Businesses that are able to select the best data to analyze for a given process or situation will be able to make optimal decisions over the long run. If your business is sophisticated enough to allow the data to speak for itself, decisions may be made that don't have the human element. In the end, the data—and any associated decisions that help to put customers first so that the business can thrive—is what will separate the best from the rest.

INCREASING YOUR MANAGEMENT COMPETENCY

1. In Chapter 2, you were introduced to a technique for creating an organizational connection chart. After reading this chapter, try enhancing that chart using the sources and uses of data template from Figure 6.1. This will enhance your ability to understand how data moves across the organization. It will also offer you clues about data requirements and cadences.
2. Related to the previous item, make sure that you are always enhancing your network of professional contacts who can provide information and support when needed. I'll remind you that people's willingness to help you is dependent on your willingness to help them when needed. Your network may be inside and outside of your company.
3. In Chapter 5, you learned that processes guide work activities. Many of those activities require data. As in item 1 above, try to use the sources and uses of data template to determine how data is used to stimulate a process, carry out work

activities, and evaluate the progress of work. This will be useful when I discuss business performance management later in the book.

4. Refer to areas in the Business Acumen Assessment related to critical thinking, systemic thinking, and problem solving. If you can relate what you've learned thus far in this book, you may notice that you're more effective in surfacing problems or making decisions.
5. Consider what happens when you're working with others to solve a problem and you feel you may not be getting to the heart of the issue. In this instance, persevere and probe more deeply to ensure that you have the best facts and data. Also, use other resources to expand your perspective to verify that the data is as complete as possible.
6. Check in with your manager to see what you can do to expand your scope of understanding about data in your company so that you can improve your analytical ability and your decision-making effectiveness.

Action Planning

In this chapter, the following characteristics were either explicitly or implicitly revealed. You may wish to identify where these were mentioned to reinforce your understanding of how they might be applied in your own work. You can also utilize the following template as a way to associate what was discussed in this chapter with your scores from your Business Acumen Assessment. From this, you can create an action plan for yourself or work with your manager to come up with specific goals and plans.

- Defining processes
- Making decisions
- Adapting to changing situations
- Deriving market insights
- Critical thinking
- Strategic thinking
- Solving problems

- Presenting persuasively
- Listening attentively
- Observing actively
- Taking action
- Earning credibility

ACTION ITEM + GOAL	STEPS TO BE TAKEN	OUTCOME PRODUCED	WHAT YOU LEARNED	WHAT YOU WILL SHARE

CHAPTER 7

MASTERING MARKETS

After you read this chapter, you should be able to:

- Evaluate market segments and customer types within a segment.
- Illustrate how customer needs and motivations are uncovered.
- Describe the purpose and structure of a customer value proposition.
- Explain how market insights are vital to the strategy of a company.

> *We see our customers as invited guests to a party, and we are the hosts. It's our job to make the customer experience a little bit better.*
>
> —JEFF BEZOS

Imagine waking up one day and feeling ravenously hungry. You open the refrigerator, and surprise—it's empty! It's time to head to the supermarket. You enter the store with your cart and proceed directly to the dairy department because you want to purchase eggs, milk, cheese, and yogurt. You arrive at the refrigerated egg display, where you notice many different varieties: white eggs, organic brown eggs, large eggs, jumbo eggs, and so on. Some are packaged in polystyrene foam, others in plastic, and still others in recycled cardboard. You're an environmentally conscious person, so you pick the organic brown eggs in the cardboard package. You didn't notice that those eggs were 50 percent higher in price than the large eggs in the polystyrene container. It's a simple process you've repeated many times.

Consumers are moved into a state of need based on a trigger event. In the case above, you were hungry (the need) and, thus, motivated (driven) to go to the market. In the store, you chose among competing products and brands. You made your selections based on what you could afford, what you value, and perhaps an image from a recent advertisement.

What's described here, in the simplest of terms, are the dynamics of a *market*. When the goings-on of any market are so visible, a lot is taken for granted. Nonetheless, there's a lot that goes on behind the scenes. Consider that each product on the shelf of a supermarket is a profit-making business for some company. Many well-run firms invest significant sums to research and assess what motivates customers and drives competitors. They do this so they can figure out which customers are most appealing to them, which products will resonate with those customers, and which competitors they will face.

In your personal life, you are a customer of some company every day. In your work life, you work in a business that produces a product or service for its own customers, and your company competes against an array of competitors. I want to make these market dynamics easy to understand by offering you a guide to learn how markets are evaluated and insights are derived.

MARKETS

When I speak to business leaders, they tend to talk a lot about their intent to focus on the market and on customers. However, some of the terms most commonly used to communicate this intent have numerous designations. These include terms such as *market focused*, *customer focused*, or *customer oriented*. Oftentimes, people substitute one of these terms for another, not truly understanding the difference between them. To eliminate confusion, it is crucial to have a firm definition of the word *market*. Simply put, a market is where buyers and sellers come together. If an organization is market focused, then it devotes its efforts to understanding the dynamics of those interactions. Buyers are customers, and sellers are competitors. A particular market area where buyers and sellers come together is called an *industry* or *sector*. Therefore, to be market focused is to comprehend the dynamics of a given market area and to concentrate business strategies on the fulfillment of unmet needs for customers in that market space.

THE IMPORTANCE OF MARKET INSIGHTS

Market insights are formed in the minds of people who have an almost intuitive awareness and appreciation of goings-on in a given market area, which can include a geography, population, or other segment. Insights can be an impetus for one person, such as a founder of a business, to take action. Insights can also inspire leaders in a larger business to create or update strategies and resultant plans. However, insights don't magically appear. They are realized as an outgrowth of ongoing market surveillance and research. Market insights are broader than insights about competitors, the industry environment, or customers. To shed light on the work involved in producing market insights, refer to Figure 7.1.

Based on my own studies, I've realized that when firms invest in the people and processes needed to conduct market research that corresponds to the speed of market movements, they are more successful

Figure 7.1 Market Insight Development

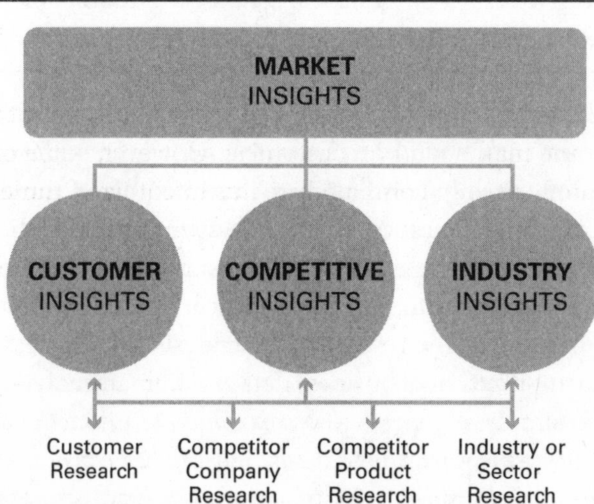

in guiding their businesses. An executive in a media company explained to me that her firm had dozens of people working as customer insight analysts who could be dispatched anywhere to observe people consuming information. What these analysts learn contributes to decisions about the products that get produced and the customer experience that gets created. Moreover, the analysts must be able to predict who will respond to specific messages so they can convey this to the advertisers they seek—and ultimately make money. Another executive I interviewed worked as the leader of product design at a mobile phone manufacturer. His team of more than 200 traveled the world observing people in social situations to better understand human behavior, including how individuals communicate with one another and how they use their mobile devices. After all, wouldn't you want your next smartphone, tablet, or other device to make your life easier based on what you do?

At the other end of the spectrum, there are many companies for which the market data needed to steer the business is either outdated or in short supply. There may be insufficient financial or human resources dedicated to doing the research, or those dedicated may not be deeply skilled in research practices. In many of these firms, there seems to be a belief that when a customer describes what he wants or a competitor takes a given action, the business must react. Although these seemingly automatic responses to market movements may have positive short-term effects, they often result in poorly considered product and market investment decisions that ultimately have negative long-term consequences.

To reinforce my points in the previous chapter, consider that successful businesses work like finely tuned automobile engines. Engines run on fuel and air. Businesses run on market data and insights. To be competitive, a company cannot afford to have its engine just sputtering along; it needs to ensure the engine is getting a steady supply of the proper fuel. Many well-run firms invest in powerful systems and analytical tools to capture and process huge amounts of transactional market data. Often this data is assimilated by these systems, and executives take action based on tabulated findings. The research and analysis I advocate for involves the timely harmonization of business data and human analytical thought. The reason is simple: *managers who can combine transactional, observational, and other timely, relevant data are more likely to produce innovative ideas and purposeful strategies.* Of greater importance for those who wish to excel, when you pursue the evaluation of market goings-on through self-study, you'll earn credibility and will also be seen as a self-starter.

LEARNING ABOUT CUSTOMERS

It's a known fact that when businesses do not have sufficient understanding of their current customers or their intended customers, they cannot be successful. When you don't know who your customers are and what motivates them (and when), you can't possibly create a product they will buy at a price they're willing to pay.

Many start-up founders who dream of great products are taken by surprise because they cannot see the world through their customers' eyes. By the same token, large companies that sell products that customers recognize and buy regularly may be caught off guard when a competitor finds a better way to meet customers' needs.

At some point in your business career, you'll likely need a solid perspective on customers and customer needs. Therefore, to help you to understand customers and their universe more deeply, I'll provide explanations of the essential building blocks of the customer's world. However, before doing so, I want to distinguish between *consumer markets* and *business markets*. You can refer to Figure 7.2 as you read along.

Figure 7.2 Business and Consumer Markets

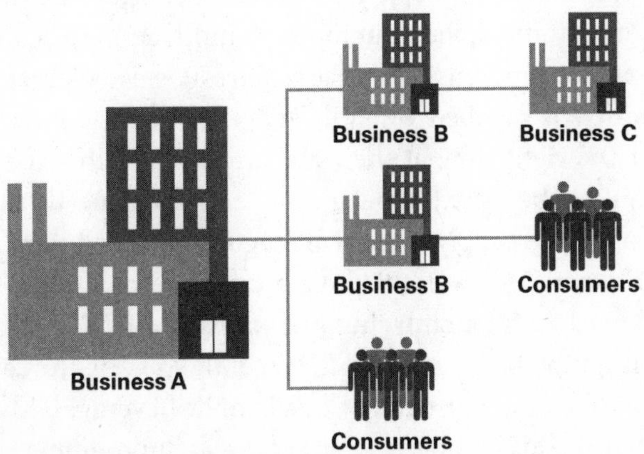

Consumer markets are those made up of people like you and me who buy food, houses, clothes, gadgets, and the like. Business markets are made up of businesses of all types in one or more locations. Businesses purchase goods and services so they can ultimately make products to sell to consumers or to other businesses. In the jargon of business, companies that sell to consumers are known as *business-to-consumer* (B2C) firms. Businesses that sell to other businesses are *business-to-business* (B2B) firms. B2B companies sell their products to businesses that then sell to customers, other businesses, or even government agencies. One of the important common denominators is that businesses are not people per se, but they are referred to in their entirety as customers and personified. The reason is that different types of people work in businesses: users, purchasers, decision makers, and influencers. The same can be said of a consumer household. The main point I want to make is this: If you know who the desired target customers are, regardless of where they reside or work, you will have a better chance to understand what motivates them and to target products or solutions toward their needs.

The other area I want to discuss involves the expression *customer needs* as it relates to what actually triggers, or motivates, a customer to act. Have you ever watched a television advertisement with an announcer saying something about meeting your unique needs? Or has a salesperson ever asked you, "What keeps you up at night?" These broad assertions or selling techniques may miss the mark because they don't take into account the true definition of the word *need* and the fact that customer needs, for the most part, are transient. Even with needs that come and go, astute business people know that by considering the habits and cadences of customers, they can induce a motivation to act.

A manufacturing business that requires a steady stream of parts to make products is satisfied when its suppliers provide the right number of parts at the right time at the right price. (Note that the company is now personified because the business overall has a need.) However, one interruption in the supply chain will magnify the need significantly, with workers idle and orders unfilled. Consumer needs, on the other hand, exhibit themselves frequently: hunger, warmth, safety, and so forth.

One last point on the term *needs*: I recently spoke with a category manager who worked for a distributor of alcoholic beverages. My goal was to learn about how his company's market research programs characterized customers and sized its markets. I asked if he had a model that mapped out market segments and customer targets. Although he described the demographic profiles, he also said that in his business, marketers weren't permitted to use the word *needs* due to its implications and the markets on which they focused. He said they use the term *motivational state.* My eyes lit up—motivational state! That's a term that I can get my mind around because it suggests that the motivation or inspiration to buy a product, or to do anything for that matter, is characterized by a basic stimulus of some kind. A business leader may be motivated to increase the efficiency of her employees so that time savings translate to greater profits. A consumer motivated by a need for status among her peers may purchase a luxury car, even though all he needs is a way to get to work in the morning. In sum, in a company, all key business stakeholders must focus their lenses on the most desirable customer populations and be able to explain what motivational states can emerge for those customers, when, and why.

MARKET SEGMENTS AND CUSTOMER TYPES

In basic marketing terms, customers who are grouped together based on common needs or motivations compose a market segment. As I described earlier, a business can focus its efforts on other businesses or on consumers. However, there are segments within each of those areas. Businesses may be segmented based on geographic area, vertical industry or sector, or the size of the business. Consumers may be segmented based on geographic area, demographic profile, or even values or beliefs. Figure 7.3 visualizes this for you.

These market segments are simple to understand from a theoretical point of view. However, in practice, businesses have to look deeply at customer preferences and behaviors—and before doing that, they must identify which customers to target and in which segments. Figure 7.3 shows that both the consumer and business segments are divided into subsegments, or *populations*, based on the roles people in those groups play in a business or a household.

In the early 1990s, Volvo knew that its automobiles were purchased by households that valued safety first. However, it did not understand that

Figure 7.3 Business and Consumer Market Segments

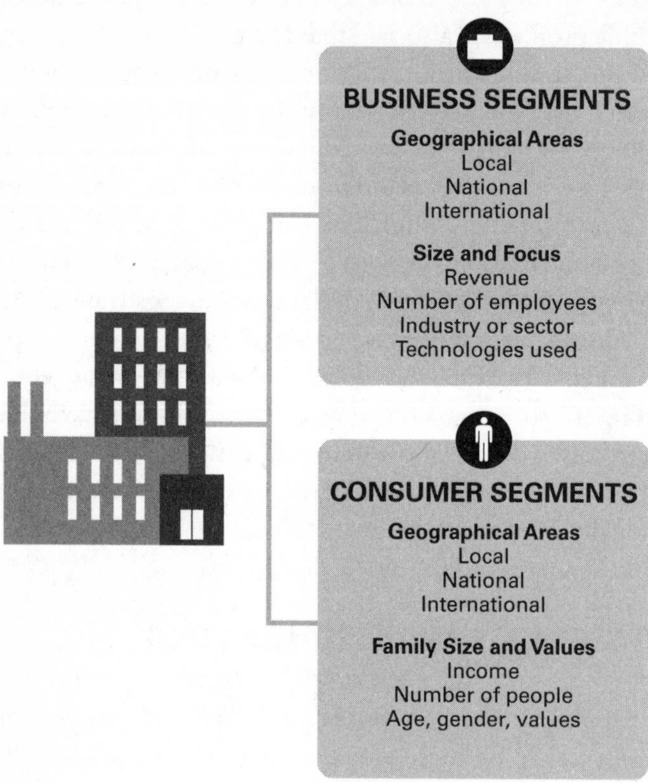

U.S. families were spending more time commuting and shuttling their kids to sporting events. These families brought their coffee or other drink cups into the car. The cup holder, a nearly ubiquitous feature in cars today, was shunned by Volvo engineers. Eventually, however, the company incorporated a cup holder in its model 850 sedans. I owned one, and I found that when the automatic gear shifter was in the "park" position, the cup holder wasn't able to emerge from its hidden compartment. Volvo understood that it had to include this feature, but not how the customer would actually use it; the company's engineers misunderstood the need behind the need.

Business people must be able to see that segments are divided into subsegments or customer types. Note that in Figure 7.4, customer types are characterized only by the role they play in a business or a household. These broad designations include buyers, users, influencers, and decision makers.

Figure 7.4 Market Segments and Subsegments

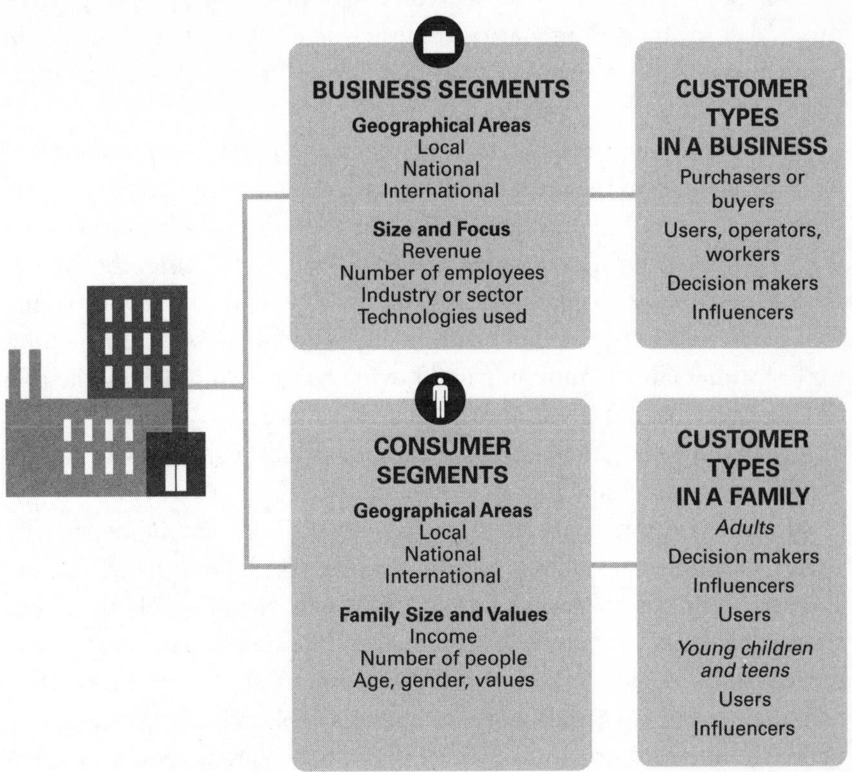

Each subsegment or population can be further divided according to the various roles individuals might play in a business or household. Many firms have found success in defining products around customer models called *personas*. A persona is a good way to distill the characteristics, motivations, affiliations, and other traits of a subsegment of *customer types*. For example, in the United States, the term *soccer mom* is used to refer to a woman who shuttles her children to sports events, rehearsals, and other activities. If you wanted to characterize a soccer mom, you might say she's middle income, drives a minivan or SUV, and is always in a rush and stressed out. Reflecting on this persona, what problems do you think she might have? She may not have time to make breakfast for her kids. She may have a lot of errands to do during the day. She needs to be on time for the afternoon's activities. Now, if you were a marketer or other business person, what would you do with this information? How much additional research would you do, and what ideas could you come up with for new products? If you worked in a marketing department or in an associated business role, you might be called upon to portray these "day in the life" scenarios of desirable customers. Doing so will help others to see what you see—and it may inspire them to follow your lead.

The creation of realistic, usable personas requires some serious legwork. This involves the creation of several customer profiles. *A customer profile is a detailed characterization of the customer's daily journey, and it accompanies your description of a day in the life of a customer.* To create these customer profiles, researchers spend time in-market or making field or site visits. In the retail business, mystery shoppers abound, studying consumers in the shopping and buying process and playing the role of shopper. Imagine going into a local store and just watching people doing what they do. It's like being an ethnographer, a person who studies people and cultures.

Today, customers are smarter than ever. They are influenced by advertising and care about specific brands. They do research online and ask friends or colleagues for advice. Moreover, apps and other tools allow consumers to compare prices online while standing in a brick-and-mortar store. Some of these consumers even work in businesses. They take their shopping knowledge and ability to research competing products right into the corridors of where they work. They are conditioned to do a lot of research, carefully examining specifications, studying competing products, and following prescribed purchasing processes.

It's also worth noting that in a B2B company, purchasing isn't just done by procurement people. In businesses today, there is a lot more interaction between the various customer types in a customer company: influencers, users, and decision makers. As mentioned, these individuals are also household consumers who are socially savvy and astute shoppers. They know how to use ratings and customer reviews for products sold online. They know how to "like" something and examine the likes, rants, and raves of other customers. The term *convergence* is used when two methods or phenomena come together. People in businesses and people in households use similar techniques to evaluate products for purchase—and are drawn into these techniques at home and at work. Figure 7.5 provides a visual representation of this convergence. What used to be a cascading model is now circular. As with many visuals, this one is easier to understand after studying it. There may be some challenges in uncovering the connection points between an influencer in a company and a user in a household—both the same person. As you study customers, you'll want to keep these dynamics in mind.

Now that I've explained the world of market segments, I imagine that, at some point, you may be called upon to pitch an idea for a product or to secure funds for a marketing investment. You'll have to consolidate your insights and ideas and describe the characteristics of the segments on which you wish the company to focus. In business terms, you are describing *market attractiveness*, which should be characterized in the following ways:

- *The degree to which the segment is growing.* For example, if you've studied people who are in their fifties and sixties, you

Figure 7.5 Customer Convergence

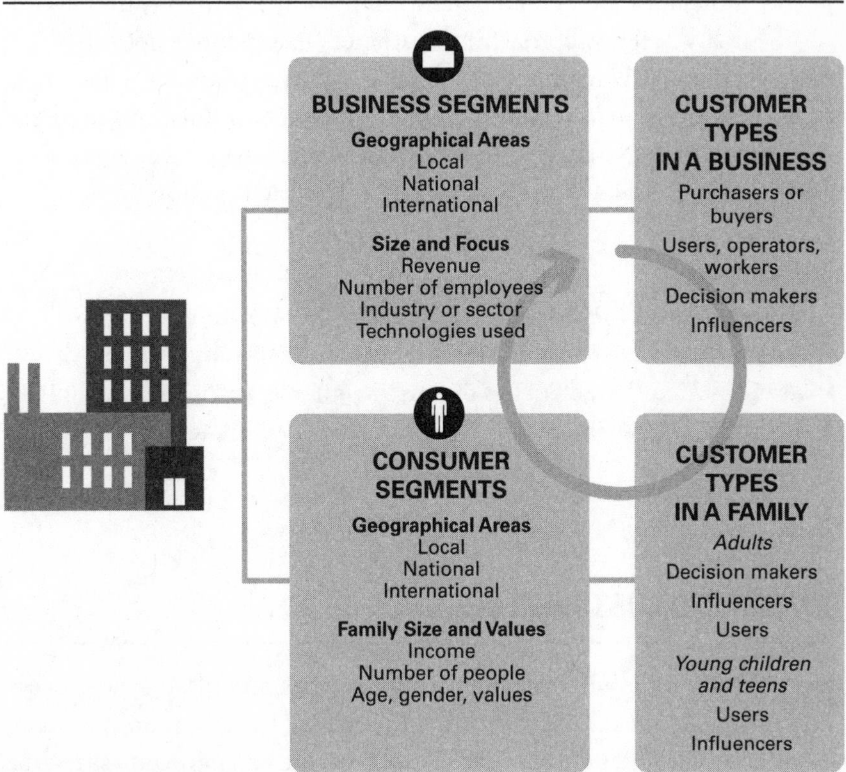

know that this segment represents sizable opportunities for companies that offer services based on convenience, travel, and healthy lifestyles. This segment is also attractive because demographic data suggest that a tremendous amount of wealth is possessed by this part of the population. You can use words such as, "The population in this segment is growing at 12 percent annually compared with the other segment, which is hardly growing at all." With clear insights backed up by reliable data, you'll find it's easier to justify in your own mind—and in the minds of your funders—that you've done your homework and that you have a fighting chance to win.

- *The number of competitors vying for the space.* It's said that when large companies consolidate, there's no room for smaller companies, and entrepreneurs might become discouraged. Others see these market dynamics through opportunistic lenses because large companies move slowly and small firms are more agile. You could defend an investment when you know that you'll be approaching customers in a manner not easily attainable by competitors to obtain market share.
- *The profit to be gained by bringing products and services to those segments.* No matter how attractive or accessible the segment, if it won't make enough money, it isn't attractive enough.

EXERCISE

Using Figure 7.4, create a market segment model for your company. Create short characterizations for each dimension and describe characteristics of those segments as if you were preparing a presentation to demonstrate your work to your managers.

DEVELOPING CUSTOMER INSIGHTS

I've had thousands of conversations with customers of all kinds. Every time I think I "get it," I learn something new. Even if you do have conversations, what should those be? What questions should you ask? What should you look for? With the structures described thus far, it's time to explore what's required to draw the insights needed to fathom the depths of customer needs and motivations.

A number of years ago, I was having trouble with my new car. When I went to pick up the car, the service representative said I'd be receiving a survey and that I should give him high marks. I dutifully filled out the survey, which was simple to do; it asked if it was easy to make an appointment and whether I liked the experience. After I got the car home, I realized the problem wasn't fixed. I called the dealer and brought the car back. Again, at pickup time, he asked me to fill out the survey. When I received it, I looked for a specific question: "Did we fix your car to your satisfaction?" It wasn't to be found. I had to take the car back to the dealer five times for the same problem before it was fixed. The dealership wanted to know the easy stuff so it could advertise its great service attitudes and environment, not what was real to me, the customer. A vital point for you is this: *You cannot hope to listen to the customers' voice if you don't give them a chance to communicate. Further, if you cannot find their true voice, who will? Your competitors.*

Although most firms use both qualitative and quantitative methods, I prefer qualitative research to gain the best perspective. I sometimes use quantitative research to validate findings. I don't have a strict rule in this regard because each business is different. However, something that you may know now, or learn in the future, is that customers don't know what they don't know. At the same time, they are burdened, unknowingly, as our guides and teachers. *Customers may say what they want and complain as they will, but what they believe they need is not always what they really need.* If your company creates products around what people think, or what the customers directly ask for, the company's products may miss the mark.

Successful companies are able to determine how to get inside the heads of their current customers or desirable new customers. To garner customer insights and listen to customers, market researchers, business analysts, and others follow a simple process:

1. Goal: What do we want to learn and why?
2. Inputs: What data do we have, and what data do we need?
3. Activities: What will we undertake to gather and assimilate data?

4. Outputs: What will we do with the data?
5. Evaluation: Did we learn what we needed to, and can we apply this knowledge?

To expand on these steps, refer to Figure 7.6, the customer insight development process. As you can see, the goal is to produce customer insights. These can be carried out through visits, interviews, evaluations of complaint data, and so on. As you review activities, a team can brainstorm or use other means to synthesize the inputs so that the relevant outputs can be put into perspective. Notice that the outputs directly reflect some of the items discussed earlier: segmentation models, customer types, and the like.

Let's extend that automobile service story I shared earlier. Suppose you work for an automobile company and you notice that the dealer satisfaction reports show great results but your business data shows decreasing market share in certain geographic areas. If you are able to do some research, you might look past the data from the dealer reports of friendly service advisors and combine that data with the repair data reports. If you were able to compare an increasing number of repairs for a given problem, or you reviewed spare parts inventory statistics, you might learn that there was a quality problem with a component. From another vantage point, would it be possible to compare the number of repairs done with the number of customer surveys completed? If you had spent

Figure 7.6 Customer Insight Development Process

Goal →	Inputs →	Activity →	Output →	Evaluate
Produce customer insights	Customer visits	• Brainstorming • Developing and testing hypotheses • Building customer work flow models	• Segmentation models • Desirable customer targets and personas • Customer needs • Value proposition • New product ideas • Ideas to improve customer service • Pricing models • Promotional ideas	Evaluate and improve visit protocols
	Customer interviews			Fine-tune interview questions
	Customer complaints			Improve customer service process
	Customer report card			Add additional sections to report card
	Satisfaction surveys			Improve survey tools
	Product repair data			Analyze product components

time spot-checking the dealer reports by calling up some of the customers, you might have exposed the problem sooner.

Many people use the term *voice of the customer* to discuss gathering insights about customers. Sometimes you must go where the customers are. Customers don't always speak with their voices per se, but they speak through their actions and behaviors. Have you ever had to wait for a person to help you in a retail store and no one was around? You vote with your feet and walk out the door—and no one knows because no one heard. If it was your store, you'd not only miss hearing the voice, you'd lose the sale.

Getting closer to customers to hear their voice might involve a visit to a store, listening in when customers call into your company, or even the mystery shopping I mentioned earlier. Listening means observing visually or hearing what's said. Either way, you can more easily listen to customers when you're attuned to do so. When you do, it's easier to discern anger, pleasure, happiness, or frustration.

Online discussion groups established by consumer products companies can capture information based on questions posed by customers or comments they make to one another. Here, the main idea is to be able to witness firsthand customer behaviors and interactions with your company or product.

In a B2B situation, a way to gain access to a customer company is to arrange an on-site visit. While you may not have to do this as part of your job now, you may have in interest in doing so in the future. To achieve this, many firms use a formal *customer visit plan*. Salespeople use a similar technique to chart which customers they're going to visit and in what sequence, but this is not quite the same. A business person can plan a visit with a salesperson or account manager. Procedurally, this planning should not be done directly with a customer because the salesperson's domain needs to be respected. When a visit team has a clear plan for what's to be accomplished during a visit (especially one requiring travel), odds for success are improved when a formal visit plan is submitted for approval. This will include the purpose, who will participate, who takes notes, and how information will be shared when the team returns. In my corporate life, my best visits occurred when I had one or two others with me because what we saw and heard was filtered through different lenses. When the time is right and you wish to plan a formal customer visit, use the template shown in Figure 7.7.

Figure 7.7 Customer Visit Plan Template

OBJECTIVE

- Describe the purpose of the visit. What do you want to learn and why? Will you visit one or many customers?

CUSTOMERS TO BE VISITED OR MARKET AREAS TO BE COVERED

- Identify companies and names of people in those companies. Describe why these particular people are targeted.
- If you are doing a field visit, where do you intend to go, and why? Who do you expect to encounter?

PREPARATION

- Which customers will be selected and why?
- If current customers, what products do they use? What revenue have they provided? What issues have they encountered in the past? If prospective customers, in which segments do they exist and how are they characterized? Do you have an organization chart to understand who's who in the customer company? Will the team review any relevant research about the customer's company?
- Will a presentation be required?
- If there are interviews to be done, who will create the interview guide?
- Will any supplies be needed? Easels, projectors, cameras?

GUIDELINES/PROTOCOL TO FOLLOW

- Who will make arrangements?
- Are there any documents to sign, such as non disclosures?
- Will any permissions be needed to record (audio or video)?
- Is there a dress code? How will introductions be made and by whom?
- Will anyone on the customer side be asked to prepare a presentation or arrange a tour?
- Do any local authorities need to be notified?
- What are the transportation requirements?

TEAM MEMBERS TO PARTICIPATE AND ROLES TO BE PLAYED

- Identify names and titles of people and the department in which they work (e.g., R&D and Marketing).
- What will each person do? Take notes, conduct interviews?

AGENDA FOR EACH VISIT

- How much time will be required?
- Will tours be needed?

BUDGET REQUIRED

- How much money is required for travel and other expenses?

HOW DATA WILL BE CAPTURED

- Who will record notes or capture information on video or audio?
- Will you have the ability to take a time-out to review what was learned so that nothing is left to chance?
- Who will verify that what's been learned is consistent with the established objectives?

WHEN AND HOW THE DEBRIEF WILL BE DONE

- Who on your team will consolidate the data into a unified report?
- What other team members will be needed to listen to the read-out?
- How will findings be combined with other research?
- When and where will the read-out take place?

In preparation for any visit, especially if arrangements are made to interview people, a set of questions should be prepared in advance in an interview guide. When a visit team is properly prepared, the visit will flow more smoothly and efficiently. Also, when interviews are properly organized and carried out, the analytical process is hastened.

The key to customer interviewing is to help customers call upon their experience and allow them to talk. Open-ended questions are best in situations when the team is trying to achieve the following:

- *Establish visualizations or images that help portray a given situation or experience.* For example, "If you could imagine the perfect day in your office, what would it look like?" Notice that this is an open-ended question that allows the person to creatively reflect on what works well and what doesn't.
- *Determine the factors that contributed to a poor experience.* One might ask, "When the product didn't work, what were you trying to do? How did you feel?" Or, "When you logged into the website and couldn't complete your order, what happened?" Another variant might be, "Who else was affected by this when you couldn't complete your task?" Or, "Has this happened at other times?"
- *Provide input for future product or service improvements or for new product offers.* Sometimes, the team is just hunting for new features or capabilities or that next innovation. A question like this might be posed: "Could you show me how you process that customer request on your system?" Or, "May I sit with you and watch you work for about an hour?" That might open the door for you to ask, "Why did you do that?" Or, "When you sighed after the phone call, what happened?" In one of my roles as a product manager, I would often visit an operations center just to watch how people did what they did. I would then ask questions of different people based on what I saw. Sometimes, I'd draw work flows or simple process charts to map what I saw. This would help me figure out if any efficiency could be gained.

As interview guides are developed, questions should be sufficiently open ended so that the customer doesn't feel forced into a right or wrong answer. Asking a customer to describe what happened or how something took place allows an interviewer to find out about feelings and attitudes. It also opens the door for follow-on questions that help clarify the situation. If you ask "why" questions, you may be able to get to the heart of the matter. "Why" puts the customer into a diagnostic state, which is really what's needed.

As you can see, customer visit data is just one input into the customer insight development process. Garnered insights will contribute to the creation of the customer profiles I mentioned earlier, and when these are consolidated and discussed with concerned teams, the "ahas" will start to become apparent.

EXERCISE

- What are the techniques used to garner customer insights in your company?
- What are the main needs or motivations for any of the customers within the chosen market segments of your company?
- Can you describe how customer needs or motivations have evolved over the past several years and what might happen in the future?

CUSTOMER RESEARCH AND INSIGHTS APPLIED TO THE CUSTOMER VALUE PROPOSITION

The *customer value proposition* is one of the most important tools used in business. The customer value proposition refers to the perceived benefit a customer will recognize from buying or using a product. This can be calculated arithmetically, as in efficiency, time savings, or cost savings. Alternatively, it can be viewed as helping a business to increase revenue. Some benefits are perceived without an arithmetic calculation because they can relate to good feelings or prestige, as in owning luxury items or visiting certain restaurants. Value propositions are built into advertisements aimed at inspiring targeted customers to buy your firm's products. To clarify this, Figure 7.8 shows a simple template I've created to lay the foundational building blocks of a value proposition. You'll notice that it combines all of what I've discussed up to this point.

Figure 7.8 Building Blocks of the Customer Value Proposition

IDENTIFY THE CUSTOMER

- Define the segment and target group so it's perfectly clear. Use facts and data to defend your customer characterizations.
- If you have multiple customer types or target groups, you will need to create a separate value proposition for each group. You can consolidate these and build on the common denominators as you develop a deeper understanding of those customers.

THE CUSTOMER'S MAIN NEEDS/MOTIVATIONS

- Describe the customer's problems, when those problems are present, and why. Because there may be more than one, list each separately.
- Clarify the motivational state that exists for each customer type.

CONNECT NEEDS TO FEATURES

- For each need, associate a feature that is, or should be, built into the product.
- Make sure that each customer's need is represented separately.

DEFINE THE BENEFITS THAT THE CUSTOMER WILL RECEIVE

- Will the customer save time or be more efficient?
- Will the customer be able to earn more money or a profit?
- Will the customer associate a feeling of affiliation with your product or brand?

WHY A CUSTOMER SHOULD SELECT YOUR PRODUCT OVER A COMPETITOR'S

- Determine key points of differentiation: "Ours is better, and here's why..."

Value propositions not only clarify the benefits to the customer but also reinforce what a business will promise to its customers. Some companies use the term *brand promise* as a way to convey their commitment to solving customer problems better than the competition. These businesses use the value proposition as a way to make sure that everyone in the company who is facing the market projects the ideals of the benefits a customer will receive.

EXERCISE

Pick a product in your company and compose a value proposition. As an extension, pick a product that's similar but sold by a competitor and compose its value proposition. Where are the similarities? Are there points of difference?

THE INDUSTRY ENVIRONMENT

If you worked for a sporting goods company that made products for tennis players or skiers and you didn't like skiing or tennis, you might find that you were less enthusiastic than someone who loved those sports. I feel that it is important for business people to associate (almost passionately) with the domain in which they work, and to deeply understand the market influences on that area.

Within the definition of *market* as described earlier, buyers (customers) and sellers (competitors) meet on the playing field of a particular industry environment. Therefore, in an industry (sometimes called a sector or an industry vertical), similar companies compete for the hearts and minds of similar types of customers. For business people, it is important to note that *industries are dynamic because the forces that drive them are always changing.*

For further study, you may wish to refer to external industry classification standards established by the Global Industry Classification Standard (GICS), as published by Standard & Poor's and MSCI Barra (www.msci.com). Here, you'll find 10 broad sectors, 24 industry groups, 68 industries, and 154 subindustries. As a quick example, some sectors include Energy, Materials, Health Care, Financials, etc.

What's critical to your understanding about industry dynamics is this: there are external influences that can change the profile and prospects of any industry area or domain in a heartbeat. Think back to times when the financial services industry or the oil and gas industry had issues and how those impacts caused changes in economic policy, government regulations, and other items. To help you analyze each of these influences, I'll share with you a model I derived. It goes by the acronym PRESTO, which breaks down as follows:

> *P = Political influences.* These are the outcomes of policies created by governmental agencies. In any geographic area, whether a country or a province, certain attitudes and beliefs are expressed in policies and guidelines.
>
> *R = Regulatory influences.* These are the regulations established in a geographic area or a country that serve to set boundaries and rules for businesses. For example, in most countries, financial

services, insurance firms, food manufacturers, and pharmaceutical companies, among others, are subject to these laws.

E = Economic influences. Simply stated, when people are employed and feel good about the economic environment, they tend to spend. At the same time, if goods are plentiful when demand is present, prices will tend to be reasonable. In simple terms, the state of any economy in any area will dictate willingness to buy—or to not buy.

S = Societal factors. In market segments, demographics and preferences change over time. Whether it's a focus on environmental sustainability, renewable resources, or trends in fashion or design, societal factors must always be considered.

T = Technological influences. The state of technology evolves continually, and it influences various sectors at different times. Innovation tends to increase when conditions in the other PRESTO factors are favorable.

O = Other influences. In many market areas, there are various business behaviors that don't fall under any umbrella. For example, if there is a trend for companies in an industry such as airlines or financial services to be merging to achieve scale economies, that's an "other" category.

PRESTO provides the framework to carry out industry research and uncover trends. Business people who put up their industry radar will be able to secure a steady stream of data that can be used to formulate market insights, as I showed you in Figure 7.1. Some business people provide direct input to the product management group so that the products can be altered to reflect those market needs. Well-run firms establish groups of people who share market data with each other based on things they learn. Because so much information is available at a moment's notice, it's important that no one person become the knowledge center. Moreover, we all interpret signals from different perspectives, and these need to be unified so they can be acted upon.

A business person can capture PRESTO indicators and discover the interrelationships among these factors using the PRESTO matrix, which is shown as a template in Figure 7.9. In each cell, information, narratives,

Figure 7.9 PRESTO Framework for Industry Analysis

INDICATOR	TWO YEARS AGO	LAST YEAR	THIS YEAR	NEXT YEAR
Political				
Regulatory				
Economic				
Social				
Technology				
Other				

and insights are recorded to portray what happened in each time frame so that trends and issues can be surfaced. It's a great technique to use to be more confident about goings-on within the industry or domain. Your inputs can be fortified through studying industry journals, business periodicals, governmental or regulatory agency reports, university research, and field research as well as through attending industry conferences. One of the things I do is establish automatic alerts that are triggered by specific keywords for areas in which I'm interested. Then, I have easy-to-reference resources about activities that are taking place in any industry area.

INDUSTRY ANALYSIS AND MARKET FORECASTS

The last thing that's done with industry information is to understand the size of an industry and its growth rates by area or geography. As you might surmise, market segmentation models should be tightly integrated with the industry analysis. Ratings agencies, such as Standard & Poor's, provide some of this. In addition, you can go to most economic development websites for any country to gain context around these statistics. This is important because your firm's business investment in products or in market expansion is dependent on the favorability of any business environment. If someone is pitching to an executive team or a venture capital firm and cannot define the market size and revenue potential for the investment, it's likely the pitch won't gain any traction.

Without proper forecasts, it's impossible to determine market potential. After all, every business has to figure out how it will invest its scarce resources. To adequately organize your thoughts around forecasting, I'll provide some additional building blocks. Recall how market segments are broad and then narrowed into subsegments and then targets. Forecasting parallels this. Suppose you want to create a forecast for a new product. You'll want to be able to figure out and convey the following:

1. *How large is the total market?* If every customer in every segment could buy what you want to sell, and there were no competitors, how many customers would that amount to? This is known as the total addressable market (TAM).
2. *If there are competitors, and other segment divisions where customers make different choices, what portion of the customer population might be available to buy?* In other words, what could you hope for now, and in the future? This is known as the available market share (AMS).
3. *How many products can you sell?* You can't always figure this out yourself because your company may have salespeople, a website, distributors, and so on. There's got to be sufficient capacity in the business to get a product from where it's produced to where it's used. Therefore, the sales forecast serves to validate the rate at which a firm might penetrate any given market.

When it comes down to what could possibly be sold, additional points of validation are needed. If you're directly involved in the forecasting process, you can consider an examination of how well your business has performed in various market segments. Alternatively, you can look at how your competitors have fared in the past. If your last product introduction sold at a specific rate, and your new product forecast is double that, but your business infrastructure hasn't changed, you'll want to rethink those numbers. If you work in a publicly traded company, consider having conversations with your company economist or other analysts to secure their opinions.

In summary, these three steps represent the basics of forecasting and are the result of careful analysis of market segments and industry categories. Forecasts are based on accurate, timely market data and, ultimately, solid assumptions about the future.

CHARACTERIZING THE COMPETITIVE ENVIRONMENT

Up to this point, the information I've imparted relates to customers, their main motivations or needs, and the industry environment in which market segments are situated. However, your company is probably not the only entity looking at those particular customers. If an unmet need is observed, it's likely that others are seeing the same thing. Without a doubt, when you're choosing one product over another, you're doing some kind of competitive analysis. However, the competitive environment is quite complex. There are three main reasons why business people must understand the competitors in addition to the industry environment (or domain) in which products are sold:

1. Competitive advantage is critical to success, and if a business loses its competitive edge, it may fail.
2. An ongoing stream of competitive intelligence provides executives with the wherewithal to come up with strategies that direct purposeful actions and positive business results.
3. No matter how much work is done to understand markets, your competitors are essentially doing the same thing (or if they're not now, they will be) because everyone's vying for the same business!

As you are well aware, all competitors in an industry space are attempting to position themselves in the most favorable light. Businesses build their brand through the pursuit of profit, market share, and prestige. Specific performance comparisons are needed in order to determine whether your firm is competing vigorously and winning in the market. In sports, how can a team know where it is in the standings if it doesn't know where its competitors are?

To compare the market position of competing firms or competing products, you will need to apply specific measurements. Revenue and profit comparisons, as well as market share comparisons, abound in publicly traded companies. Sometimes you can evaluate your own firm's number of products against a given competitor's number of products. In competitive analysis, you will always want to know where you stand in relation to others.

Many companies become obsessed by this to the point that they follow every move of every competitor. This is probably not as healthy as you might think. You always want to gauge your position, but only to establish your strategic goals. *If your company is always reacting to competitor actions, you'll quickly find that your company will be falling behind.*

To start your work, find out if there's a competitive intelligence or market intelligence group in your own company. In larger firms, these departments do exist, even though their outputs may not be visible to everyone. If you don't have sufficient formality in your company and you want to adopt a more competitive mindset, you can start by creating your own competitive intelligence repository. Here's what you'll want to include:

- A list of key terms for your industry
- A series of files or dossiers for each competitor firm
- A list of any associations where competitor firms might be visible
- Advertisements that are conducted by competitors
- Government or other industry reports that capture activities of competitor firms
- Lists of products that are produced or sold by each firm
- Target markets on which those competitors focus

Competitive intelligence is all around you, and it's yours for the taking. Here are some simple steps you can take:

- Study the job board on your competitor's website.
- Speak with your salespeople to see which competitive products they are seeing in the market.
- Take a walk through a store to see who's selling what and how they're packaging or advertising.
- Read trade journals to find out where competitors are advertising and what they're saying.

As you do your industry and competitive research, you might visit the websites of regulators to see what companies might be affected by specific regulations or policies. You can also visit the website of the U.S. Patent and Trademark Office (www.uspto.gov), the European Patent

Office (www.epo.org), or even the Thomson Reuters site (www.thomsonreuters.com) for scholarly and scientific research done by people who work in various companies or institutions. Seek and you shall find! When your competitive radar is up and operating and scanning the horizon, you'll invariably be attuned to what's going on so that you can contribute to conversations about innovation and in building competitive advantage for your company.

ANALYZING COMPETITORS

When you gain the necessary insights about your competitors, it's easier to derive focused positioning—and it's easier to influence the formulation of definite goals and strategies. As mentioned earlier, a competitor profile might be a great way to capture this information. Figure 7.10 illustrates how you might organize this profile. When you use a tool like this, you are equipped with a methodology that allows you to compare competitive firms in a more consistent way. Further, when you have a blank space, it makes it clear that you, or others, must obtain the data to complete the profile.

Once the competitive profiles are done, the analysis can finally begin. Whether you're leading this or someone from the competitive intelligence department is, concentration is directed to the clarification of how competitors do what they do and why. How do they deliver value to their customers?

You may already have some of this information for your own company based on what you've gathered from the book thus far. Think about items such as organizational structure, processes, and customers. These allow for the construction of competitive comparisons that help you draw the most important conclusions about what they're up to and what direction is possible. Also, you can use other resources (either in your own company or elsewhere) to uncover how competitors do what they do. After information is recorded from the profiles and study of competitive company business models, it can be consolidated into an analytical format that better enables side-by-side analysis. Refer to Figure 7.11 to review how these integrated findings might be assembled.

Now, I'd like to wrap up my discussion on the competition and describe why competitive product comparisons are an important element of this analysis.

Figure 7.10 Competitor Profile Template

Name of competitor	
Date of profile	
Address of main office and other locations	
URL	
Public or privately held	
General statement about the company's or brand's reputation in the market	
General observations about the financial condition of the firm—any relevant financial data at the product level or at the level of the division of that company where your products compete	
Divisional or business unit structure plus a description of each division's market focus, market segments, and market share; additionally, include key customers and/or key wins, if relevant	
Relevant organization charts and key executives supporting the divisions that sell the products you compete with	
Number of employees (by division)	
Names and model numbers (or other identifiers) of every product with which you compete. Include feature, function, and other attribute comparisons	
Market segments on which competitor focuses	
Key accounts or customers to whom the firm sells (especially B2B)	
Pricing strategies and discounting activity for each product	
Channels used to move products from source to customer	
Promotional mix profiles (how does the firm advertise and promote, where, and when)	
Selling models (direct sales force, web, etc.)	
Value propositions represented for those products	
How the competitive products are positioned against other competitors as well as your own products	
Employee morale or other employee indicators	
Key strengths for the products with which yours compete	
Key weaknesses for the products with which yours compete	
Known competitive strategies of this competitor: What are the most visible activities of this competitor over the past year or two, and what might you expect in the future?	

Figure 7.11 Competitive Company Comparisons

	YOUR COMPANY	COMPETITOR A	COMPETITOR B
Vision			
Goals			
Strategies			
Structure			
Systems			
Processes			
Customers			
Competitors			
Products			
Results			

As the battles for the hearts and minds of customers take place, astute business people must know if and how their product is different enough from the competitors' products to inspire a customer to buy. When you shop for a refrigerator, what do you look for? You assess the desired attributes such as size, color, layout, and capacity. After that, you might look at a consumer publication to evaluate ratings based on laboratory tests or the opinions of other customers. Ultimately, you'll select the product with the benefits you want and the value you place on that product.

When a company wants to undertake a comparison of a tangible product, it may purchase one and bring it into a laboratory to be *reverse engineered*—or broken down into its parts so that those parts can be studied. Each part can be evaluated in terms of how much each might cost to procure so that a bill of materials can be created. Engineers can also put the competitor product under stress tests, usage tests, and other evaluations to see where the points of comparison can be made. In my corporate life, a vendor of one model of computer operating in our data center asked to "rent time" on a competitor's computer, also running in our data center, to run benchmark tests or to see how given applications would perform under equivalent conditions. For intangible products, becoming a user of a service, or hiring consultants to use a competitor service, is a way to draw comparisons.

The main idea behind this competitive product analysis is to be able to compare how your company's product functions in relation to competitors' and how the features of your product compare to those of the competitors. This can be done from the perspective of performance, capacity, safety, security, usability, maintainability, or the overall customer experience. Once this is done, the next step in the process is to understand how each company positions its product in the market. All things considered, positioning is part of a company's strategy to communicate the value and benefits of its product in relation to others available to customers so that it can win in its chosen markets.

SUMMARY

In the final analysis, managers in a company must understand the market environment and its dynamically moving parts. Throughout your career in business, regardless of the firm in which you work, you must keep on top of market activities and the associated insights that result from your study. You will find that if you want to formulate a strategy, produce a business case, launch a product, or defend a business investment, you must have the best market information possible. Starting with the market first is the most efficient way to approach the process. If you start with the product or idea first, you may spend a lot of time forcing it into a market that does not have an appetite for it.

As you might surmise, this work can be a full-time job—and then some. In fact, in many firms, it is; market intelligence functions do exist. If you're a manager who works in an operating department and you need to get work done, you might need to communicate with people in a market intelligence department or equivalent function. If you speak the language of "market," regardless of where you work in a company, you'll earn that much more credibility and improve your business acumen.

INCREASING YOUR MANAGEMENT COMPETENCY

1. Find out who is responsible for the existing segmentation models in your company. You may need to meet with several people from marketing, sales, and product management. Ask them to explain the research that was undertaken to assemble the model and how the segments have changed over time.

2. If the segmentation model is not available, you should be able to create a model out of information that you can find out from various stakeholders who understand the customers your company sells to.
3. Who are key customer types within each market segment? Can you describe people who play roles in a customer company such as decision maker, influencer, and user?
4. If an upcoming customer visit is planned, try to attend. Use the customer visit plan template in Figure 7.7 to find out if there's a formal protocol or if the visit is informal. If you can play a role as note taker or information recorder, you'll greatly enhance your understanding of the customer's world.
5. Make it a point to study the products of your company, and write a value proposition for those products. Assess whether those value propositions demonstrate what's required of an effective value proposition.
6. Study your competitors' products, and create a value proposition for each of their products, as if you were writing it from the customer's perspective. Use this as a way to compare your value proposition to others so that you might fine-tune yours.
7. Establish a number of online alerts from keywords that are germane to the industry environment in which you work—or areas you want to study.
8. Create a list of industry or trade periodicals and analyst organizations that are the most relevant to your company. Subscribe to as many as you can to improve your perspectives about the business environment or domain.
9. If you've never done a market share forecast, talk to your manager or your peers to learn about forecasting activities that have been carried out within your organization.
10. Find out about the forecasting cycle in your company. Who is responsible for what forecasts? Perhaps you can approach those people to learn how they do what they do.

Action Planning

In this chapter, the following characteristics were either explicitly or implicitly revealed. You may wish to identify where these were mentioned to reinforce your understanding of how they might be applied in your own work. You can also utilize the following template as a way to associate what was discussed in this chapter with your scores from your Business Acumen Assessment. From this, you can create an action plan for yourself or work with your manager to come up with specific goals and plans.

- Defining processes
- Being a self-starter
- Deriving market insights
- Evaluating the industry and domain
- Entrepreneurial thinking
- Listening attentively
- Observing actively
- Developing customer relationships
- Developing external relationships
- Being a reliable team player

ACTION ITEM + GOAL	STEPS TO BE TAKEN	OUTCOME PRODUCED	WHAT YOU LEARNED	WHAT YOU WILL SHARE

SETTING DIRECTION WITH STRATEGY

After you read this chapter, you should be able to:

- Explain how strategies are formulated using a strategic planning process.
- Understand the required market data and other inputs that shape strategies.
- Analyze and synthesize data to uncover strategic opportunities for the business.

It is not the strongest or the most intelligent who will survive but those who can best manage change.

—CHARLES DARWIN

When I was a kid, I read Jack London's *The Call of the Wild*. I was taken by his description of the dog Buck, who became a masterful animal who "perceived and determined and responded in the same instant." Buck transformed from a docile pet to a survivor, and he had to deal with whatever situation arose, without advance notice.

Could you imagine yourself in a business role operating from moment to moment, not knowing what's coming next? Probably not. Yet, sometimes it seems like that's what happens. A competitor introduces a new product, and everyone runs around trying to figure out what to do. A customer demands that you provide a new service, interrupting the plans you all just agreed upon. Disruption abounds, yet everyone's supposed to adhere to the playbook.

People who work in a business, just like people who play on a sports team or who perform in a show, need to know what they're working toward and why. Everyone needs a goal and a path to achieve that goal. Good business people realize that there are unexpected bumps along the way and adapt with aplomb. This is the essence of strategic planning and execution. In this chapter, I introduce you to the fundamental principles of strategy, and I discuss what's required to set your mileposts for success. In doing this, I cover the following areas:

1. Foundations of strategy
2. Dimensions of the strategic planning process
3. Techniques to analyze and synthesize data so you can pivot with agility
4. Transformation of your acquired perspectives of your business into a model for the future

FOUNDATIONS OF STRATEGY

From a broad standpoint, strategies are essentially game plans that establish parameters for achieving competitive advantage. *Strategies are built on the goals of what's to be done along with the activities and actions that spell out how it's to be done.*

Strategy has been, and always will be, an important topic for discussion, debate, and academic study. People who include Alfred DuPont Chandler, Peter Drucker, Igor Ansoff, and Michael Porter have contributed greatly to the field of study and positioned strategy at the forefront of business success. As senior executives will attest, well-developed strategies and flawless execution create competitive advantage.

In most firms, the first step in creation of a strategy is to envision a future state that reflects what the firm wants to do and how it wishes to be viewed by customers and others. Some say that vision is a reflection of the heart and soul of a company. When a vision is brought to light, it should be easy to establish achievable goals to fulfill that vision and drive the business. Right? Well, perhaps not. Many years ago, after I was promoted to my first product management job, my boss's boss asked me about my vision for my product. Mind you, I'd only been on the job for a couple of months. I was caught off guard. Although I knew what he was asking for (after all, I did study strategy in graduate school), I was not equipped to answer his question. You can probably imagine how I felt! What would you say if your boss asked you to describe your understanding about the vision for the company? One thing is for sure: you would need an answer! Unfortunately, many business people don't have ready access to the company vision at the tip of their tongue or in their back pocket. To ultimately be successful in business, you must be able to convey the vision for the company as set forth by its leaders. In its simplest form, a vision represents a firm's core values. Here are some examples of vision statements:

- Amazon's vision is "to be the earth's most customer centric company; to build a place where people can come to find and discover anything they might want to buy online."
- Starbuck's vision is "to share great coffee with our friends and help make the world a little better."

Vision is not something that you're likely to have to come up with unless you're starting your own company or leading a business. However, in a business, we all must work toward a vision because it serves as our anchor to the firm. In my prior leadership roles, I would often have directors who reported to me create a vision statement for their group or their product line. I wanted them to be able to internalize the overall company vision and values that would serve to inspire others—including customers, salespeople, and so on. The exercise would ultimately have to be written from the perspective of a business journalist writing about their "mini-business" two years in the future. I also wanted them to envision what they wanted their future customers to say about their products.

Next, let's talk strategic goals. A sports team may aspire to win the championship trophy at the end of a season, just as a company may aspire to have the most recognized brand name in a category. More specifically, a business may seek to attain 50 percent market share in a geographic area. Goals are vital because they're where a company can take aim and, thus, deploy its resources. In a competitive environment, business people should be able to develop (or contribute to the development of) explicit goals and associated performance targets that will fulfill the vision.

Once the vision and goals are established, the strategies or game plans are set forth. As indicted earlier, the strategy describes what's to be done and how it's to be done. Business leaders generally set the goals and strategy, which invariably determines the investments and resources that are allocated to achieve the goals. Refer to Figure 8.1 for a visual of this simple hierarchy.

To put this into perspective, I'd like to provide you with an example for a new business:

1. *Vision:* In a world that is increasingly busy and stressed out, I want to help people achieve a greater level of calmness so they can relax, reenergize, and see things more clearly. I want to be known as the person who brings mindfulness and relaxation to busy business people.
2. *Strategic goal:* To build ten 20-Minute Stress-Saver Salons in Manhattan within the next 18 months.
3. *Strategies:* The salons will provide massage, guided meditation, and other efficient stress reduction programs, with each service

Figure 8.1 Strategy Hierarchy

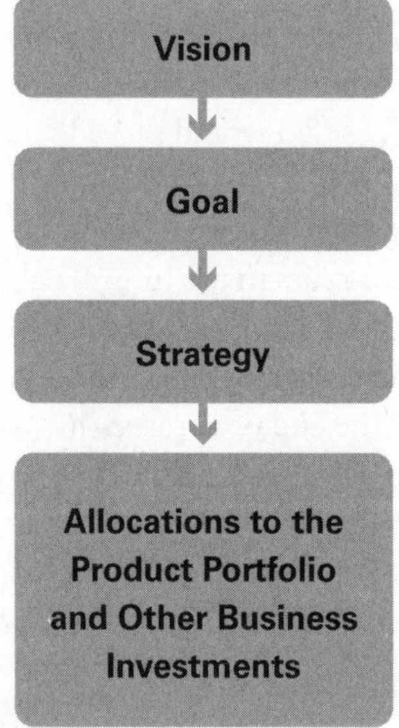

lasting 20 minutes. Our salons will be situated in locations with heavy foot traffic and will operate before, during, and after normal working hours.

4. *Investments:* $6 million in real estate and other setup expenses, $500,000 for new products, and $1 million for advertising.

EXERCISE

- What is the expressed vision for your company?
- What are the top goals established by the leaders in your firm?
- What is the stated strategy for the business?
- How does the strategy guide the work that's done in your department?
- How can you assimilate these into your day-to-day job?

Strategies should also establish the *parameters for execution*. Well-formulated strategies set the stage for robust, ongoing planning and decision making for the business and its products as they evolve in chosen markets. Note that I use the word *ongoing*. This means that businesses run every day, and business people must be alert so they can better anticipate what might happen and respond to unforeseen events when they do happen.

In conducting research for this book, I learned that senior leaders in major firms believe that poor business performance is a result of poor execution. This is true even in firms where it's believed there is a solid strategic plan in place. Executional shortfalls abound, and there are several reasons for these:

1. People in various departments are unclear on what they're supposed to do, with whom, and when—even with clear goals. This goes beyond role confusion. Sometimes managers or individual contributors don't have the requisite skill or know-how. Other times, the work required cannot be done with the current resources due to other commitments.
2. Insufficient attention is paid to the cultivation of business people who can ensure that the work of others gets done and

that the appropriate handoffs between departments are carried out seamlessly.

3. An organizational paralysis can occur as a result of overplanning and underperforming. Some people just cannot seem to mobilize themselves beyond spreadsheets and presentation decks. In certain environments, people who work remotely slow things down considerably because face-to-face collaboration is required to move things along quickly.
4. Even when people are executing the plan, they can fail to adapt to the unanticipated situations that arise on a day-to-day basis, or they can fail to communicate to leaders. This lack of agility, especially to market changes, will cause a business to lose ground to competitors.

In several parts of this book, I discuss the importance of working across functional boundaries in order synchronize work and achieve goals. I urge you to take these seriously as you aim your sights on creating realistic goals, achievable strategies, and the wherewithal to execute those strategies.

THE STRATEGIC PLANNING PROCESS

If you review business literature, then practically every day you will read something about remarkable innovations from Apple or Google. They do a great job and earn the profits that allow them to experiment and tinker. It's part of their strategy. And they make for great benchmarks. On the same plane, we can see the work of people who have been successful in their creation of newer business models. Richard Branson's Virgin Airlines broke the mold on the legacy airline model. Steve Case offered direct access to the Internet using AOL. Their passion, vision, and strategy are to be admired.

As business people, we might feel frustrated that we can't be as notably successful as some of these entrepreneurs. Most of us, however, start out in an existing company. We may contribute to the strategic plan or devise one for a product or a foray into a new market area. Regardless of the work ahead of you, and because leaders want business people to think

Figure 8.2 Basic Strategic Planning Process

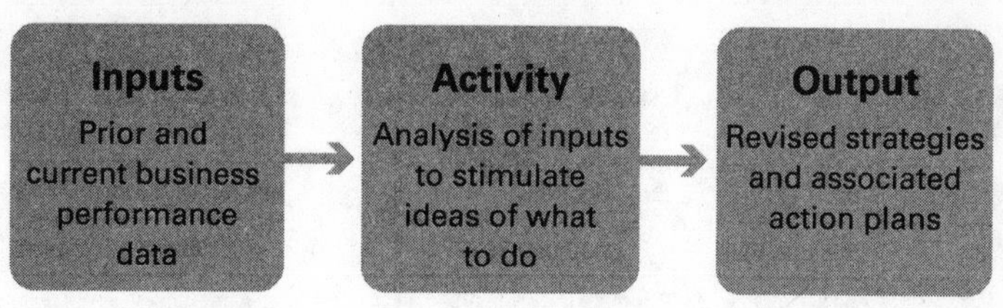

strategically, I want to simplify what's required. Like all processes, the strategic planning process is made up of inputs, activities, and outputs, as shown in Figure 8.2.

The strategic planning process serves to establish and manage the steps that represent the vision for the business. This process leads to explicit strategic goals and sets the stage to articulate the game plans or strategies that will be used to achieve those goals. In your thought process, you should consider the following questions:

1. What path has the business followed to this point?
2. What are the future-state vision and goals for the business?
3. What specific strategies and plans will be used to achieve the vision and goals?

The flowchart in Figure 8.2 provides a visual representation of these process steps.

While this is fairly straightforward, a lot of input data is required. Therefore, in Figure 8.3, I expand the basic model to reveal some additional details. Mind you, this is a time to take good notes and focus on the homework required to put any strategy into perspective.

EXERCISE
How does the strategic planning process in Figure 8.3 compare to what's used in your company?

The strategic planning process should consider what's been achieved and what's been a challenge when it comes to inspiring a plan of action

Figure 8.3 Expanded Strategic Planning Process for an Ongoing Business

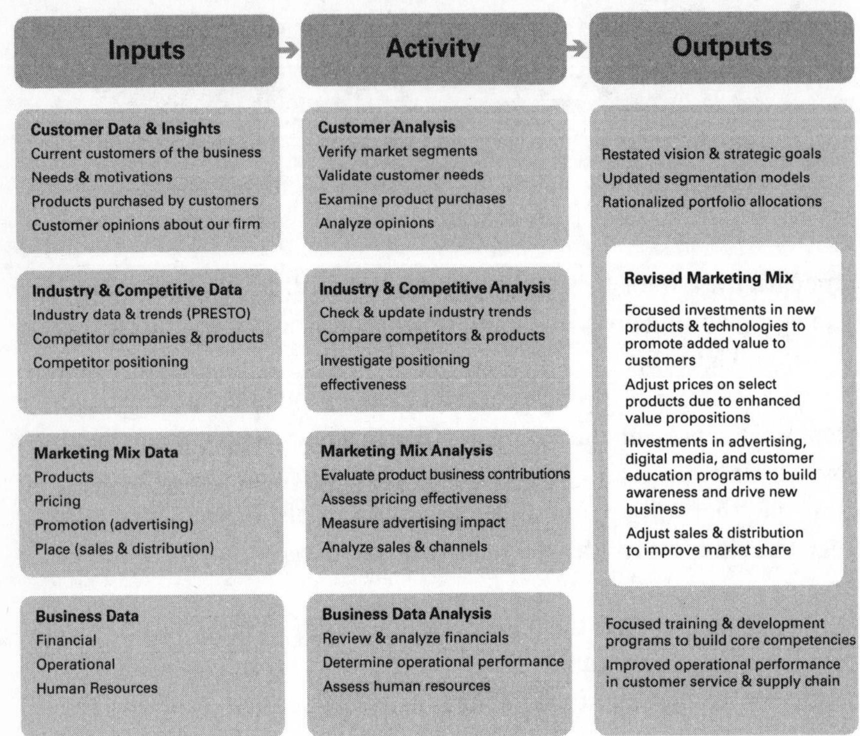

over a future time frame. As can be seen, there are a host of dependencies on data, which include market, financial, operational, and product data. Let's take a look at the main buckets that reflect each other as inputs and activities in Figure 8.3.

Customers. Chapter 7 offered important guidelines for understanding your customers. Knowing who they are and what motivates them is an essential part of the business formula. In strategic analysis, you must ensure that you have an accurate picture of the market segments you're targeting and the customer needs you're fulfilling. When you can describe how segments are changing (growing, shrinking, or staying the same), you can figure out where to focus the strategy for the business.

Industry and competition. Also in Chapter 7, I showed you how to assess industry trends and competitive activity. As you track those areas and come to understand how they affect the business, you can calibrate your organization's positioning. In other words, your strategic advantage is tied to where you want to be situated in the field of competitors and how you want to be seen in the eyes of your customers.

Portfolio and other investments. When a strategy is developed or revised, leaders in those firms must rationalize investments made in product portfolios and other areas of the business. Eventually, the investments cascade to smaller parts of the business—business divisions or product lines. Regardless, each part of the business operates in a more balanced way through the use of a marketing mix model that's periodically revised based on stated goals. I'll describe the components of the model and then explain how they're combined.

Marketing mix. The marketing mix is made up of four ingredients:

1. Products and their associated capabilities that provide value for customers
2. Prices that reflect what's paid by customers for the value received
3. Promotional programs that advertise the benefits to chosen customers, educate those customers, or encourage conversations that spur customers to buy products
4. Place, which describes how products are sold or distributed so they can move easily from the point of creation to the point of use

Here's an easy way to look at this: When you want to bake a cake, you have to combine flour, sugar, eggs, milk, and butter. Then, you blend the ingredients together and put the batter in the oven, where a chemical reaction yields a sweet result—the cake. When you run a business, you have to mix several business ingredients in order to produce a business result. You don't just devise and build a product and hope someone beats a path to your door. You devise the product based on understood customer needs, and you ensure that the product provides value for those intended customers. However, no customer will ever know about the product unless the business creates awareness and interest. Thus, to complete the job, you have to get the product to the customer. In a nutshell, that's the marketing mix, and business leaders must alter the ingredients of the marketing mix consistent with the goals they establish in order to produce the desired revenue and profit.

The marketing mix represents a critical dimension for any business. The more complex the company, the more important it is to track the performance of products and product lines across their life cycles. After all, product sales provide the revenue and profit for the business. Without products, there is no business.

There are many resources that you can use to study products and product life cycles. My own book, *The Product Manager's Desk Reference* (2e), provides comprehensive coverage of the topic. Another resource is Theodore Levitt's classic article from the November 1965 issue of the *Harvard Business Review* entitled "Exploit the Product Life Cycle." As a quick review, there are four main life cycle phases: introduction, growth, maturity, and decline. Each life cycle phase is tracked based on product unit sales, unit pricing, product revenue, profit, cash flow, market share, and other relevant metrics. Although the textbook representation looks like what's shown in Figure 8.4, note that each metric should be tracked and visualized to portray the product's life and to explain what's going on with the product's business during that stage. This information is central to the strategy because the overarching goals of the firm require clarification on given segments that will be served with specific products. If the product portfolio is filled with products that are mature, then there

Figure 8.4 Product Life Cycle Curve

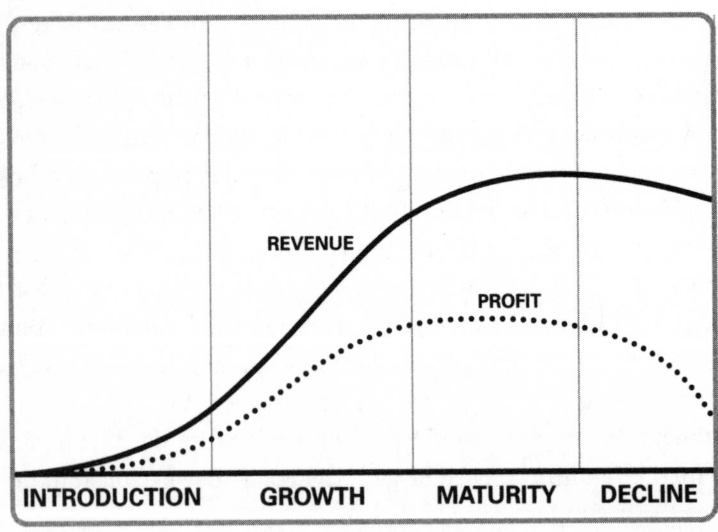

may not be sufficient future revenue from new products to sustain the business. Likewise, if products have very short life cycles and are not replenished as fast as the market is moving, again, there will be insufficient revenue to operate the business in the future. If there is sufficient balance in the portfolio between new and current products, and significant profit is being returned to the business, then the business leaders will have more money and more choices for strategic investments in the business. Imagine running a business without this data!

Other investments that the company makes also can have a dramatic impact on overall outcomes. The marketing mix model may apply to organic business growth to increase revenue or market share. However companies also invest in "inorganic" growth initiatives. These may include mergers and acquisitions as well as the creation of new business divisions. As an example, the EMC Corporation, once a company that only made computer storage products, transformed itself from a hardware-only business to a company that provided hardware, software, and services. During this transformation, senior leaders realized that they did not have the requisite talent to operate those new divisions, so they invested in executives from outside the firm with the requisite expertise to help fulfill the company's growth-oriented strategy. As you study companies and how they've engineered their growth initiatives, you will ultimately learn that large-scale inorganic initiatives are complex and don't always succeed as planned. Nevertheless, it's important to put these into perspective as you gain an understanding of the growth-oriented investments made by your company.

Now, we still have to evaluate all of the data from the various inputs, but this can't be done alone. A number of people from different functions have to be involved during the data analysis in order for the revised strategies to be considered and agreed upon. This collaboration is important because each functional leader will ultimately have to provide resources to fulfill the agreed-upon goals.

ANALYSIS AND SYNTHESIS: THE PIVOT POINT

Because markets are so dynamic, a lot of data needs to be collected and synthesized. Once this is done, it's easier to anticipate what might happen next and what needs to be done to work toward the goal. Data must be collected, organized, and synthesized so that future strategies and action plans can be set forth for further execution. It's also imperative that those involved (a cross-functional team) in the analysis and synthesis understand the intricacies and complexities of the organization in order to obtain the best perspective on what's next. This means:

1. Looking at the broad business horizon to derive the most suitable strategic goals
2. Linking those goals to anticipated changes in markets
3. Deriving and integrating the best marketing mix model consistent with the strategic goals
4. Establishing tracking metrics to determine success

I cannot reinforce this enough: the best goals and plans will be rendered useless unless these four items can be carried out. Implicit in this statement is the fact that execution will be stymied if the gears of the organization cannot appropriately come together.

All data must be analyzed as separate pieces, and then the interrelationships must be studied. For example, if I understand what motivates a customer to buy my product, I can create advertising programs to communicate the value. However, if the economic environment is poor, then the customer will not necessarily buy my product. Alternatively, if there's an influx of competitors in a favorable economic environment, my product's value proposition may be called into question and sales may be lost—even with a high-quality product. At some point, a *snapshot of the business* has to be taken. This freeze-frame captures the moment when the moving parts of the business are viewed together as a whole and not in motion, just as the gears of a watch can be viewed while not moving. Once we take the snapshot, we can study the business in more detail and determine what the pivot point must be. That's where synthesis or integration of the data comes into play.

When business people synthesize data, they need a canvas on which to paint their snapshot of what's happened thus far. This business data canvas is divided into two areas: business results from market activity, which are external to the firm, and business actions and outcomes from inside the walls of the business. See Figure 8.5 for a visual representation of how this *external* and *internal* data is captured on the business data canvas.

Figure 8.5 The Canvas to Capture External and Internal Business Data

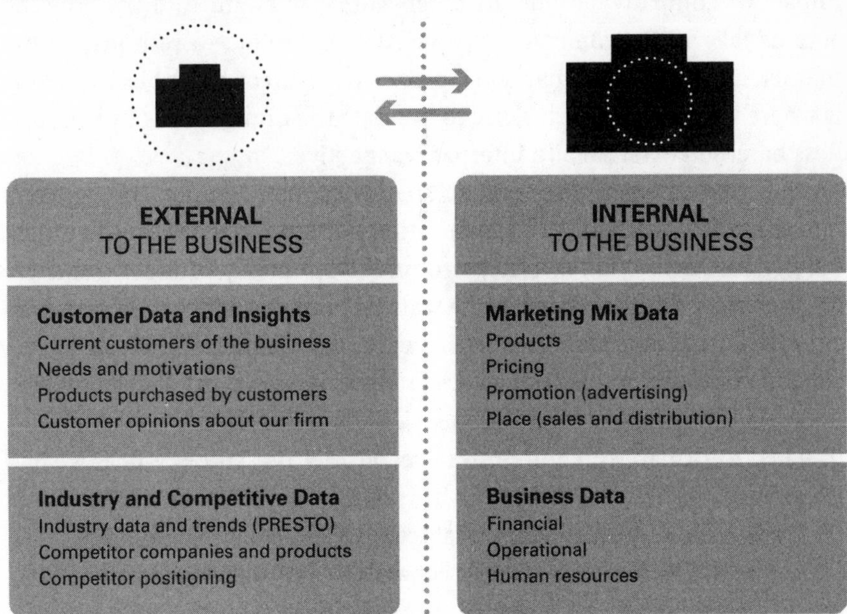

When business people examine the data from any of these perspectives, they have to look at a number of cause-and-effect impacts. For example, consider a software company that knows its customers are global, with employees everywhere who need up-to-the-minute data. If it capitalizes on that trend and produces products for remote workers that are better than those of competitors, it can likely charge a premium for its products, which then shows up as more revenue and profit for the company. With this, notice the interplay between the external and internal environments. However, in any company, making the connections between cause and effect can be problematic if data is insufficient or missing. In such a case, it's like assembling a dinosaur skeleton with half the actual fossils; you have to fill in the blanks, yet come up with a cohesive, logical image.

At the intersection of those external and internal data points, business people can utilize a SWOT analysis. SWOT is an acronym for strengths, weaknesses, opportunities, and threats. Like many tools used in business, SWOT is simple to understand yet often complex to deploy. To help you bridge the gap between theory and practice, I'll provide some guidance.

The main idea behind SWOT analysis is to evaluate the market impact of company actions. In other words, we want to learn how the actions taken by a company have worked to produce a response in the market, and how those market responses have affected the business. This is where it makes so much sense to evaluate the dimensions of your business based on external and internal perspectives.

Furthermore, SWOT analysis "snapshots" can be updated over time by people who work in your organization, regardless of function. A number of years ago, I had a strategy room set up for my product team. We had a SWOT diagram drawn on a wall that was covered entirely with an erasable whiteboard. Anyone on the team could write notes on the board based on data that might have been collected or observations made. Every couple of months, we'd take a quick snapshot to see if the accumulated information required us to reconsider our strategy, or if we had to make a midcourse correction. This collaborative approach catalyzed and motivated our cross-functional team. The team members knew their contributions were being considered, and it demonstrated that the ongoing analysis of business data is required to gain the proper perspective—and to think about strategic planning as an ongoing effort. From time to time, based on the cadence of your market, you have to take a snapshot to see what's going on or to recalibrate. When your cross-functional colleagues are involved in the process, everyone is inspired to move in the same direction—and collectively, they will maintain the equilibrium required to execute.

To organize the SWOT model for your business, you have to populate each quadrant with relevant insights that are supported by good data. Take a look at the SWOT template shown in Figure 8.6, where I've included the definitions in each quadrant. Notice that the strengths, weaknesses, and threats involve actions that led us to this this snapshot of the business. The opportunities, however, focus on the future. Therefore, opportunities should only be considered after a careful analysis of the inputs to the overall process. Refer to the strategy planning model where opportunities are, in fact, the outputs.

In addition, review the examples shown in each quadrant. These are fairly general, but the most important thing is that they must be supported by accurate data. If you're suggesting that one of the company's strengths is its good reputation, what research or surveys support that? If

Figure 8.6 SWOT Analysis Template with Quadrant Definitions

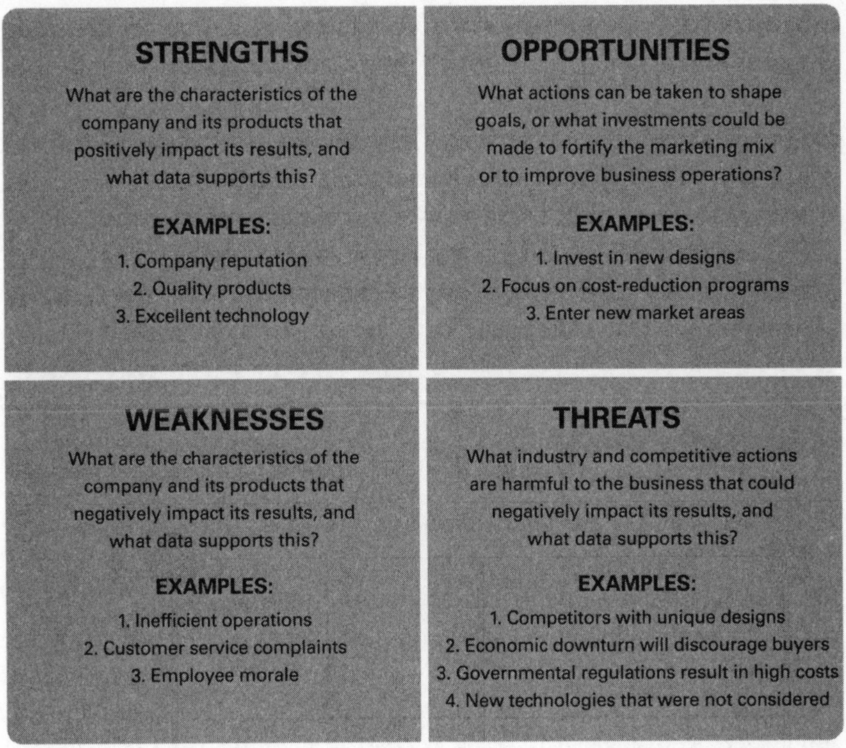

STRENGTHS	OPPORTUNITIES
What are the characteristics of the company and its products that positively impact its results, and what data supports this? **EXAMPLES:** 1. Company reputation 2. Quality products 3. Excellent technology	What actions can be taken to shape goals, or what investments could be made to fortify the marketing mix or to improve business operations? **EXAMPLES:** 1. Invest in new designs 2. Focus on cost-reduction programs 3. Enter new market areas
WEAKNESSES	**THREATS**
What are the characteristics of the company and its products that negatively impact its results, and what data supports this? **EXAMPLES:** 1. Inefficient operations 2. Customer service complaints 3. Employee morale	What industry and competitive actions are harmful to the business that could negatively impact its results, and what data supports this? **EXAMPLES:** 1. Competitors with unique designs 2. Economic downturn will discourage buyers 3. Governmental regulations result in high costs 4. New technologies that were not considered

you indicate a weakness in terms of operational efficiency, where would that data have materialized, and what would the impact be on the business? You and your team must be focused on these many variables in order for ideas and opportunities to gel in your minds. To reinforce an important point, you cannot just look at the parts; you have to see how they come together to form that big picture.

When I described my strategy room before, I indicated that we would take a snapshot from time to time to see how things were trending. Recall that I said we used a wall-sized whiteboard. After a while, we'd have to capture everything so we could erase the board. In doing so, we would put this information into a presentation we called the state of the business. One of the methods used is reflected in the template shown in Figure 8.7 entitled the *strategic game board*. This tool delivers a series of

Figure 8.7 Strategic Game Board Template, Current and Prior Years

BUSINESS DIMENSION	SNAPSHOT FROM TWO YEARS AGO	SNAPSHOT FROM LAST YEAR	SNAPSHOT FROM THIS YEAR
Vision			
Goals			
Overall business strategy			
Market segments			
Market share			
Company positioning			
Product strategy			
Pricing strategy			
Promotion strategy			
Place/channel strategy			
Revenue			
Profit			
Efficiency metrics			
Quality metrics			

snapshots over time, providing any business team with a multidimensional perspective. It also serves as the focal point to tell the story of where we've been, where we are, and where we're going. Ultimately, this is really what the entire strategy formulation process is about.

Although it's impossible to fill in each cell with data, you can use the strategic game board template to make sure that the data, insights, and conclusions are provided for. Anywhere there's a gap, you have to either get the data or default to the creation of assumptions—which may not sit well with the bosses. Make sure your team is involved in crafting the state of the business, always keeping in mind that you have to weave an impactful story through a detailed study of internal and external business data and how that was synthesized in your SWOT model. When you and your team work on as many cause-and-effect statements as possible, you've sown the seeds for great brainstorming that will help expose your future vision, goals, strategy, and marketing mix model. The following are some cause-and-effect statements for you to use in a template form.

1. We did ________, and as a result, here's what happened.
2. We learned ________ along the way, and continued to fine-tune what we did.
3. We fell short because of ________, so now we have to focus on ________.
4. Our competitors did ________ because of________.
5. The economy is growing in ________ [country], and it's time to expand our market share.
6. After evaluating our competitors' products, our R&D team came up with a new technology. Now, it's time to integrate this technology into our product platform.
7. Our research tells us that customers now prefer ________, and we altered our product to meet those customers' needs.
8. More customers find value in using our products to do ________, and because the products are in short supply, they're willing pay more.

STRATEGIC OPTIONS: GOING FORWARD

Now that you've completed your snapshot and state of the business story, it's time to move forward with an integrated strategy. As I've discussed in this chapter, your strategy should describe the activities that will be undertaken to create competitive advantage in the market and sufficient revenue and profit for the company. For most business people, this is completely logical. Whether you're playing a role on a strategy team in a company or plotting your way forward in a smaller enterprise, your strategy must simply state what you want to do to create value for your business and its stakeholders, as well as why you want to do it.

Michael Porter, in his book *Competitive Strategy*, describes three main approaches to strategy. He believes that a firm should focus on one of the following:

1. Employ a *cost leadership* strategy that focuses on cost management in a given market area. The U.S. retailer Costco manages the number of products it sells, obtains the best prices from its suppliers, and marks those up by 15 percent. To maintain cost leadership, it continuously tries to optimize

aspects of its business. Costco is famous for its $1.50 hot dog. However, when this was first introduced, it purchased the hot dogs from an outside company. Over time, the company learned to produce its own hot dogs, which allowed it to save cost and keep the price the same.

2. Adopt a *differentiation* strategy so that your company and its products are unique relative to the competition. Consumer beverage firms create unique products based on taste or image. German luxury automakers often differentiate themselves based on style or technology.
3. Use a *market niche* strategy based on having lower costs or more appealing features or specifications than rivals do. Many hotel operators have divided their properties to focus on different kinds of travelers. Marriott has many different brands that focus on a market niche. For the lower-cost market niche, it developed its Courtyard properties to focus on price-conscious business travelers and its Residence Inn to focus on price-conscious business travelers or families who need a longer-stay experience. It uses a *market niche* strategy based on *differentiation* from other competitors. To extend the Marriott example further, its Edition properties offer one-of-a-kind modern luxury properties to appeal to travelers who value a sophisticated experience and contemporary design.

In short, there are numerous resources you can use to study the work of great contributors in the area of business strategy. However, I don't want you to think about strategy from a just a theoretical standpoint. Business people must consider what needs to be achieved based on a vision from the leaders of the firm as well as the ensuing steps that must be taken. Once the vision is set, the game board template can be used to encapsulate goals and the other important components of the strategy. Notice that in Figure 8.7, the game board template only considers the past and the present. Now, we need to link the past and present with the future.

I'm sure you've heard people say that just because you achieved certain performance levels in the past doesn't mean that you'll attain the same levels in the future. Although that's a truism, it's important to use the same performance categories for the past, present, and future. This is

Figure 8.8 Strategic Game Board Template—the Complete Picture

	SNAPSHOTS			OPPORTUNITIES	
BUSINESS DIMENSION	TWO YEARS AGO	LAST YEAR	THIS YEAR	FOR THIS YEAR	FOR THE YEAR AFTER
Vision					
Goals					
Overall business strategy					
Market segments					
Market share					
Company positioning					
Product strategy					
Pricing strategy					
Promotion strategy					
Place/channel strategy					
Revenue					
Profit					
Efficiency metrics					
Quality metrics					

evidenced by the game board template in Figure 8.8, which includes two additional columns to point to the areas in which opportunities can be articulated for next year and the year after.

The template offers you a great blueprint to use in creating your future strategic story. In addition, use the following example to think about how you might knit your strategic story together:

> *Our vision for next year is ________________, and because of that, our goals include ___________ and ____________. Based on our vision and goals, our overarching strategy is to _____________. This strategy will enable us to focus on _____________ segments, where we hope to earn market share of ________, a ____ percent improvement. Our product investments will provide improvements from new technologies and increased functionality, which will also dramatically improve overall quality. By doing so, our customer value proposition will allow us to improve our pricing power. Furthermore, because we*

can competitively differentiate our products, we can focus our promotional activities to communicate through our advertising programs and sales training. With all of these, we expect to increase revenue by _____ percent over the next three years, with a corresponding increase in profitability.

SUMMARY

Most business people have applied the philosophy espoused in Lewis Carroll's well known quote: "If you don't know where you're going, any road will get you there." The moral of that story is this: without a strategy, a business is rudderless and, thus, more reactive to market forces. A strategy contributes to the future direction of the business in order to maintain the firm's competitive advantage.

I strongly recommend that you invest sufficient time to learn about the strategic planning process and how your efforts contribute to its outcomes. Doing so will also increase your knowledge of your company's business and its operations, which, in turn, will lead to greater levels of business acumen. It will also alert you to how different dimensions of the business operate and interoperate. When you involve people from other functions along the way, you'll develop deeper working relationships because you'll foster an environment of trust, sharing, and transparency. Further, the more intimately you understand how your business works, the more you can get your mind around things that can be done to move the business forward in areas such as new markets, new processes, or new product innovations.

INCREASING YOUR MANAGEMENT COMPETENCY

1. Take the time to understand the strategy of your organization and how people are aligned around that strategy. Identify the work that you do that supports the strategy.
2. If you work in a larger organization, locate the firm's vision statement. If you don't understand it, ask how it was developed and how that vision is associated with the strategic goals of the firm.

3. If you want to do some competitive analysis, compare the vision of your business to the vision of other firms. Where are the differences? Search for areas of competitive differentiation.
4. Try to keep current on what's happening with other companies in your industry. Read through the *Wall Street Journal*, the *Harvard Business Review*, and other publications to learn how other companies create and communicate their strategies.
5. Refer to the external and internal business canvas template shown in Figure 8.5. Using resources in this book, come up with a comprehensive list of items that will help you clarify the "what" and "why" for each item. You'll be able to easily apply what you discover to the SWOT analysis as well as to the strategy game board.
6. Create a strategic game board template for your business, similar to the one shown in Figure 8.8. Use this to craft your own story about the past, present, and future of your business.
7. Use the SWOT analysis template to analyze your own company. Then, use the SWOT template to analyze your competitors. From this, you will be able to pinpoint exactly where your business is situated. If, for example, you feel that there's an external threat from competitor actions, use the competitor SWOT to find areas on which you can focus to create strategic opportunities that can be turned into strengths.
8. When the time is right, involve other people from different departments in strategic analysis and planning. Recall my use of the strategy room. When others are involved in this process, they will be more likely to engage and provide valuable input. Also, when they buy into the future, they're more likely to assign resources and work toward agreed-upon goals.

Action Planning

In this chapter, the following characteristics were either explicitly or implicitly revealed. You may wish to identify where these were mentioned to reinforce your understanding of how they might be applied in your own work. You can also utilize the following template as a way to associate what was discussed in this chapter with your scores from your Business Acumen Assessment. From this, you can create an action plan for yourself or work with your manager to come up with specific goals and plans.

- Managing
- Defining processes
- Making decisions
- Critical thinking
- Strategic thinking
- Systemic thinking
- Entrepreneurial thinking
- Deriving market insights

ACTION ITEM + GOAL	STEPS TO BE TAKEN	OUTCOME PRODUCED	WHAT YOU LEARNED	WHAT YOU WILL SHARE

CHAPTER 9

UNDERSTANDING PRODUCTS

After you read this chapter, you should be able to:

- Explain why products are the lifeblood of any company.
- Describe how product investments are justified using a business case.
- Utilize a make-versus-buy analysis as part of a business case.
- Consider the impact of design thinking on products that create the desired customer experience.
- Use project management as a technique to efficiently plan and monitor work.

Don't make something unless it is both necessary and useful; but if it is both necessary and useful, don't hesitate to make it beautiful.

—SHAKER PHILOSOPHY

Have you ever seen one of those TV shows that feature a passionate inventor who's trying to convince an investor to finance her innovation? Alternatively, have you ever had the privilege to observe an entrepreneur pitch an idea to a venture capital firm? I have, and I can safely say that the passion of almost every innovator is undeniable! However, a silence always follows the questions from the investors that include, "Have you made any money?" or, "How much does it cost to produce?"

In the world of entrepreneurship, ideas for great new innovations abound in an unconstrained landscape. This is because entrepreneurs are usually visionary, socially aware, and have quick-thinking minds that rapidly experiment, fail, adapt, and ultimately succeed. In larger companies, people and processes are required to select the right products to bring to life. Much needs to be considered as each investment is carefully evaluated. Most studies conclude that products fail because of insufficient knowledge of customers and products that are not strategically important to the business. In my own research, I find that people across functions are not aligned around what's supposed to happen and when. They also overlook details because they don't see the bigger picture of a product within the context of an ongoing business. *Success in companies today requires people who can think and act like entrepreneurs to get the gears of the organization to move more quickly, because markets are moving faster.*

This chapter is designed to help you establish important linkages between market insights, strategic planning, and the ideas for innovative new products or enhancements to existing products. To achieve this, I'll concentrate on these topics:

1. What you should know about products
2. How product ideas are processed and evaluated using a business case
3. Within the context of a product business case, how design thinking is used to create the best customer experience
4. How to pitch a product business case to management
5. How project management techniques keep things moving smoothly once the investment decision is made
6. The role of intellectual property management and how it contributes to a product's differential advantage

WHAT YOU SHOULD KNOW ABOUT PRODUCTS

Although the three symbiotic pillars of a business (people, processes, and products) may seem easy to comprehend, they can be challenging to integrate. Therefore, it is important for someone in the company to ensure this happens. That person may be a CEO, a general manager, or a product manager. As I've mentioned throughout this book, business people who understand the interconnection of these three pillars, and other more detailed connections throughout the organization, will have a greater impact on business outcomes than those who do not.

To concentrate your attention, I want to provide the definition for a product: *a product is anything that's sold.* Many people distinguish between tangible and intangible products: tangible products are "made" (e.g., a computer), and intangible products are "experienced" (e.g., a service or mobile app). However, such a debate can be a distraction from the foundational constructs required for a successful product. Ultimately, a product represents value to a customer who's willing to pay for a perceived benefit.

Although products represent one of the three pillars, they can vary based on what a customer might actually purchase. Within a business context, a product is not always a single, stand-alone item; instead, within most companies, there is a *hierarchy of products and services.* A product may be part of another product or product line, packaged with a group of products, or offered as a *solution* or system to meet broad sets of customer needs.

Products and product lines are usually part of a larger product portfolio—either in a single firm or in a division of a larger company. For example, a business that sells to a business (B2B) may sell a complete product or a product component, such as a subassembly or software module. The next firm in the chain (as in business-to-business-to-consumer) may assemble the components or modules into a more complete product to be sold to a consumer. This is true for complete products such as automobiles, smartphones, computers, or even bank accounts. Figure 9.1 provides a visual of this product and portfolio hierarchy.

Business people should know that for any product to be successful, it must solve a customer problem or meet a customer need. Many products have a variety of features or attributes that contribute to how they work and the experience they produce for the intended customer. Therefore, in order to ensure that products deliver what's expected, they must be linked back to the explicit customer target within a market segment. To remind you about this important connection, refer to Figure 9.2.

Figure 9.1 Product and Portfolio Hierarchy

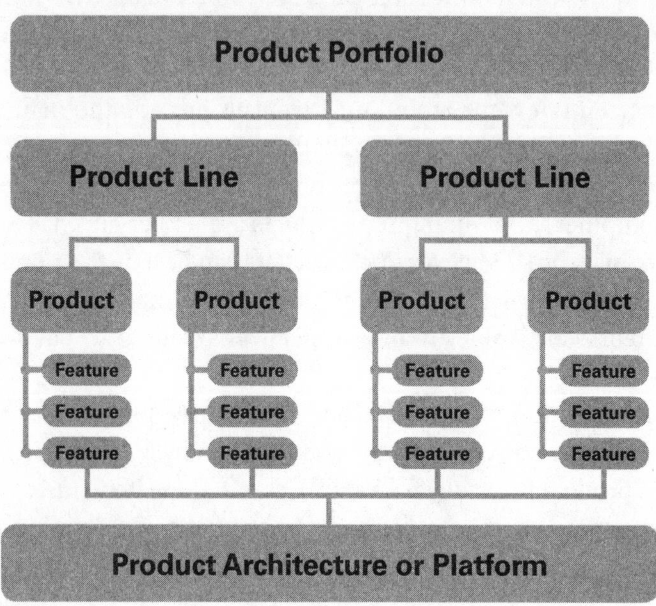

As a final step to reinforce the point of how linkages are created from desired market segments to the ultimate experience, I've prepared an example shown in Figure 9.3

As you review that table, put yourself in the role of a product manager at a bank where your goal is to create a mobile application. Hopefully, sufficient research would be available to understand the habits and behaviors of the customers within each segment. In the example shown in Figure 9.3, what would happen if your bank didn't offer a mobile application for the person in charge of managing the family money? It's likely that other competing banks would figure it out, which would likely cause the customer to defect and do business with a competitor who offers that product.

Figure 9.2 Translating a Targeted Customer Need into a Feature and a Customer Experience

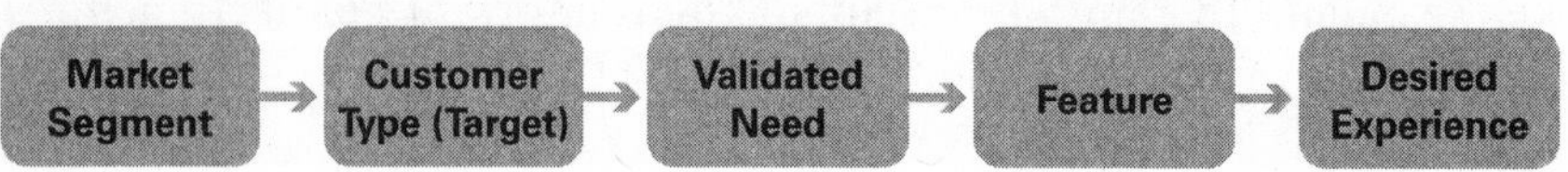

Figure 9.3 Work Template to Associate a Need with a Feature

MARKET SEGMENT	CUSTOMER TYPE	VALIDATED NEED	PRODUCT FEATURE	DESIRED EXPERIENCE
Affluent family	Bill payer and investment manager in the family who travels a lot	Wants instant information on family financial status	Mobile application offering snapshot view of bank balances	The customer must be able to quickly recognize the app icon and use the app to find the correct information. Also, the information must be easy to read and logically organized.

EXERCISE

Use the table in Figure 9.3 as a template to determine how the feature of a product in your company meets a specific customer need and inspires the desired experience.

PROCESSING IDEAS AND OPPORTUNITIES

In most companies, ideas for new products and updates to current products are often uncovered from many sources. It's not uncommon for senior leaders to insist on finding ideas that are innovative or distinctly different from anything that might be available on the market. These firms use an *ideation* process to put as many product ideas on the table as possible. These ideas come from market research, customer insights, and other market-sensing activities to derive ideas that stand out among the competition. Purposeful ideation programs are conducted in the form of structured customer visits, focus groups, or the use of customer advisory boards. In my own experience, I've learned a lot about customer preferences when I've been able to establish relationships with customers who want to be involved in product planning and idea validation. These *lead customers* are open to providing feedback and reviewing samples or prototypes and can add tremendous value in the ideation process. Another method that has been shown to have merit is patent mapping. Using this approach, R&D people or others may review others' patents to identify areas of potential competitive activity, which can validate some of the new ideas under consideration.

In reality, due to resource limitations, there will always be more ideas or opportunities than any one business can evaluate. To get ahead of the curve, many companies use a process to quickly evaluate a lot of ideas using a simple set of decision criteria. They evaluate the idea to determine if it is strategically important, has true market merit, and is technically feasible. Evaluations also must consider if others in the organization can come together to produce the product, launch it to the market, and then manage it along with all the other products of the company. Even if you work in a smaller company with one or two products, eventually the challenge of evaluating and prioritizing will become evident.

Figure 9.4 Phase-Gate Process for New Product Development

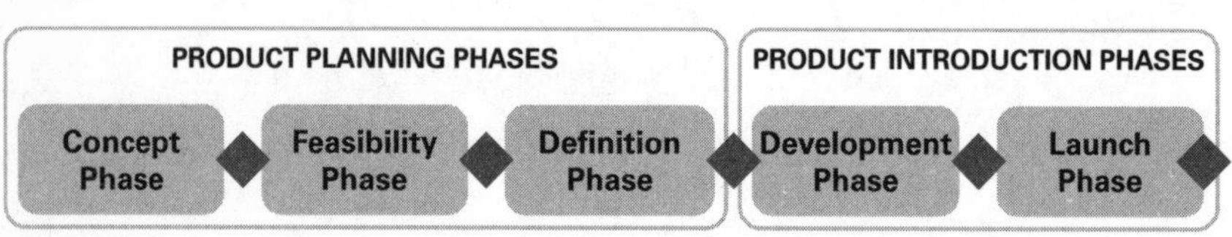

The majority of firms use a new product development (NPD) process to evaluate and select product investments and to ensure that chosen product investments can be effectively brought to market. The NPD process is organized into two main work areas: product planning and product introduction. It also comprises a series of phases and decision gates that allow for the appropriate level of study needed to make a decision about what to invest in and what to avoid. Refer to Figure 9.4 for a basic overview of the NPD process.

Planning phases include:

1. *Concept:* Many new ideas are rapidly reviewed and recorded in a brief opportunity statement or concept document. However, most are eliminated. The main idea is to decide on what makes sense to study further in the subsequent phase.
2. *Feasibility:* A limited number of ideas are studied in more detail, and a business case is started that serves to justify the investment to leaders in the company.
3. *Definition:* An even smaller number of ideas are fully assessed, and the product's functionality and features are finalized using

a *product requirements document*. The business case is also finalized, and the go/no-go investment decision is made.

New product introduction phases include:

1. *Development:* The product is actually built or sourced, and tested.
2. *Launch:* The product is brought to market.

Like most processes, the NPD process is illustrated as linear. However, markets are constantly changing. Sometimes, it's like trying to figure out what to do during an earthquake. On one day, an opportunity assessment seems logical, and in the blink of an eye, the economy takes a dive and options need to be reconsidered. Some people who work on these product projects become overly wedded to the process and develop emotional attachments to their ideas and won't let go of them. And by the way, it's a characteristic that is shared with entrepreneurs who have lots of great ideas! Leaders in well-run companies realize that the NPD process is a guideline for the work to be done so that decisions can be made about whether to continue assessing the opportunity or to stop work if the opportunity does not make business sense.

To summarize, finding the proper pace is a great product planning challenge. Business people should know that a linear model is used to ensure that the necessary work gets done by all concerned people, but work should proceed apace to stay in front of any competitors. Accordingly, phases may require compression (speeding up) if there's enough data to make a good decision, or extension (slowing down) if additional research is needed. In the end, business people must leverage the process without being overly constrained—very much the way an agile start-up might operate. Even if things are moving along, if a prototype reveals a gap in the product's composition, a product team may have to double back if it's felt that additional research or analysis is required. Planning phases are used to ensure that the proper level of study is done so that the chances of rework or failure are minimized. I'll share with you what one executive expressed to me on the topic of rework: "If you don't have time to do it right during planning, how will you have time to fix it later, when you're too busy with other things?"

EXERCISE

- What techniques are used in your company to uncover ideas for new products?
- How is the NPD process used in your company?
- Is your company using a sequential product development process or an iterative process? What's the benefit for using one product development process over another?

USING A BUSINESS CASE TO JUSTIFY A PRODUCT INVESTMENT

As you continue your learning journey in any company, you'll learn that many standard documents and templates are used to guide thinking and ensure consistency in doing work. When it comes to product planning, one of the most important documents is the business case.

The *business case* follows a standard methodology and is used to justify investments in new products, enhancements, and other business initiatives. The business case is assembled collaboratively and evolves during the product planning phases. It's important for you to know that its believability is tied directly to the realistic achievement of its intended outcomes. A business case is composed of the following sections:

1. *Executive summary:* This is a one-page summation of the entire document.
2. *Framing:* Every good story needs a strong context. This section sets the stage for everything to come. It includes a discussion of how the opportunity came about and why it's important to the business.
3. *Business need and/or strategic fit:* This section describes how the business will benefit from the investment and how it's directly linked to the strategy of the company.
4. *Market assessment:* Data and insights based on market research are included in this section. It should be constructed to clearly demonstrate that the product addresses the customer need, solves the problem, and is competitively differentiated.

5. *Product description:* This section must convey the characteristics of the product that are connected to the customer's needs. The description includes functionality, features, designs, performance characteristics, and customer experience requirements.
6. *Project plan:* All work done by people in different functions must be spelled out with regard to the development of the product as well as the support needed once it's in the market.
7. *Assumptions, forecasts, and financials:* Scenarios should be included that tell stories about future situations that might arise. Each scenario will include forecast volumes, prices, costs, expenses, and profit.
8. *Operations and implementation:* In order to put the investment into action, several puzzle pieces must come together to get the product ready and into the market at the right time. Organizational connection charts (as mentioned in Chapter 2) can be used to identify roles and contributions from people in various departments to fortify this section of the case.
9. *Risk analysis and contingency plans:* The business case should represent the best possible proof that an investment will deliver the promised return to the business. This section is often structured around questions such as, "What if the technology doesn't work?" "What if the right people aren't available?" "What happens if we can't get the product to market on time?"
10. *Recommendation:* Every case reaches a conclusion; the team must recommend either a go or no-go for the investment that considers the facts and data presented to defend that decision.

Within the boundaries of a business case for a product, there are two very important areas that must be included: the customer value proposition and competitive positioning. A *customer value proposition* is used to prove that the proposed product delivers a real benefit to the target customer. A relevant value proposition requires an understanding of the target customer and verification of the customer's problem or need. It also requires qualitative and/or quantitative proof that the product solves that problem. Saving time or money or helping a customer be more efficient can be quantified through a mathematical calculation that shows a before-and-after profile. Other benefits can be on a more emotional level, such as the association with a brand or perceived prestige. *Competitive positioning* is used to distinguish the product from its competitors. Effective positioning describes how you want your target customers to perceive your product. You've likely heard examples on television advertisements that use phrases like, "unlike others, ours is better, and here's why." Competitive differentiation is crucial, and it must be easily communicated to customers in sales and marketing materials.

The cross-functional team that produces the business case must prove that team members or other designated people from various departments will work together to carry out what's contained in the case, once approved. Very often, good ideas go bad when the capacity of the organization is insufficient to support the work at hand. Therefore, each function should detail its contribution to what's contained in the case. Here are some examples:

- *Product development or engineering* must be able to design and produce the product. It must ensure that it has the right technology and understands how to meet industry standards, achieve quality requirements, and produce the product.
- *Marketing* must be able to create the plans and programs for advertising, promotion, customer education, and sales training. It must also play an integral role in the product launch.
- *Customer service* must be able to deal with order taking, complaint handling, and other work activities on the front line of customer interactions.
- *Operations* must ensure that there is sufficient capacity in the company based on physical work locations, IT and supporting systems, and installation or deployment.
- A *supply chain* organization may be involved in physical product or component procurement. It must support operations, development, or other departments that require externally sourced items.
- *Manufacturing or assembly* may be required. Parts and components are brought together in a facility for production and delivery. Manufacturing works closely with supply chain, operations, and development in order to meet its obligations to the business.

EXERCISE

- Determine if there's a standard business case template in your company. If so, study its contents and compare them to what's listed in this chapter. Are there similarities? Differences?
- Locate a business case for a product from your company. Ask the person who led the team that produced the case to review for you the work that was done and the outcome.
- If you cannot locate a business case for a current product in your company, try to compose a case for a product sold by your company as if you were doing it from the beginning. You can call this a retrospective case, which will add to your perspective on the method used to justify a product investment.

I've illuminated many areas in this book that will ultimately be used in the assembly of a business case. This includes the involvement of people in other departments and use of processes, strategic context, and market insights. I hope that you'll take note so that when the time is right, you'll contribute to the success of a product business case.

THE IMPORTANCE OF PRODUCT DESIGN

Throughout the book, I've talked about the importance of understanding what customers do and why. Not only is it important in defining and defending product investments, it's important to know how your company translates market information into inspiring designs.

Design thinking is a methodology that helps people involved in the creation of a product to think about the product across a broad spectrum of customer needs and associated customer or market problems. In a book called *Design Thinking for Strategic Innovation*, author Idris Mootee defines design thinking as "the search for a magical balance between business and art, structure and chaos, intuition and logic, concept and execution, playfulness and formality, and control and empowerment."

Design thinking is useful when it examines the world in which customers operate. In this way, it helps to refine the product's definition—how it looks or feels—and contributes to the creation of a positive customer experience. Additionally, design thinking centers on what is technically feasible and what appeals to the value system of a customer.

The benefits gained by adopting this type of mindset cannot be underestimated. For instance, the management of a product, once in the market, requires a significant amount of data and the ability to evaluate various aspects of the business that support the product. If the complete environmental perspective is not considered, a lot of time will be spent fixing problems and reworking the product instead of thinking of ways to improve market share and make more money.

One of the most important undercurrents in product planning is verifying that what's envisioned will appeal to the desired customer and gain market traction. *Prototypes* can be actual models of a physical product or a mock-up of a working (or nonworking) set of screenshots for an application. In my prior corporate life at Oracle, if a product manager wanted to pitch an idea to me and my leadership team, he or she would be required to create a nonworking demo to show the design, layout, and navigation from the customer's perspective to present with the business case. If you were a clothing designer, you would create a sample, both to verify your vision and to show to prospective buyers in the retail channel. Prototypes allow business people, developers, designers, or others to use their creativity to bring their ideas to life.

When the *Wall Street Journal* first launched its application for the iPad, the development team actually worked on mock-ups in the lab. They created storyboards to capture a day in the life of the paper's readers and how those readers might interact with the content on the device. They created working models that were tested internally. Then, when sufficient progress had been made, they took the app loaded onto an iPad to the streets of New York City to get first reactions from people on the street! They took videos of the people so they could see how potential users would react. From there, they worked out some of the design problems and then brought the product back to the lab for rework so that the product could be readied for launch. The product was a great success, and it opened the doors to new and exciting business opportunities.

EXERCISE
Meet with people who are responsible for product design and development to find out which aspects of design thinking are used in the products produced in your company.

PRODUCT PACKAGING AND LABELING

Like you, I'm a consumer. Companies that market their products to us want to move us into a buying mood as fast as they possibly can. Sophisticated consumer products companies conduct research that examines our eye movements, response to colors and shapes, and other parameters that inspire buying behavior. Notice how website design, detergent packaging, book covers, and even editorial content are presented to people (as in the use of infographics). And it's not just consumer firms that are focused on packaging and labeling; industrial B2B companies pay attention to these as well. For example, in the oil and gas industry, there are a few companies that produce oil drill bits. Some firms use a distinctive color, and people who work on a rig will refer to the bit by the company's name brand and perceived reputation in a positive way. Another example is from a company that produced chemical sensors used in airport passenger screening. This company had the greatest market share of all firms in that space. One of this company's competitors changed its product design and the box in which the product was packaged and delivered. That competitor who came up with the new design gained greater market share. In this case, the most distinctive design won.

Product packaging and labeling should not be an afterthought for any business. People in marketing, product design, and other areas should focus on this during the NPD process. Here are a few points that are important to remember if you are ever involved in this work:

1. The job of packaging is to *stand out from others*. Colors, designs, use of fonts, and other items are designed to attract the attention of a buyer. The next time you're in a movie theater, look at the coming attractions posters for a clue.

2. An advertising friend of mine once told me that *simpler is better*. She was working on a campaign for a vodka producer and showed me some of the creative pieces used in the pitch. She explained that her job was to present a pleasing package that reduced the noise of the visual and drove attention to the product. Simplicity could also apply to the ease of product access. How many times have you purchased a product that's encased in rigid plastic and requires a chain saw to open? Good for the producer, not for the consumer.
3. Your package should trigger an *emotional response*. When you watch Coca-Cola advertisements during the holidays and see the cute polar bears frolicking and holding up those red and silver cans, you get that warm fuzzy feeling that bonds you to the brand.
4. Consider your *market segments*. If you're appealing to environmentalists, don't use polystyrene packaging. Sustainability is the watchword in many areas, including packaging. If you're appealing to technology geeks, deploy the shiny objects. If beauty is in the eye of the beholder, know your beholder.

In addition to the packaging in which the product is placed, the actual labeling must also be considered. Make note of international (in-country) requirements for language and color. Overall, make sure you're keeping a watchful eye on your company's products and your competitor's products so that you can provide input when needed, or guidance and leadership when required.

SOCIALIZATION AND THE PITCH

The business case must be properly presented to management. The leader of the cross-functional team is usually the person who has to deliver that presentation. On the surface, this is logical. However, in an organization, there are a number of back channels and political levers that need to be adjusted. Savvy business people know that they have to manage up, down, and across the organization. They keep leaders informed and updated on the progress of the case because they know that ultimately, they'll be asking for money for the project in much the same way a start-up founder seeks funding from a venture capital firm.

In Japan, the nemawashi business practice is used by people to engage in conversations in either a formal or informal setting to discuss an idea or plan of action. In other words, in Japanese business culture, all decisions are made by group consensus, and it's impossible to get anything accepted if the leaders of the organization are not properly briefed in advance. In Western businesses, we refer to this as *socialization.* Oftentimes, these "meetings before the meeting" obviate the need for a formal presentation. This technique can be applied in any environment where there are many functional leaders who have their own agendas and metrics. The best product idea will go nowhere if you can't get everyone on board in advance.

Over the course of my career, I explored the world of start-ups and met a number of angel investors and venture capitalists. I also observed a number of pitch presentations by people who seemed to believe they had great ideas. I learned a lot from these sessions, and from speaking with the investors as well as those who were pitching their great ideas. As you might imagine, very few ideas seem attractive to funders, and there are important reasons why.

In business, the person doing the pitch must have the skill, credibility, personality, and passion to do an effective job. Wherever you work, I recommend that you follow the business practices needed to socialize the ideas in advance. Throughout this book, I've provided you with all of the ingredients for a successful pitch. Your job is to weave an impactful short story that imparts:

1. A precise portrayal of the dynamics of the market (size and potential) and your clear understanding of the customer's problem or challenge.
2. A description of the product, hopefully with a prototype or sample to show or demonstrate. Focus specifically on how you'll solve the customer's problem.
3. A compelling value proposition and defensible competitive positioning, including how your company or product will win in the market.

4. Why the time is right, and when the product needs to be in the market.
5. How much money you want, for what, and over what time period.
6. When you will receive your first orders and what you project your cash flow to be. Clearly express the return on investment (ROI) so that it can be easily understood by the leaders who are to provide funding.

Another great tool to use to augment the pitch is a *press release*. In my corporate life, I would ask my product managers to think of the product launch and an internally oriented press release that would be used to announce the product to the sales and marketing departments if the product was to actually be launched. Essentially, this document would summarize information from the business case and explain the customers' situation (what's their problem) as well as why this product would be attractive to them (the value proposition) and better than competitive offerings (positioning). I would also ask them to present the kinds of customer testimonials that they would hope to find in product reviews (in online forums or other areas).

MAKE-VERSUS-BUY ANALYSIS

When it comes to building a product—whether it's tangible or intangible—it may be more cost effective to have an outside company do the work. The following sample case sheds some light on how to make such a decision.

You work for the Happy Healthcare Company, which produces monitors and sensors for health-conscious people. These include heart rate monitors, sleep sensors, and other products. Your CEO believes it's important for the company to manufacture its own products in order to maintain high quality and control over production. Although the executives on the leadership team agree that it's imperative to increase capacity, there's limited space for this expanded production. Each time the production line is reconfigured for a different product, valuable time is lost and unit costs increase. Currently, the most important product is the

Figure 9.5 Make-Versus-Buy Analysis

	CURRENT	PROPOSAL 1 IN-HOUSE	PROPOSAL 2 VENDOR A	PROPOSAL 3 VENDOR B
Unit volumes	65,000	85,000	85,000	85,000
Selling price per unit	199.00	199.00	199.00	199.00
COST OF GOODS SOLD (COGS)				
Materials - per unit	34.00	34.00		
Labor - per unit	18.00	16.00		
Overhead- per unit	28.00	19.00		
Total COGS per unit	**80.00**	**69.00**	**58.00**	**53.00**
OTHER EXPENSES				
Production line configuration (annual)	354,000	90,000	--	--
Software production (in-house work)	620,000	620,000	620,000	620,000
Hardware and software integration and test	431,000	391,000	250,000	283,000
Transportation and logistics	732,000	732,000	821,000	698,000
Quality control inspector	--	--	91,000	--
Inventory carrying costs	195,000	134,000	62,000	97,000
Product documentation	58,000	58,000	58,000	58,000
Total Other Expenses	**2,390,000**	**2,025,000**	**1,902,000**	**1,756,000**
SUMMARY				
Revenue	12,935,000	16,915,000	16,915,000	16,915,000
COGS	5,200,000	5,865,000	4,930,000	4,595,000
Gross Margin	7,735,000	11,050,000	11,985,000	12,410,000
Expenses	2,390,000	2,025,000	1,902,000	1,756,000
Net Income	**5,345,000**	**9,025,000**	**10,083,000**	**10,654,000**
Net Income %	**41.3%**	**53.4%**	**59.6%**	**63.0%**
Full cost per unit (COGS + expenses/volume)	116.77	92.82	80.38	73.66
Minimum production run volume	5,000	--	--	--
Minimum order quantity	--	--	10,000	7,500
Experience in this business	High	High	Moderate	Low
Verified references	--	--	Yes	No
Influence in materials selection	--	--	Yes	No
Production in U.S.	Yes	Yes	Maybe	Yes
Willingness to allow on-site inspections	--	--	Yes (at our cost)	No

sleep sensor, which is made up of physical product components and a smartphone app. Software development is done in-house. Volumes and revenue have grown nicely, even though gross margin has been shrinking. The firm currently sells 65,000 units per year, and the strategy for the next two years is 85,000 units per year.

Your make-versus-buy team members represent product design, manufacturing, operations, development, and supply chain. Together, you created a request for proposal (RFP) that was issued to five firms, but only two firms made it to the short list. Figure 9.5 outlines the essence of the two proposals. It also contains one from your team, which has some ideas about production expansion and cost management—and wants to keep things in-house.

As your team evaluates the information, there is a lot of debate. The comparison is not as simple as you thought it would be because there are a number of variables. Each vendor provided only one cost per unit, so it's not clear what is included in the cost. Your team members feel that the in-house option offers greater transparency and more control. They may have a point; Vendor B wouldn't allow you to inspect or influence materials. That's a major issue for you because your company wants to ensure exceptionally high quality. Vendor B can help your company make more money, as it offers you the best net income percent of all choices. However, that doesn't mean it's the right firm, especially considering the fact that it has very limited experience in this sector.

The team members debated all the issues and ultimately settled on staying in-house. Despite some of the political implications that weren't put on the chart, they offered to construct a small facility on the property to house one of the other product production lines and allow for greater capacity on the current line. They felt that if they were to run a part-time shift with lower-wage workers, they could reduce labor costs. Also, as a result of the increased capacity, the supply chain group found that it could earn some solid discounts from its suppliers.

As you can see, there are many ways to evaluate this model. Merely looking at the numbers doesn't tell you the entire story. You have to dig into other areas, such as the people and processes. The CEO was pleased with the decision because it was consistent with her vision while allowing the company to grow and keep local people employed. Her reputation in the community was worth the compromise on profit.

At some point in your career, you may encounter the opportunity to conduct a make-versus-buy analysis. The matrix shown in Figure 9.5, and the preceding analysis example, should equip you with the ability to facilitate robust discussions that argue business and strategic merits—as well as the financials.

MAKING THE DECISION TO INVEST

Earlier in the chapter, I introduced you to the phases of the NPD process and described the need to make a decision at the end of each phase. In Chapter 6, I demonstrated how a decision matrix could be used to compare a number of opportunities based on a set of decision criteria. As an opportunity progresses through each of the product planning phases, an increasing number of decision criteria will be applied, reflecting a wider set of issues that business leaders need to consider. These criteria should focus on the following:

- Is the investment strategically important to the achievement of your goals?
- Does the investment contain a valid, proven customer value proposition?
- Is the product distinctly different from and can it be properly positioned in the market against competitor products?
- Does your firm have capable, available resources to work on the product if approved?
- Is the investment affordable, and does it provide the required return to the business?
- Have you considered all of the main risks before making a final decision?

To make the best decision possible, you must have sufficient data. Data you perceive as current may be out of date in short order. Therefore, even after the decision to invest is made, you should constantly recheck all data sources for accuracy and completeness, just in case any of those items change.

FACETS OF PRODUCT DEVELOPMENT

One of my favorite hobbies is woodworking. As a craftsman, I abide by a guideline that woodworkers have followed for centuries: measure twice and cut once. As described earlier, a lot of work goes into the planning phases. Think of product planning as the "measuring" part of woodworking. Once the decision to invest is made, it's time to "cut," or in other words, to execute and build the product. The main players in product development may work in engineering, R&D, or even IT.

In many firms, concerned business people may be responsible for the oversight of product development projects, and in doing so, must anticipate that things will go wrong. As a point of reference, think of how a general manager or CEO might get involved in reprioritizing work or in negotiating trade-offs for critical product projects—that's how you might envision business interventions during the development phase.

As development projects are undertaken, people who work on those project teams complete their work and orchestrate handoffs along the way. In some cases, business people may get directly involved to expedite those handoffs and interactions between different departments or with resources outside of the company. As an example, some business people may be assigned the job of ensuring that regulatory approvals and/or certifications for local or international product deployments get done so that the product can be marketed, sold, and supported domestically or internationally. Overall, the more you're involved in the business or exposed to products that are in development, the more familiar you'll become with the ebb and flow of these activities. That's where project management is important.

EXERCISE

What are the interactions that take place between the people in product development and others? What are the key handoffs, dependencies, and challenges?

PROJECT MANAGEMENT AND PROGRESS TRACKING

Whenever a person or group of people is assigned to produce a product, they're working on a project. Business people must be well-versed in project management methodology, which is clearly documented in *A Guide to the Project Management Body of Knowledge* produced by the Project Management Institute (PMI) (www.pmi.org). According to the PMI, project management covers "the application of knowledge, skills and techniques to execute projects effectively and efficiently." In this section, I aim to provide a high-level summary that emphasizes the importance of project management to track work activities, especially those called out in the business case.

In the realm of project management, projects are managed under what is known as the "triple constraint," which is composed of project *scope*, *time*, and *cost*. Each constraint is similar to a variable in a mathematical equation. If one variable changes, then the entire outcome of the formula will change. Successful results from the development phase are dependent on several simultaneous ongoing projects that must be completed on time and within budget. The result should be a completed product. If costs go up or the project takes too long, the product requirements will be unfulfilled and the product may fail.

A project plan is made up of many tasks that are organized and grouped under an umbrella known as a *work breakdown structure* (WBS). I like to think of a WBS as if it were a process because of how it divides work activities into tasks that are like subprocesses. Each task has a start time and an end time; thus, by default, each task has a *duration* associated with it. In addition, some tasks must be completed before other tasks can start (these are called predecessor tasks). If a predecessor task is not completed, then the following task (a successor task) can't be completed. In project management terminology, these successor tasks are *dependent* on predecessor tasks. This can delay the entire project. With some projects, tasks can be worked on simultaneously and autonomously. However, even in such projects, at some point, all deliverables must be assembled into a unified whole in order to complete the project. If you're a business person who's overseeing one or more projects, you should be intently concerned with how activities are defined so that the path from start to finish is crystal clear.

To help you understand how a project plan is constructed, consider a small project for a company involving planning for a customer service training program. The project was just assigned to Jennifer, a business analyst in the marketing department. She has to create a project plan related to the logistics for the new customer service training program. First, Jennifer must create the WBS. She's done so as follows:

WBS 5.0—Customer Service Training Program

5.1—Customer Service Agent Training Logistics

5.1.1—Service manager to select personnel to be trained

5.1.2—Marketing manager to develop training materials

5.1.3—Decide on date of training

5.1.4—Secure training facility

5.1.5—Order training materials

5.1.6—Send out invitations

5.1.7—Process registrations

5.1.8—Send over final instructions for room setup to training facility manager

5.1.9—Distribute preclass materials to attendees

A Gantt chart is a project management tool used to show how projects are organized. This chart portrays tasks as a series of horizontal bars, sequenced and linked to show duration and dependencies within the context of the WBS. Some of the steps from the WBS are shown in a simple Gantt chart in Figure 9.6.

Invariably, business people will need to create project plans to schedule resources and ensure that work gets done. However, in my research, I've learned that performance tracking against plans is not done as well as it could be. For example, sometimes the plan doesn't consider how much time a person can devote to a task. Think of it this way: if you are assigned a task that needs to be completed in one day, what does that actually mean? Do you have eight hours during a week to do the task, or do you

Figure 9.6 Simple Gantt Chart

		START	END	WK 1	WK 2	WK 3	WK 4	WK 5	WK 6	WK 7
1	Secure facility	1-Apr	15-Apr	■	■					
2	Order materials	1-May	7-May					■		
3	Send invitation	5-Apr	12-Apr		■					
4	Process registrations	6-Apr	6-May		■	■	■	■		
5	Send final instructions	7-May	14-May						■	
6	Conduct training	15-May	21-May							■

complete it in one eight-hour day? If you're like me, you're involved in meetings, responding to e-mails, talking to people on the phone, and getting dozens of interruptions. Before I know it, the day's over, and I have only partially completed the task. To track performance, you need to make sure you know the identity of the assigned person and whether she can do the work in the allotted time. Similarly, when a cost estimate is provided by a functional manager, it may not be known how that estimate was derived. If the details behind that estimate are unknown, then the project is exposed to the risk of exceeding the allotted budget. It is safe to assume that actual performance won't always match the plan. Thus, to manage this inherent risk, a performance tracking tool, like the one shown in Figure 9.7, should be used. This tracking tool has very broad application; in fact, this is the same kind of tool used by major defense contractor firms in reporting status to their military customers.

Note that in the status report, there are budgeted hours for a person, start and end dates, and budgeted costs. As you can see, the report tracks hours and incurred expenses. As the project progressed through the first month, even though the employees worked full-time, they uncovered problems and encountered delays. The overall impact is a budget overrun and a schedule slip. If these were part of an important product launch, then the launch might be delayed, exposing the company to a variety of market and financial risks. As you can see, project scheduling and tracking are critical to the success of any business. The more projects there are, the greater is the need for oversight to reduce risk and improve business performance.

Figure 9.7 Sample Project Status Report

RESOURCE	PROJECT HOURS	START DATE	END DATE	BUDGET	HOURS WORKED	INCURRED SPENDING	ESTIMATED HOURS TO COMPLETE	ESTIMATED DATE TO COMPLETE	TOTAL HOURS TO COMPLETE	ESTIMATED COST TO COMPLETE	UNDER/ OVER BUDGET	EXPLANATION
Engineer	480	1-Apr	30-Jun	$43,200	120	$10,800	440	15-Jul	560	$50,400	$(7,200)	2 weeks late due to technical problem
Tester	320	1-Apr	31-May	$24,000	120	$9,000	260	30-Jul	380	$28,500	$(4,500)	Engineering delay and testing protocol problems

INTELLECTUAL PROPERTY

When products provide the needed differential advantage for the company, it's often because of an underlying technology or a proprietary feature. According to a definition found on the Cornell University Law School website, "Intellectual property is any product of the human intellect that the law protects from unauthorized use by others." Because most products or product components represent the intellectual property (IP) of the company, legal IP protection is needed. Without such protection, IP could be misappropriated by competitors, making businesses reluctant to invest in R&D or other types of innovative activity. As you traverse your career in business, you must be cognizant of the types of IP that exist and the protections offered for that IP.

In the United States, you can refer to the guidelines and information posted on the website of the Patent and Trademark Office (uspto.gov). You can search on patents and trademarks for any country to learn the rules, application procedures, and how to identify potential conflicts. I'll provide you with some simple definitions that you should become familiar with. This will heighten your sensitivity to the importance of IP—and by knowing these, you'll be equipped to participate in the conversation when IP issues arise.

- *A patent* provides legal protection for an inventor or group of inventors in a company. Note that patent protections vary from country to country. For example, there is a profound difference in the patentability of software in the United States versus in other countries. A patent provides the inventor with the right to exclude others from using what's covered in the patent itself for a specific period of time. The pharmaceutical industry offers good examples for further study.
- *Trade secrets* can cover formulas, service models, or compilations of information used by a business to create its products and services. A trade secret should be protected if it's not generally known to others or if the creator of the secret takes special precautions to keep it a secret. If, for any reason, the secret "leaks out" and is available to others, it's fair game and is no longer

protected. For example, if a competitor reverse engineers a publicly available product and manufactures that product using what's thought to be the trade secret, then it's as if the trade secret were publicly available. Legal protection is only available when someone has protected the secret and that secret was improperly obtained. For example, there are current challenges and legal proceedings between very visible smartphone makers.

- *Trademarks* are symbols, words, devices, sounds, scents, or a combination of items that exclusively identify the source (company) of a product or service. Trademarks are owned by the people who invented and used the mark first. Trademarks should be registered to ensure protection, and proof of first use is required. If someone develops a similar trademark, the battle lines are drawn based on who can prove first use or that the businesses are not in conflict. Moreover, trademarks require consistent use to be kept in force.
- *Copyrights* represent a form of legal protection granted to a person or an entity (an originator) for the protection of their work. A copyright will cover "original works of authorship," including literary, dramatic, architectural, pictorial, graphic, and audiovisual presentations. Copyrights do not protect ideas, processes, titles, or slogans. As an employee, work that you create during your employment automatically belongs to your employer, and the employer is considered the author. For more information, visit www.copyright.gov.

If IP rights are not considered before and during product development, then the leaders of the company may be in for a surprise at the most inopportune time. The IP issue should be surfaced in the business case and be verified during the development process. The best way to do this is to engage either the company's legal department or the services of a patent attorney. If the product is deemed to contain IP, then it would be up to the executives in the company and the legal team to ensure that efforts are undertaken to register and protect the IP. Business people may or may not be involved in this process, but they should be cognizant of the need for IP protection.

SUMMARY

There's no shortage of product ideas. The deeper your involvement in all things "market," the more ideas will emerge—from customer suggestions, salespeople, competitive activity, and elsewhere. The challenge for most business people is the sheer volume of ideas. The faster you can dismiss the ones that don't have strategic or market merit, the greater the time available to concentrate on the evaluation of meaningful opportunities. The fact remains that many wonderful product ideas won't ever see the light of day, while others may slip through to the market only to fall flat.

Business people have an opportunity to be more impactful if they're more mindful about the myriad gears that spin both from inside and outside the company. You can gain this mindfulness when you understand each and every step that is involved from the time an idea materializes, how it's processed, and what goes in to the decisions made to invest—or not.

When you concentrate on innovative ways to solve customer problems, through new methods or unique designs that deliver the most compelling experience, you'll have more winning products. As we all know, winning products provide your company with the financial resources to continue to invest and grow.

INCREASING YOUR MANAGEMENT COMPETENCY

1. Create a product and portfolio hierarchy for a product or product line in your own company. Model it after the one shown in Figure 9.1. You may need to interact with people in different areas, such as product managers, engineers, or salespeople. You can also refer to your company's website. Further, consider creating a competitor product and portfolio hierarchy, and use it as part of a competitive analysis.
2. To learn how ideas are brought into your company, you can meet with people in sales, marketing, customer service, and product management. Try to find out how those ideas are organized and how they're handled.
3. Meet with your company leaders to find out if they employ any creative methods for ideation to uncover opportunities.

Try to see how these are linked to the opportunities that may emerge from the strategic planning process.

4. If you'd like to focus some of your attention on creative idea generation, you can use market research and other information to uncover market patterns or trends. Delve into and research the many sources of market information: review trade journals and business publications, visit customers, scan your daily informational feeds, read synopses from your competitive intelligence group, review relevant blogs, and check into any other sources you may have. And don't forget to share what you learn with others in your organization!
5. Find out if your company uses a phase-gate, or similar, process. Is there a process owner you can talk to, or process documentation that you can review? This can help you understand how ideas are uncovered, evaluated, and documented.
6. Does your company use any specific templates or tools for documents, such as a business case? If so, where are they located? Find out who has worked on those cases, and talk to them about the process they followed and the outcomes they achieved.
7. If your company produces a tangible product, arrange to take a factory tour. If your company produces software, ask to spend an hour with a software developer to see how his work results in providing product functionality or a feature.
8. Take a class in project management to learn the basics and speak the language of project management.
9. Investigate the business oversight required in your company for product development projects. Which people are involved? What do they do? Is it documented?
10. Ask your manager if she can introduce you to a person or team who's been involved in a make-versus-buy analysis. Hopefully you'll learn much from the work that was done and how the decision was made.
11. Make an appointment with a member of the legal department and ask him to explain the kind of intellectual property protection that is used in your company.

Action Planning

In this chapter, the following characteristics were either explicitly or implicitly revealed. You may wish to identify where these were mentioned to reinforce your understanding of how they might be applied in your own work. You can also utilize the following template as a way to associate what was discussed in this chapter with your scores from your Business Acumen Assessment. From this, you can create an action plan for yourself or work with your manager to come up with specific goals and plans.

- Making decisions
- Defining processes
- Deriving market insights
- Understanding products
- Systemic thinking
- Strategic thinking
- Entrepreneurial thinking
- Developing organizational instinct
- Exercising political judgment
- Presenting persuasively
- Listening attentively
- Influencing others
- Negotiating
- Developing external relationships
- Being results oriented
- Evaluating business performance

ACTION ITEM + GOAL	STEPS TO BE TAKEN	OUTCOME PRODUCED	WHAT YOU LEARNED	WHAT YOU WILL SHARE

CHAPTER 10

MARKETING: THE FULCRUM OF THE ORGANIZATION

After you read this chapter, you should be able to:

- Explain the role and importance of marketing in a company.
- Characterize the structure and operating model for marketing.
- Describe the marketing cycle in your company.
- Understand the elements of a go-to-market strategy.

The only limit to our realization of tomorrow will be our doubts of today.

—FRANKLIN D. ROOSEVELT

I've been a business traveler for a long time. Airport terminals in the past were utilitarian and unfriendly. Today, many airports are designed for travelers who shop, dine, and conduct business. This is marketing at work.

From a broad standpoint, *marketing is about inspiring dialogues with or between customers, attracting customers to your company and its brand, creating a remarkable experience, and producing information to educate customers so they can make buying decisions.* With this, it's easy to conclude that marketing activities are geared toward the visible, as presented in advertising and promotional programs. However, marketing isn't only about what's visible. Marketing *ensures that there's adequate market data and insights to help set strategic direction, which then contributes to the creation of outward-facing programs that drive business activity.* Therefore, the success of the marketing function hinges on its ability to have a positive impact on the results of the company.

As a business person, you'll need to be familiar with the marketing department in your company as a hub of activity and orchestrator of business. You'll need to understand its structure, subfunctions, and cross-organizational impacts. It's important that you consider the marketing function as part of an interconnected whole, not just a stand-alone department. To that end, in this chapter, I discuss the following topics:

1. The role of the marketing function
2. How the marketing function is organized
3. The purpose and importance of the marketing cycle
4. The importance of marketing in driving go-to-market activity

THE ROLE OF THE MARKETING FUNCTION

Marketing is one of the most dynamic functions in a company based on the sheer volume of energy used to catalyze activity. It's in a continual state of evolution. As any consumer can attest, brand building and advertising are expanding rapidly. Whether it's because we are an increasingly mobile society or because we're using so many devices, the increasing presence of marketing output is undeniable.

When you look "under the hood" in any company, you will see an organization that is in flux. I've been witness to dozens of reorganizations in marketing departments, and I'm sure you will see these, too. Through those experiences, I've observed that senior leaders are intent on ensuring that there's a solid mission and purpose of marketing—that its goals are clear, its processes are well defined, and the structure of the department reflects its mission and goals. Further to this, I've learned that marketing leaders are vitally concerned about the collection and management of data, the continual improvement of the customer experience, and an environment that inspires creative collaboration with people across the enterprise.

As I conducted research for this book, I spoke with many marketing leaders. One theme connecting all of those conversations is the *importance of data*. One chief marketing officer (CMO) said that her company has more customer data now than it has ever had before. Its current challenge is to harness that data more completely in order to fine-tune the company's messages to people in specific market segments. This is exemplified by a Nike advertisement I saw recently. It was for their Nike+ Running app. When I looked at the Nike website, I read about the app and what it does for runners in terms of keeping track of total runs, average pace, and other statistics. Interestingly, Nike now has the capability to track all of the users of this app, along with their habits and preferences. Further, it's created a community of runners who can benchmark their performance against others and focus on raising their game! It's a remarkable feat for a company to capture the power of a continuous stream of data from people in a market segment. The term "know your customer" cannot be underestimated here. When you work in a company that creates this kind of focus, you'll know that its marketing machine is humming on all cylinders.

Another area that has become the focus of energy and resources is the creation of *unique customer experiences*. I've referred to the importance of this many times throughout this book. In my own experience with L.L. Bean, the company that sells clothing and other outdoor gear, anytime I call, I can quickly speak to a human being. This is important to me in my interactions with a company. I like the total experience, from purchasing a product, to receiving the goods when the shipping is free, to the high-quality feel of the clothing and the ease with which I can send something back if it's not up to par. To me, this is the total experience I care about. Whether it's L.L. Bean, Zappos, or any other company that stands apart in the market, those that are easiest to do business with have a leg up over the competition. As a business person, you must take notice of what your company does, or doesn't do, to deliver the kind of complete experience expected by customers. When you observe what other companies do and make comparisons to your own company, you'll know where your company excels and where it falls short.

Today, marketing plays a more important role than ever in catalyzing collaboration across the organization. To reinforce a central theme of this book, cross-functional participation is critical to the success of the company. Even though people are distributed across the country and around the world, marketing leaders want to ensure that the right people are working together toward common business objectives. As a C-suite leader, the chief marketing officer (CMO) is instrumental in aligning the efforts of marketing with the strategy of the business and the work of all concerned functions. When this happens, roles and responsibilities are clearer for all. Finally, business people who work in marketing, such as product managers, brand managers, or category managers, become the cross-functional integrators who orchestrate the work of others so that goals can be more easily met. Additional clarity on these cross-organizational interactions is provided for you in the next section.

THE MARKETING ORGANIZATION

As I mentioned earlier in the book, when you're navigating any company, it's a good idea to use an organization chart to find your way around. The marketing department is a function for which this matters a lot. To ease the way, I've created a simple chart so that you're familiar with some of the roles in the marketing organization. Refer to Figure 10.1 to gain this perspective.

As you come to understand the operational model of the marketing function in your own company, you'll see that the marketing department does not operate in isolation. In learning about the interconnections between the marketing subfunctions, and how marketing interacts with

Figure 10.1 Simple Marketing Department Organization Chart

other functions of the company, you will also gain great insights into the overall operation of the company.

One of the most important relationships for the marketing function to nurture is that with the sales and channel areas ("place" in the marketing mix model). Salespeople in B2B companies are integral to the success of the *direct* channel strategy. These people are responsible for finding new customers and maintaining relationships with current customers to keep orders flowing into the company. To find new customers, they rely on the marketing function to carry out programs designed to find those prospective customers or sales leads. In addition, marketing must provide adequate and frequent enough communications to the marketplace to drive customers to stores or websites as part of the *indirect* channel strategy. In the business-to-business-to-consumer model, a salesperson may call on a retailer (such as a buyer or purchasing agent) who will procure the company's products. However, the company that produces the product will often invest in advertising programs to encourage customers to buy products in the channel of their choice, such as retail or online.

Another important relationship in the marketing department is the one between product management and other marketing subfunctions. For example, a product manager will define not only the product's functionality and features, but also the value proposition for the product as well as competitive positioning so that marketing can plan and orchestrate the proper promotional campaigns that will ultimately drive product revenue. Moreover, when products need to be launched to the market, an entire cross-functional team must be involved to ensure that all needed players are focused on the product launch. Consistent go-to-market activities cannot be achieved without precise collaboration between marketing, product management, sales, operations, and others.

A third significant relationship is the one between marketing and the information technology (IT) organization. Interestingly, the IT group is a service provider to any business function that utilizes technology systems—and today, that means every business function! The value it provides is vital, and the marketing department should be one of its best customers. One such system managed by IT is the customer relationship management (CRM) system. This system is a crucial company database that includes customer records. It may track which products customers own, the frequency of product usage, and the amount of money spent by those customers.

A popular metric used by B2B companies is *customer lifetime value*, which indicates the total amount spent by customers over the course of their relationship with the firm. In my research, I learned that high-value customers who call a company's customer service department are often identified by their telephone number, as the call is recognized by the telephone switch. These customers are routed more quickly to a customer service representative, whereas customers who spend less may wait on hold for a few minutes.

Sales and marketing people also use the CRM system to keep track of promotional campaigns and lead-generation programs. Customer service people use it to keep track of customer complaints (as "cases") or reported problems with products. In a company, the CRM system is a critical work tool.

EXERCISE

- What CRM system is used in your company?
- Who is responsible for the interactions between IT and marketing to ensure that the CRM system is kept up-to-date?

In addition, the IT function is responsible for various other systems that may be associated with the work of multiple departments. For example, accounting and financial systems keep track of revenue, costs, and expenses. They also manage and maintain supply chain systems to monitor purchasing, usage, transportation, and logistics. The data produced by these systems is harnessed to produce business performance metrics, such as revenue by product, product costs, and gross margins for those products. For example, they can track the data associated with the quote-to-cash process described earlier in the book.

The marketing organization continues to evolve, and I can't emphasize enough its importance to the company. In your firm, you may encounter an organization chart similar to the one shown in Figure 10.1. However, there are other ways to depict the marketing department's subfunctions. In Figure 10.2, the CMO is depicted as leader and orchestrator. With such great responsibility, the CMO must ensure that the subfunctions are also completely aligned around the marketing strategy.

If the marketing organization is a critical lynchpin that supports the growth of the company, then its role and purpose must be clearly known

Figure 10.2 The Marketing Organization as an Organizational Hub

by everyone—including people in all business functions. Nowhere is it more important for business people to understand that the more aligned people are, the greater the chances to achieve great business results. Therefore, I want to extend the visual from Figure 10.2 to reflect a broader perspective. Figure 10.3 characterizes how the hub of marketing influences other internal functions (finance, IT, customer service, and sales) and external stakeholders (industry analysts, external partners, advertising agencies, and other consultants).

The most important message I want you to take from this section is that the structure of the marketing organization must fit its purpose in the company. As you link various aspects of the company's structure to the results it produces, you will see that marketing plays a vital role.

EXERCISE

- Use what's covered here to create the organization chart for the marketing function in your company.
- Make it a point to learn about the work produced by people in each subfunction.

Figure 10.3 Expanded Focus of Marketing as an Organizational Hub

THE MARKETING CYCLE

The work of marketing in a company can be thought of as an ongoing cycle of activities aimed at processing large amounts of data that are used to shape the strategies that grow the business. This marketing cycle can be viewed as a major process, complete with inputs, activities, and outputs. In this marketing cycle, the inputs are referred to as inbound marketing and the outputs as outbound marketing. During processing, the inbound inputs are synthesized so that logical, focused programs can be devised and carried out. I provide a visual for this in Figure 10.4.

Inbound marketing refers to the efforts devoted to securing data and information from a variety of sources so that it can be used to guide marketing plans and programs. Inbound marketing subfunctions include customer research, competitive intelligence, and industry analysis, which I discussed in Chapter 7. Inbound marketing acts as the radar on the marketplace. People who carry out inbound marketing activities often operate in a market research role (or equivalent) under the umbrella of the marketing department. They are constantly scanning the horizon of

Figure 10.4 The Marketing Cycle

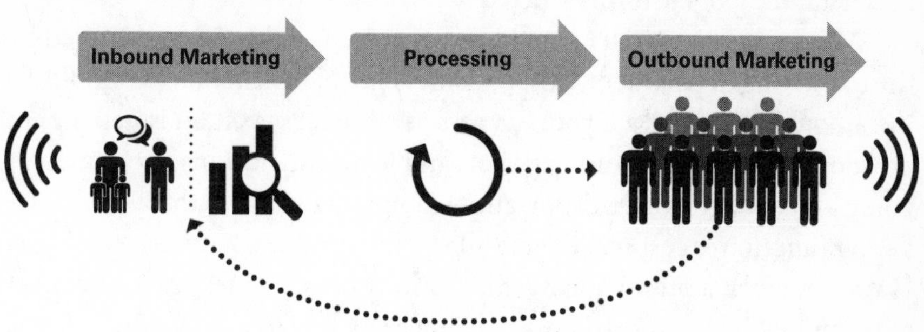

the marketplace to identify market-based issues, such as general trends, economic signals, customer preferences, and competitive activity.

You can focus your discovery of inbound marketing activities by understanding the key roles and responsibilities of people who work in this area. In some firms, *market intelligence* may be the name of the subfunction that handles all research and analysis. Alternatively, the department could be called *market research*. Often, you'll find that the subfunctions are divided into areas with titles such as customer research, customer insights, competitive intelligence, and industry analysis. Regardless, I suggest that you spend some time analyzing the marketing organization in your company so that you can fully appreciate the efforts that are undertaken. In your discovery process, aim to identify the following:

- How industry, customer, and competitive research is done
- Who plans, coordinates, and conducts such research projects
- What output documents are produced (e.g., research reports)
- How others are made aware of the findings
- Where the documents are stored for access by others or for further study

It's important for any business person to fully understand inbound marketing efforts and outputs because these are applied elsewhere in the company. Strategic plans cannot be formulated without relevant market context, and products cannot be conceived or launched without a solid understanding of customers' needs.

Although market data should be organized, collected, and shared by the marketing department, other business people are not off the hook! As I've frequently conveyed, your success as a business person is dependent on your own ability to study markets and form conclusions about market goings-on. At a major transportation company I studied, the global marketing function is responsible for all the inbound work described above. However, when a brand manager is working on a business case, she must also conduct her own market surveillance as a way to validate the insights that support her position. In an interview I conducted, a brand manager expressed that she wanted to ensure that the market intelligence from her research department was accurate and consistent with her position. She indicated that to sell her idea, she had to effectively represent these market matters to her leaders in order to get them excited and persuade them to follow her lead. When I asked her what she did to stay on top of things, she said that she usually scanned industry and business periodicals and visited customers. Further, she indicated that she frequently created presentations or wrote summaries for others to share her findings or insights.

Outbound marketing encompasses the work activities carried out to create programs that communicate the company's message to customers or analysts using advertising, public relations, customer education programs, events, and others. Outbound marketing programs are organized around campaigns that are designed for a specific purpose and targeted at a defined segment. For example, a webinar produced by a software company may be deployed to educate prospective users about the benefits of that software or system. Outbound marketing may also include programs to augment the selling and delivery of products.

In my opinion, this is where definitions of marketing can become fuzzy. There are many types of outbound programs that are delivered through almost as many means. Outbound programs you likely experience every day include the advertisements you view on websites, TV, or billboards. Because people are so mobile, companies must focus on where the customer is at any moment. I may read the *New York Times* on my smartphone, tablet, or the physical newspaper. It depends on where I am and what I'm doing. Therefore, the advertisers must figure out who

I am (they want to know the customer) and where I'm likely to see the advertisement, and act accordingly.

In sum, *the marketing cycle must have a constant stream of inbound data that is rapidly synthesized and translated into programs that will stimulate demand for the company's products and services.* With the proper planning and monitoring, money will be optimally directed to areas most likely to have the optimal impact on business results.

GO-TO-MARKET PLANNING

If the overall business strategy describes where the company is going, marketing contributes to how the company will get there. Go-to-market strategies, driven by marketing, ensure that all the right business functions work together to sustain and grow the business. This cross-functional set of initiatives is often contained in the *marketing plan* to provide the right context for those go-to-market activities. The plan is based on the data, observations, and findings from inbound marketing activities, and its content enables everyone to know who the customers are, what they value, and the experience they desire. It spells out the products that are to be sold, the channels that will deliver those products, and the programs that will communicate that value.

In Figure 10.5, I've provided a general marketing plan template that you might find in your company. However, my goal for this section is to introduce you to the areas that are most important for you to apply namely the elements of the marketing mix and the product launch (items 5 and 6 in Figure 10.5). More important, I want you to see how many of the aspects of the plan draw on topics discussed in this book—in particular, what was shown in Figure 8.3 in Chapter 8 on the topic of strategy. To be clear, when you make connections between the strategy and the go-to-market plan, you'll be equipped to see how the gears of the company work to satisfy customers and make money.

EXERCISE

Locate a marketing plan that's used in your company, and compare its content to that of Figure 10.5.

Figure 10.5 Marketing Plan Template

Marketing Plan Template

1) Executive Summary and Introduction
2) Planning Assumptions
3) Strategic Context
4) Market Environment
    a. Industry and competition
    b. Market segments
    c. Target customers
5) Go-to-Market: The Marketing Mix
    a. Product information
    b. Pricing strategies tied to the value proposition
    c. Advertising, promotion, branding, and customer education
    d. Sales and distribution channels
6) Go-to-Market: The Product Launch (if applicable)
7) Sales Training
8) Customer Service Training
9) Budgets and Financial Projections
10) Performance Metrics
11) Risk Management and Contingency Plans
12) Appendices

THE MARKETING MIX

In 1948, a professor at Harvard University by the name of James W. Culliton wrote an article entitled "The Management of Marketing Costs." In it, he suggested that the business executive was a "mixer of ingredients" and specifically "order-getting ingredients" such as communications, channels, pricing, and other items. Then in 1953, fellow Harvard professor Neil H. Borden wrote his "Note on the Concept of the Marketing Mix," in which he coined the now-common phrase to describe how components were assembled for a marketing program. These included product, pricing, branding, channels of distribution, selling, and advertising. Although the concept has been studied by many over the intervening decades, the main thrust and intent of the mix model remains largely intact. The basic marketing mix model is based on the four Ps: product, price, promotion, and place (or channel). These are the control levers for effective marketing execution.

The first area of focus for the marketing mix is the *product.* To summarize what I covered in Chapter 9, *a product, whether tangible or intangible, is designed to solve a problem or deliver a benefit that a customer is willing to pay for.* Essential elements of the product description include the value proposition and its competitive positioning. These are considered when attempting to calculate the *price* of the product. Therefore, price represents the value or benefit that the customer will receive.

Within the marketing department, people who focus on outbound programs are also concerned about *advertising, promotion, branding,* and *customer education.* This part of the mix model depicts details of the programs that will *communicate* the value and benefits that will be realized by the targeted customers. These promotions drive demand, interest, and, hopefully, customer action. To put these into perspective, think of promotional programs as an integrated set of tactical activities that can be divided into individual *campaigns.* Each campaign is focused on a particular market segment, with its own goal, call to action, budget, and metrics.

To go the distance, the plan spells out how products move from the point of creation to the point of use through direct or indirect sales, physical distribution channels (e.g., wholesalers or retailers), or websites. These pathways have traditionally been unidirectional—that is, from the company to the customer. Now, customers often seek to purchase a product on their own terms. Therefore, it's up to the company to *make products accessible* through the most convenient channel or device preferred by the customer. Any channel or combination of channels can be referred to as a "channel mix." Each firm's channel mix is guided by the strategy of the company and its investments to move, sell, and deliver products. Although this may seem simple enough, sometimes the pricing and advertising groups don't talk to each other, leading customers to find one price in a store and another price online. If you discover this as you learn about marketing operations, you'll see the benefit of clear lines of communication across marketing subfunctions.

The conceptual foundation of the marketing mix is fairly straightforward to understand. However, its application is rather complex. It's often referred to as a model, implying that there are scenarios for which the model can be translated into an integrated go-to-market strategy. Further, if the subfunctions in the marketing department are not well integrated, then some "lever" of the model might not be pulled to produce the outcome. Therefore, in the development of any marketing mix model, all subfunctions must be integrated and focused on achieving a desired goal (or set of goals).

If you worked for a company that operated a chain of food stores (the store is the "channel" for the food products) and your CMO said that an increase in retail traffic is required to fulfill the revenue goals of the company for the upcoming year, how would a marketing mix model be prepared and developed? First, prior-period store traffic patterns would have to be studied to establish a baseline model. This would involve evaluating the number of people who visit each store every day and how much each customer spends on her "basket" of products. Then, advertising and promotional spending would have to be assessed to determine if previous advertisements drove people into stores. The data would also have to be analyzed against the economic picture that was in place during the study period as well as seasonal factors such as weather and holidays. If you noticed that there was a decrease in sales in the Northeast stores in the month of January, you might ask if it was due to a harsh winter or because people spent a lot during the December holidays and were cutting back. If your marketers decided to invest in promotional campaigns and price reductions in a subsequent January, would that encourage more customers to go shopping? Alternatively, if the store operated without advertising in the past, would future advertising create demand? If so, which type? Would television, radio, social media, or a combination of these be appropriate? Additionally, if a promotional program were undertaken, would it need to be accompanied by selective sales price reductions on specific products? As an interested business person and a consumer, consider questions that you might ask the manager of a supermarket chain in your own town to understand what's done to drive business and track outcomes.

As can be seen from this simple example, the marketing mix model has to be adjusted frequently enough to drive customers to purchase products and, ultimately, steer the business. Thus, the astute business person should be cognizant of the complex goings-on in marketing mix planning to truly gain the best perspective on how these strategies are considered, implemented, and monitored.

PRODUCT LAUNCHES

From time to time, the company will introduce new products or enhancements to existing products. The marketing function plays a key role in the orchestration of a successful launch. In exploring how your company operates, you will learn that the product launch is another cross-functional project. It is carried out over a specified period of time and culminates with a final announcement to the market. I conduct a lot of research on this topic, and I've learned about a the activities that separate good launches from poorly executed launches. These firms are successful with their product launches because:

1. They establish a *market window*, which represents when targeted customers are most likely to buy. Companies that launch products in the autumn in time for the holiday season provide evidence of this practice.
2. The CMO stays closely involved to ensure that all functions are collaborating and fulfilling their obligations to the launch team. They also serve as voices to industry analysts or journalists if the products are envisioned as vital to the firm's future.
3. They align all assumptions with what is contained in the business case.
4. They produce creative marketing materials, sales training, press tours, and other events that engage the target audience and catalyze business.

I recommend that you become familiar with product launch protocols in your company. At some point, you may work as a team member on a launch team, or you may carry out other work as required through your own organization. Regardless of your role, it is worthwhile to gain some experience associated with a product launch. Also, pay close attention to goings-on in your company that might include internal launch events, interviews with journalists, or other publicly visible activities.

EXERCISE

- What are the product launches that have been most memorable to you, and why?
- Find out about a recent product launch in your company and who the assigned launch leader was. Ask that person to describe the launch project and what made it memorable.

SUMMARY

It's generally known that executives who are aligned around the goals and strategy of the firm are adept at creating optimal organizational structures. Nowhere is this more evident than in the marketing function. You will find that effective CMOs know what it takes to create the plans and programs that attract and retain customers in order to stimulate business growth. However, this broad view requires a deeper understanding of the marketing function and how it operates as a hub of activity around which others can rally.

It may seem easy to understand this larger picture of what marketing does and how it affects the business. The fact remains that contemporary companies are becoming more complex, and resources are in short supply. It is, therefore, incumbent on managers to broaden their understanding of marketing and to be able to understand how the various parts must come together to create rational, effective go-to-market strategies.

However, I don't want you to get so wrapped up in the organizational part of marketing that you forget what your company is about—its customers. Every company must understand the dynamic needs and motivations of customers, and how those customers can be reached when and where they need to be. It's a two-way street, where customers who hunt for or receive the best "signals" from a company at the time and place most suitable for them are more likely to engage and buy. A well-oiled marketing machine is the best way to go for the gold.

INCREASING YOUR MANAGEMENT COMPETENCY

1. If you're deeply interested in marketing, make it a point to understand how the marketing function is structured in your company. If you work in a multidivisional firm, you may find that there are corporate marketing functions as well as those that operate at a divisional (or business unit) level.
2. One way to review the activities of a marketing function is to review marketing plans. If you're learning to navigate the organization, try to arrange some meetings with key marketing people to see if they'll share some of their prior or current marketing plans with you. Perhaps you can compare their structure with the outline I shared earlier in this chapter.
3. Find out which people in your company are responsible for relationships with advertising agencies. Ask if they'll spend some time discussing those relationships and how information flows between your company and the agency. Ask if they will show you a *creative brief*. The creative brief is a document prepared by someone in your marketing department to communicate to an advertising agency creative team about an envisioned advertising campaign. It portrays the market environment in a way that will inspire the agency to come up with creative approaches for reaching the targeted audience and inspiring the desired response.
4. Make it a point to speak with people who work in sales to find out about their interactions with marketing in your company. Do they feel that they're adequately trained in the products? Are they informed about upcoming promotional activities?
5. Speak with people in marketing or product management to find out if they'll show you their launch plans and launch documentation. Find out if there's a close connection between the marketing and product people.
6. Some universities have used marketing mix model simulations to help students understand the interplay between those elements. As these simulations have evolved using gaming techniques, these learning situations can expose business people to many different inputs and outcomes. Find out if these tools are used in your company, either in your company

training group or in the marketing department. Although theoretical in nature, this may be a helpful way to learn about the complexity of managing the marketing mix, especially when various stakeholders own different elements of the mix.

Action Planning

In this chapter, the following characteristics were either explicitly or implicitly revealed. You may wish to identify where these were mentioned to reinforce your understanding of how they might be applied in your own work. You can also utilize the following template as a way to associate what was discussed in this chapter with your scores from your Business Acumen Assessment. From this, you can create an action plan for yourself or work with your manager to come up with specific goals and plans.

- Being a self-starter
- Defining processes
- Deriving market insights
- Understanding products
- Evaluating the industry and domain
- Strategic thinking
- Systemic thinking
- Entrepreneurial thinking
- Developing organizational instinct
- Writing clearly and concisely
- Observing actively
- Including others
- Improving business processes
- Earning credibility

ACTION ITEM + GOAL	STEPS TO BE TAKEN	OUTCOME PRODUCED	WHAT YOU LEARNED	WHAT YOU WILL SHARE

CHAPTER 11

ASSESSING BUSINESS PERFORMANCE

After you read this chapter, you should be able to:

- Consider financial and nonfinancial measurements used in a company.
- Explain why it's important to view a host of metrics from an integrated, holistic perspective.
- Treat performance management as integral to strategic planning and execution.
- Use a performance scorecard to evaluate a dimension of a business.

You may never know what results come of your action, but if you do nothing, there will be no result.

—MAHATMA GANDHI

The old proverb "nothing succeeds like success" suggests that the attainment of success leads to further opportunities. For most leaders of publicly traded companies, success is driven by financial performance. However, true assessments of company performance should not be based solely on financial data. Instead, success must be viewed holistically as the aggregate of all activity.

People who own retail establishments are always "keeping an eye on the store" to guide their business decisions. They don't walk around with a laminated playbook, the way a football coach might. Their days are filled with customer demands, administrative issues, and numerous unexpected interruptions. At the end of the day, they tally up the money from the cash register, take inventory so they can replenish their stock, think about their customer interactions, and feedforward to set things up for the next day. Applying this small business operating model and mindset will benefit you regardless of the size of the company in which you work. When I'm facilitating workshops, I encourage participants to imagine that they're the business owner, spending their own money. This reminds them to consider their work in a company from a more personal vantage point, and it is something I recommend you consider as you tackle various roles in your management career.

This chapter is designed to integrate much of what's been discussed in this book to bring business performance to the forefront. As I've suggested all along, company leaders want their managers to view the many facets of the business from a holistic, systemic perspective in order to understand how the company produces positive returns. Whatever role you play, I want you to become a business employee who's viewed by leadership as a prized asset. Therefore, to contribute to your understanding about business performance management, I focus my attention in this chapter on the following topics:

- The importance of having a performance management mindset
- How metrics and key performance indicators are used
- Commonly used metrics in marketing and profit-impacting activities
- Putting performance management into action by using a scorecard

THE PERFORMANCE MANAGEMENT MINDSET

Throughout this book, I've described why it is important to evaluate markets, formulate strategies, utilize financial tools, leverage processes, and work effectively with people across the company. In the end, however, everything boils down to execution and profits earned. Precision analysis and a keen eye allow business people to associate independent observations with data-driven measurements in order to bring the state of the business into clear focus.

When publicly traded companies report their results to stock market analysts and shareholders, they're revealing snapshots of their actual performance against established goals. This puts a very strong emphasis on *financial achievements*. Those leaders are also encouraged to provide sufficient guidance on how expenditures being made now are expected to influence results in the next quarter or fiscal year. Insightful leaders focus on identifying what contributed to current achievements and what's needed to be a major player in the long term. That's the *balanced perspective* business people need to really think about. Arriving at this vantage point takes some work.

When I worked as a financial analyst during my corporate life, I often found myself "crunching the numbers" to find relationships between various aspects of the business so I could present logical conclusions to my managers about what happened and recommendations for what to do next. It took time to train myself to be an astute analyst of business performance, and it may not happen for you overnight. Thus, I want to encourage you to be cognizant of the effort required to gain this mindset. Treat this area of work as you would physical exercise: the more you do it, the healthier and stronger you become. The reason is simple: without exception, *executives want business people to speak the language of business (i.e., efficiency and productivity) in order to contribute to positive business results.*

MEASURING BUSINESS PERFORMANCE

Metrics are vital to the operation of any company and provide leaders and other business people with the means to assess how well the business is doing. Metrics are essentially *measurements of business results* and are made up of both financial and nonfinancial data. They allow leaders and others to understand what's happening in the business.

In your company, you're likely to hear the term *key performance indicators* (KPIs). These are nonfinancial measurements that illustrate a firm's progress toward the achievement of its goals. Well-run firms that track their KPIs over time against their strategic priorities use these to make business adjustments as required. Here are some examples of where KPIs are used:

- An airline tracks *on-time departures* to figure out how to improve on-time performance. Some airlines put people into boarding queues to ensure that they can get everyone on the plane as quickly as possible. When combined with other ground operations activities (e.g., cleaning the plane and refueling) to speed things along, the airline will free up the plane to take more flights and earn more money.
- An oil company will track *production volumes* for each of its oil wells. This allows it to look at capacity (or supply) versus market demand. From this, it can accelerate or decelerate production as needed.
- In a manufacturing company, managers will often track the *rate of goods produced* on a production line. Some firms have found a correlation between higher line speeds and lower product quality. By tracking this KPI, they can find the optimal production rate.
- *Employee engagement* is a way that a company can evaluate the degree to which employees are aligned with the strategic priorities of the company. If employee satisfaction (a measure of engagement) is low, leaders can create programs to involve and deepen bonds with employees to encourage greater levels of productivity.
- A software company that produces cloud-based applications might examine the number of *service-affecting outages* (those that cause customers to be unable to use the system) in order to find and fix software bugs as well as to improve overall product quality. When quality is improved, customers are happier.

When KPIs are associated with other data and/or metrics, senior executives are able to get a more complete picture of what's happening. Most leaders in a company focus on a just a handful of KPIs and/or metrics that help them to *pinpoint trends* and *derive future strategies*. This helps them to pinpoint elements deemed vital to the success of the company. These are referred to as *critical success factors* (CSFs). Examples of forward-looking CSFs include:

- Decrease production line scrap rates by 35 percent.
- Reduce product costs by 15 percent.
- Increase revenue from current customers by 20 percent.

As you progress in your career, you'll immensely benefit from continued study of business performance. You will also find that there are hundreds of metrics available for use. Although it's unrealistic to discuss all of them here, I want to provide you with a sufficient perspective on performance management by focusing on two key areas: simple *marketing metrics* and metrics that have an *impact on company profits*. These are the ones you are most likely to encounter. You can utilize these to learn more about how your company currently works and how it should operate in the future.

MARKETING METRICS

As you're aware, the market(s) in which your company operates is multidimensional and ever-changing. The term *market movement* is used to indicate that one or more market dynamics are in play at any point in time. When the makeup of a market segment shifts, customer needs will also change and competitors will take notice. For example, consider the market segment of baby boomers in the United States. As baby boomers began to reach retirement age, they arrived with a specific set of values, spending habits, and debt levels—and many of them had sizeable bank accounts. Therefore, their needs were different from those of the generation that had previously composed this segment—people who lived through a depression and were extremely conservative. Companies that did not anticipate or respond to these demographic shifts probably found that their products and services were missing the mark. To extend this example, consider how people in the boomer demographic would shift their priorities if the economy started to falter and their bank accounts dwindled. They might need to continue working, and their needs would be geared toward saving and frugality.

Using metrics to track market activity enables business people, and oftentimes the cross-functional teams they work with, to take snapshots in order to determine what's going on and how to plan their next moves. To help you gain a similar perspective, I divide this section into two parts. First, I focus on inbound metrics, including market share, customer usage, customer satisfaction, and customer profitability. Then, I cover outbound marketing metrics, with a focus on lead generation, revenue earned from promotional activity, and incremental sales from price-oriented promotions. This reflects the two types of marketing activities discussed in Chapter 10.

Recall that inbound marketing focuses efforts on capturing data so that goals and strategies can be formulated. In order to be as market-focused as possible and to ensure that the company can gain as many customers as possible, it's important to collect and assess these marketing metrics.

INBOUND MARKETING METRICS

Market share is a metric that you'll come across throughout your business career. It's significant because it describes how a company, a division of a company, or a product line is performing in relation to its competitors. Sounds simple, right? However, to derive believable market share estimates, there must be data available about the competitors. Depending on the market segment or geographic area in which your company operates, the composition of competitors and the verified number of customers may vary. Sectors that are visible, regulated, or routinely tracked (e.g., banks, insurance companies, airlines, and pharmaceuticals firms) have data available from internal and external sources (e.g., regulators' websites), making it relatively easy to track. Other industries may have players that make market share estimation a challenge. To overcome this, companies will attempt to define a market segment in terms of the number of competitors, number of products available, and number of customers.

A "big box" home improvement retailer can look at all of its stores in a given geographic area and evaluate the number of customers who purchase products from a specific category (e.g., building construction materials) as well as those who purchase a particular product (e.g., framing lumber). It can track the number of competitors (other big-box stores, building supply firms, etc.), study building permits, and even work with its suppliers to determine what to carry in stock to meet demand. From that, it can assess and monitor its market share. Although market share calculations can be complex, there are two that I'll explain. One focuses on unit volumes and the other on revenue.

1. *Market share based on unit volumes.* If you're in a business that sells tangible products or service-based transactions, you can use the following formula to judge total market growth (or contraction) by evaluating this metric over time.

$$\frac{\text{Unit sales volume (quantity)}}{\text{Total market volume (quantity)}} = \text{Unit market share (percent)}$$

2. *Market share based on revenue earned.* This is another share measurement that is associated with prices of products or fees earned by one company versus another. Because prices charged multiplied by volumes sold equals revenue earned, it's possible to calculate the revenue market share of one company in relation to all competitors. The following formula is used:

$$\frac{\text{Total company revenue}}{\text{Total revenue (all competitors)}} = \text{Market share percent}$$

   Sometimes, a company may have greater unit market share and lower revenue market share. Such a company might choose to lower prices to improve unit market share. This may reduce its revenue and profit, while opening a door to sell other products and services.

EXERCISE

- How does your company measure market share?
- What can you do to uncover this information and use it in the job you're doing now?

Customer usage is another helpful metric. It reveals how frequently a product or products are used by customers. In the world of software applications, a company might evaluate the features that are used the most. An online video streaming service monitors how frequently certain programs are viewed and collects information about customer preferences. Have you noticed the increasing variety of specialized television programming? This is because these firms understand their audiences, create content for those viewers, and use this to prove to advertisers that their products will achieve the best exposure.

Customer satisfaction is used to determine if customers are happy with the firm's products, services, and their overall experience in doing business with the company. Customer satisfaction scores can provide powerful motivations for employees to meet or exceed customers' expectations. If customer satisfaction scores trend upward, it provides positive reinforcement to people in the company that they are doing the right things for the customers, especially when satisfaction ratings directly affect revenue and profit. Customer satisfaction scores are collected in surveys that ask customers a number of questions about how they feel about the company, its products, or their experience with the firm. They are typically measured on a five-point rating scale (very dissatisfied, dissatisfied, neutral, satisfied, and very satisfied).

Another metric you should become familiar with is related to the willingness of those customers to recommend your company or its products. This customer loyalty indicator is sometimes referred to as the *net promoter score* (NPS). As a consumer, when you have a great experience with a product or a company, you probably talk it up to your friends, family, and colleagues. In fact, such recommendations are invaluable because the person is putting his own reputation on the line. As companies grow and mature, the best path to sustaining that growth is to reduce the cost of acquiring a new customer, which is where the NPS can play an important role. If your customer acquisition costs are going down, your NPS scores are high, and revenue is growing, then there's a good chance that customer recommendations are driving growth. The NPS rating is measured using a survey. Five- or ten-point rating scales are commonly used.

I'm sure you've been asked to respond to numerous surveys about whether you'd recommend a company. I get them from airlines, car dealers, and various websites. This persistence is important because companies who use the NPS need to ensure that the sample size is large and that they frequently tap into how customers' feelings may be changing. In addition to asking how likely you are to recommend them, they also ask if they may contact you for further comment. Some firms may ask, "What's the main reason for the score you gave us?" or "What could we do to rate a 10?" This constant feedback cycle contributes to the ability of a company to monitor trends and respond accordingly.

Customer profitability allows companies to determine which customers add the most value to the business. In a B2B company, it's generally rather easy to employ this metric because accounting systems keep track of sales to given customers. In the consumer world, determining the profitability of customers in a market segment can provide relevant information about business performance and some hints about competitive positioning. Conventional wisdom suggests that it's easier to make money from current customers than from new customers. Therefore, when a company engages with profitable, happy customers, it has a great chance to learn about evolving customer needs.

A metric of customer profitability that's highly desirable for management is *customer lifetime value*. This metric pinpoints how much customers have purchased over the course of their history with the company. It is updated over time as customer purchase data is collected. If a company has sufficient information about a customer, it can utilize the present value of anticipated future cash inflows from that customer relationship. Such information can help leaders to determine whether to continue investing in a particular marketing program given the activity that it drives. Firms with product or service contracts will have an easier time doing this. Today, with the advent of various service-oriented software applications as well as arrangements where monthly or annual fees are charged, a company can easily see how much money is earned from each customer.

EXERCISE

- How does your company keep track of customer satisfaction or customer loyalty?
- Which customers (or types of customers) are the most profitable to your company? How do you know?

OUTBOUND MARKETING METRICS

The outbound marketing metrics I'll cover for you in this section are those used by companies to evaluate the effectiveness of advertising and promotion programs, which often form the bedrock of their marketing strategy. Business people should be aware of how these programs (or campaigns) set the tone and timing for a variety of promotional undertakings. Some advertising and promotional campaigns can be expensive and difficult to assess, especially when the incremental revenue associated with those programs can't be traced back to the advertisement. Moreover, most companies employ a diverse set of promotional campaigns. These are delivered through a variety of communication channels tuned to take aim at the eyes, ears, and minds of customers. With so many ways to spend marketing dollars, it's vital to focus efforts on linking marketing investments to financial outcomes, which is why you'll hear chief marketing officers talk about the return on investment (ROI) of marketing expenditures. In this section, I concentrate on explaining some simple metrics used to track promotional programs that are designed to build awareness, stimulate demand, and, ultimately, increase revenue and profits.

Lead generation programs are used by a company to develop new business, as they provide a stream of customer prospects or leads. To inspire customers to engage, firms use e-mail, social media, events, content, or other means. In the end, the question is, How many new leads are being generated each day, week, or month? Viewing the ebb and flow of *new leads over time* provides a good indicator of the success of lead generation programs. An important metric is the *cost per lead* or CPL, which provides insight into the cost effectiveness of marketing campaigns that are created to find new customers. The cost per lead can be calculated by totaling up all focused marketing expenditures and dividing that by the number of new leads:

$$\frac{\text{Total spent on lead generation programs}}{\text{Number of new qualified leads}} = \text{Cost per lead}$$

Tracking over time can be done in absolute values and can be smoothed using, for example, a monthly or quarterly moving average. Once new sales leads are qualified, it's possible for a company to look at the sales cycle: the time it takes to engage a new lead until a sale is made.

If a company tracks sales cycles over time, it can use that information to fine-tune its marketing and selling activities in order to speed up revenue generation.

Revenue earned from promotional activity. People who research marketing program performance often use the term *conversion rate.* If your company runs an advertising campaign targeted at driving people to its website, what is it that they're actually being driven to do? If it's to buy something, then the path to that purchase must be as expeditious as possible. Conversion tracking can be accomplished by following these steps:

- Identify the total number of people targeted in the campaign. If your company uses e-mail, the number of e-mail addresses in the database should be easily available.
- Calculate the number of people who visited the website or store. This is easily tracked when a special landing page is used for the promotion.
- Determine how many of those people actually made a purchase.

Incremental sales (or promotional lift). As I've alluded to previously, marketers will set goals to encourage current customers to keep buying, and to acquire new customers to increase revenue. Price-oriented promotions (discounts, coupons, etc.) are used to achieve these goals. These promotions are easy to track because they have a fairly immediate impact on sales. However, if discounting is done too frequently, it's more difficult to change customer behaviors. This has been exemplified in the automobile industry, where seasonal sales events seem to be the accepted norm. If a company is not overly dependent on rampant discounting, it can calculate its average sales over time (a baseline) and then measure the incremental impact from the promotional program, which would be the revenue earned above that baseline.

PROFIT-IMPACTING METRICS

According to business authors Jim Collins and Jerry Porras in their book *Built to Last,* "profit is like oxygen, food, water, and blood for the body: they are not the point of life, but without them, there is no life."

It goes without saying that a company's financial health is measured by its profitability. When KPIs and other metrics are associated with profit, it's easier to identify cause and effect and to make optimal business decisions to positively affect profit.

In Chapter 4, I discussed the two key measures of profit: gross margin and net profit. Gross margin is a valued financial metric because it reveals:

- The amount of money being earned from sales of products and services
- The effectiveness of product pricing policies and the costs incurred to produce products
- Information about the mix of products and services that should be created and sold in order to achieve the strategic aims of the firm

When I discussed the profit and loss statement, I indicated that the expenses incurred to run the business are deducted from gross margin to ultimately arrive at net profit, or the "bottom line." However, gross margin must be sufficient to cover all of the expenses incurred to run the business and still produce a profit. To fine-tune their perspectives, business leaders evaluate various *expense-to-revenue (E/R) ratios* as metrics to define what's spent by a particular function in the production of revenue. These are also used to benchmark a firm's performance against that of its competitors. For example, a company that spends significantly on R&D as a percentage of revenue may have a greater potential to produce newer, innovative products—an important indicator of future success.

Return on investment (ROI) is one method to determine the profits that are generated in relation to monies invested. If a company invests in a new factory, the business case will calculate the monetary investment and the contribution to profit from that factory. If an advertisement is produced and its purpose is to inspire incremental revenue and profit, ROI can be used. A simple ROI formula is shown below:

$$\frac{\text{Net profit \$}}{\text{Amount invested \$}} = \text{Return on investment (\%)}$$

Return on sales (ROS) refers to net profit as a percentage of sales revenue. The main idea is to identify the percentage of revenue that's showing up on the bottom line. ROS calculations can also contribute to competitive analysis because you can compare your company's ROS to that of your competitors. The ROS formula is shown here:

$$\frac{\text{Net profit \$}}{\text{Total sales \$}} = \text{Return on sales (\%)}$$

Unit volumes provide you with a way to evaluate the number of units sold or the number of transactions processed. This helps determine the contribution value of incremental units. It also allows you to figure out how sensitive your unit volumes are in relation to the prices charged. Further, you can use unit volumes to calculate your market share or market penetration numbers and to target advertising and promotion programs that might increase unit sales. In companies that sell many products, the revenue generated by each product as a proportion of total sales is referred to as the sales mix. This information can, over time, reveal patterns in usage and be used to gauge customer preferences.

Unit volume analysis can be expanded upon when the *average revenue per unit sold* (ARPU) is calculated. ARPU is depicted in the following formula:

$$\frac{\text{Total revenue}}{\text{Total units sold}} = \text{Average revenue per unit}$$

If ARPU is tracked over time, it's possible to associate the movement of average prices based on influences such as competitor discounting or excess supply in the market. To extend my point about sales mix analysis, if ARPU shows that a company sells too many low-priced, low-margin products, its leaders might want to use advertising to stimulate demand for higher-priced, higher-margin products. Alternatively, it can reveal that its higher-priced products don't offer a compelling value proposition to its customers. (By the way, ARPU is often used in the communications industry, except it refers to average revenue per user, instead of unit, and is another way to evaluate which products are used by customers and the average price paid by those customers.)

As a way to enhance ARPU analysis for tangible products, company leaders will often evaluate *inventory turns* as a vital metric. This metric refers to the number of times inventory is sold and replenished during a given time period, as indicated by the following formula:

$$\frac{\text{Total revenue}}{\text{Total value of inventory (from the balance sheet)}} = \begin{matrix}\text{Number of} \\ \text{inventory "turns"}\end{matrix}$$

Inventory turns can be a measure of business velocity, so when a company such as a discount department store speeds up its inventory turns, it will likely increase its profit. However, this metric can be enhanced when it's paired with another metric: days of sales inventory or DSI, as shown in the following formula:

$$\frac{\text{Average value of inventory}}{\text{Cost of goods sold}} \times 365 = \text{Days of sales inventory}$$

Interestingly, DSI is really the inverse of the inventory turnover ratio multiplied by 365. With this metric, inventory management can be more easily factored into the firm's pursuit of profit.

Now, consider how the chief financial officer (CFO) must use a host of financial and other metrics to make sure there's sufficient money to operate the business. For instance, the CFO examines inventory data, expenses incurred, and cash flow to make sure there's enough money to operate the company. The senior leadership team evaluates a complete suite of metrics that provides visibility into company performance to determine where to invest and where to trim in order to grow the company and increase profits.

EXERCISE

- What are some of the profit-impacting metrics used in your company?
- How does the ROS metric impact the strategic goals of the firm?

PERFORMANCE MANAGEMENT IN ACTION

I've worked in companies that didn't grow very much and in companies that grew rapidly. It's more exciting, fun, and stimulating to work in a fast-growing firm! However, you'll find that all companies have a life cycle. Although things seem great during periods of growth, I can safely say that it doesn't last forever—unless the company stays ahead of the curve. This is why you'll often hear your CEO and others call for investments in innovation, marketing, and R&D. Moreover, leaders are motivated to grow the company because shareholders or other investors want a positive return on their investment in the company. Businesses can be effectively steered toward profitable growth when the right metrics are properly knit together for analysis and action. When this is done well, leaders can tell the story of what happened and how goals and strategies are to be verified or revised.

To obtain the best vantage point, data and metrics should be organized into a business scorecard. As a first step, refer to the simple scorecard template shown in Figure 11.1. The first column contains business elements such as stated goals, KPIs, or specific metrics. There can be many rows, depending on the depth of the analysis required. Notice that the scorecard integrates retrospective and current business information. It also contains columns to set the stage for future plans. When business information can be portrayed through the lenses of the past and present, there's a better chance of making the right connection to derive focused goals and strategies. To reinforce this, please refer back to Chapter 8 and Figures 8.7 and 8.8.

Figure 11.1 Simple Business Scorecard

BUSINESS ELEMENT/METRIC	TWO YEARS AGO	LAST YEAR	THIS YEAR	NEXT YEAR	YEAR AFTER

Now, I'd like to show you how this simple scorecard can be applied. In order to do this, I'll create a situation and populate a sample scorecard. It will contain some of the measurements that I covered in this chapter and in Chapter 4, including:

- Unit volumes
- Average revenue per unit
- Revenue
- Cost of goods sold
- Gross margin
- Net profit
- Return on sales
- Market share
- Net promoter score

My goal is to show you how the metrics might be associated with one another and how various people in an organization might interpret the information and assess those associations. Note that in the following case, I focus only on the two prior years and the current year so that I can cover the analysis as expeditiously as possible.

This is a case about a company that produces plumbing products used in kitchens and baths. The leadership team observed a deceleration of the business last year. This year, there was a slight a drop in market share and in revenue over the previous year. This prompted the executives to want to find out what was going on and what should be done. It appointed a small team made up of a marketing analyst, a financial analyst, and a business analyst to study the situation. This small team was provided with the scorecard shown in Figure 11.2 in order to undertake its analysis.

When the team members met for the first time, they agreed that it would be wise to break down the scorecard into some smaller pieces for further study, and to look for relationships between the metrics. They recorded their observations in the format shown in Figure 11.3. However, that seemed to be the easy part. As they brainstormed, they realized that they would need to conduct a more detailed analysis.

Team members agreed that they would seek out functional leaders and others in the company to analyze what happened in each area. They decided to reach out to the company economist, chief financial officer,

Figure 11.2 Plumbing Products Business Scorecard

BUSINESS ELEMENT/METRIC	TWO YEARS AGO	LAST YEAR	THIS YEAR
Units Sold: New Construction Segment	467,500	411,400	402,740
Units Sold: Remodeling Segment	906,500	1,133,125	1,152,190
Total Company Revenue	$535,860,000	$548,306,375	$545,780,430
Average Revenue Per Unit (ARPU)	$390	$355	$351
Gross Margin $	$225,061,200	$202,873,359	$202,590,000
Gross Margin %	42%	37%	37%
Net Profit $	$94,370,000	$88,456,700	$81,867,065
Return on Sales (ROS)	18%	16%	15%
Total Company Market Share	26.4%	22.3%	22.1%
Net Promoter Score	8.9	8.2	7.9
Inventory Returns	11 times	8 times	9 times

Figure 11.3 Scorecard Observations

METRIC	OBSERVATION
Sales Mix	New construction revenue is declining. What's the root cause?
Total Revenue	In the big picture, over 3 years, revenue hasn't shifted much. Why?
Average Revenue Per Unit (ARPU)	Why is ARPU trending downward?
Net Profit and Return on Sales	Overall profitability is eroding. Is there a reason?
Market Share	What caused market share to decrease?
Net Promoter Score	What is contributing to the decline in this loyalty indicator?
Inventory Turns	What contributed to a slowing of inventory turnover?

head of manufacturing, chief marketing officer, vice president of R&D, and vice president of customer service.

When the team members reconvened, they discovered that the metrics themselves were not as revealing as what was learned from each of the functional leaders with whom they met. The team members were cognizant of many of the external forces on the company, including industry trends, competitive pressures, and customer preferences. In their discussions with one another, they realized that there was a tremendous amount of knowledge in the organization that wasn't exchanged.

They found out that various people saw a number of market signals but were not adequately sharing that information. As an aside, earlier in the book, I discussed the importance of business people knowing who does what with whom, as this knowledge leads to improved communication and faster decision making. This was an important lesson learned by this project team, because if information had been surfaced more quickly, the leaders may have made different business decisions.

To continue, the team members found in their analysis that there were two underlying forces. One was that the economy was in a slight recession. The other was that competitors were taking action to meet the needs of the market but the company was not. Although this seems fairly simple to comprehend, many causes and effects were uncovered during the team's brainstorming activity. Because there were several interdependencies, the team members decided to sketch out their findings on a whiteboard in the form of a mind map. What they ultimately created is shown for you in Figure 11.4, which is titled an information connection chart.

Figure 11.4 Information Connection Chart

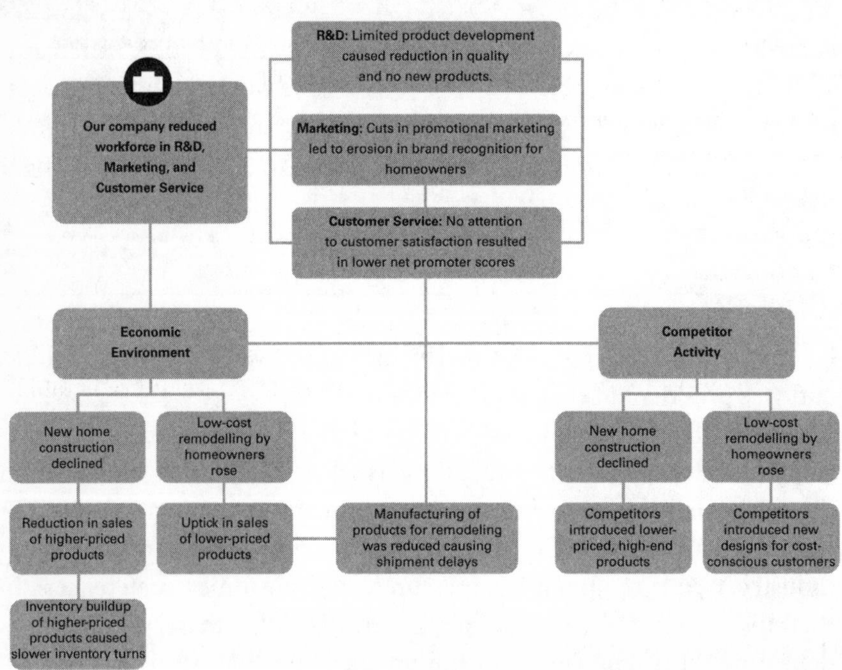

To quote an old saying, one picture is worth a thousand words! When the team presented this chart to management, it was as if all the functional walls came down. All of the leaders saw that during an economic contraction, they had focused only on the internal dimensions of the business, not on the market. They lost sight of customer preferences, became vulnerable to the competition, and as a result, did not invest sufficiently to create or update their products to meet the changing market requirements. In the final analysis, it came down to the financials—as it usually does.

EXERCISE

- Based on the analysis of the situation, what would you recommend to management in order to achieve growth?
- Try to apply the information connection chart concept when you're presented with a business scorecard or scenario requiring the analysis of many metrics.

As you may surmise from what you've read in the book and, in particular, the discussion on performance metrics, it's important to keep track of the business so that you're not caught off guard. Periodic scorecard evaluations help you to understand how all the numbers and business indicators come together to form a picture of the business. In the overall scheme of things, it's important to ensure that the business is evaluated from a holistic standpoint.

SUMMARY

One of the most predictable aspects of business is that it's unpredictable! Customers change their minds in a heartbeat. Competitors enter markets without notice. Economic conditions are upset the minute the price of gasoline changes or when exchange rates shift the balance of trade. These are just a few of the situations that can cause business leaders to lose sleep thinking about what to do next. Because these macro-level events are highly visible, everyone faces similar issues at the same point in time. However, inside the four walls of your company, the circumstances are different; there aren't immediate news headlines or leading economic indicators like the ones crawling across the bottom of your TV screen. This is because business outcomes are the result of the work of many people across the company—it's hard to track everything and keep it all straight in your head the way the owner of a small business might.

General George Patton famously said, "A good plan violently executed now is better than a perfect plan next week." Regardless of the plan, you'll quickly find that when you're on the front lines of business, it's often difficult to determine what's important and what to do next. Competitors, customers, and other market happenings are highly dynamic, with the changes happening fast! Technology has become both friend and foe, and the vast seas of data can seem to obliterate the picture if you don't have a clear mind.

But there is hope. And the source of this hope resides in the very basics of business that have been assembled for you in this book. Now that you know just how rapidly business moves, you'll want to harness the data and assemble the key metrics as fast as you can. If you do, you'll be well equipped to steer the ship of business through whatever turbulent seas lie ahead. After all, nothing succeeds like success.

INCREASING YOUR MANAGEMENT COMPETENCY

1. Visit your CMO or other managers in the marketing department to learn about the most important marketing metrics used in your company.
2. Talk with your CFO to learn how scorecards are assembled and used in the company. In addition, find out how business or company performance reporting is undertaken. You will want to learn about what's included, when results are presented, and what format is used.
3. Take advantage of any opportunity to attend a management business review. You'll get a sense of how management discusses business results and the areas deemed most important.
4. As I discussed in Chapter 5, most processes have performance metrics associated with them. Make it one of your goals to learn about those linkages.

Action Planning

In this chapter, the following characteristics were either explicitly or implicitly revealed. You may wish to identify where these were mentioned to reinforce your understanding of how they might be applied in your own work. You can also utilize the following template as a way to associate what was discussed in this chapter with your scores from your Business Acumen Assessment. From this, you can create an action plan for yourself or work with your manager to come up with specific goals and plans.

- Managing
- Defining processes
- Making decisions
- Adapting to changing situations
- Critical thinking
- Strategic thinking
- Systemic thinking
- Solving problems
- Being results oriented
- Evaluating business performance
- Improving business processes
- Taking action
- Assuming accountability

ACTION ITEM + GOAL	STEPS TO BE TAKEN	OUTCOME PRODUCED	WHAT YOU LEARNED	WHAT YOU WILL SHARE

CHAPTER 12

YOUR PROFESSIONAL DEVELOPMENT STRATEGY

Life isn't about finding yourself. Life is about creating yourself.

—GEORGE BERNARD SHAW

Imagine that you're planning a road trip. You pore over the maps to figure out how to get to your ultimate destination. As you do this, you realize there are many points of interest along the way that might be worth a visit. Once you start your journey, you find that there are indeed some great places to visit. Sometimes you get to take in beautiful vistas, experience new things, and meet dynamic people. In other instances, you may find that the upcoming stop-off isn't worth the effort and floor it to get to the next one!

Career planning can sometimes feel like a road trip. You think you know where you're going, but the destinations aren't always that satisfying. With this book, I believe you can take a more purposeful approach in the clarification of your career goals. Using the provided templates, exercises, and tips to improve your management competency, your career road map can be made simpler. I hope I've infused your mind with a greater sense of what's "out there"—particularly, to be alert to situations that might pop up when least expected, so that you can address it all with purpose and aplomb.

You could feel that there is a lot to undertake. You might want to defer to your boss who you feel should play a strong hand in your development. In some cases, this is a good idea and you'll receive great coaching from your manager. In other situations, you'll wonder what's happening when goings-on in the company seem to be moving past you at a lightning clip and you're out of the loop. With this, the best advice I can offer is to take matters into your own hands.

THE IMPORTANCE OF CAREER OWNERSHIP

During my corporate career, I was always advised to take responsibility for my own professional development. Over time, I realized that I had some great managers who shaped my raw talent and pointed me in the right direction. I also met new people who seemed wiser and more experienced in a host of disciplines, and they provided me with insights and suggestions. Those were, and are, my mentors. In the overall scheme of things, you will benefit from the advice and suggestions of the many people you work for, and dozens or hundreds of peers.

I don't want to mask the simplicity of this issue of career ownership. In today's business environment, companies are highly selective about who is hired and who gets promoted. Employers may push you hard to achieve their own ambitions, which may seem a lot to ask in a world where work-life balance is the holy grail of success. What's mentioned in this book must be learned and expanded upon. The characteristics associated with business acumen are nonnegotiable. To get ahead, you'll likely have to work longer and harder than you may have imagined. You'll have to consider yourself part of the team, while keeping a watchful eye on internal and external happenings to keep things organized in your mind, just as I described Buck, the survivor in *The Call of the Wild*.

I don't want to discourage you. I want to encourage you to embrace the challenges that lie ahead, regardless of your current level of experience or state of your career.

To take control, you need data and a *purposeful professional development strategy*. It requires you to assess where you've been, where you are, and what your next steps ought to be. It means that ongoing assessments of your business acumen and other skills must be done frequently enough so that "the product of you" offers a compelling value proposition for your employer and that you are positioned competitively against others who may be vying for the next promotion.

The data you need is contained in the dimensions of business acumen that I defined for you in Chapter 1 and the assessment I provide for you in Appendix A (or the online version which can be found at http://survey.sequentlearning.com/s3/business-acumen). Your job is to use the following template to create this purposeful professional development strategy. Why do I use this term *purposeful*? Well, if you search for a definition of the word *purposeful*, you'll find other terms: determined; resolute; steadfast. This is the mindset you need to adopt to maintain control over your business career. While there are certainly other areas on which you can and should focus, my intent here is to keep things contained within the context of this book.

The template follows the same pattern as the Business Acumen Assessment and is divided into groups with the associated characteristics. To keep it simple, I just used a few key words to remind you about the topic. There are two other columns: goals and action plan. This is where you have to get down to work. I recommend that you take the template and transfer it to another tableau—either a piece of paper or an electronic file. This will allow you to expand each characteristic and add or edit as needed. You'll want to share this with your manager to determine how to shape the goals and action plans. Alternatively, you can use your burgeoning professional network, either online or in other venues, to find out what other people are doing. Seek out mentors. Talk to managers in other departments. Read emerging literature. Work on projects that have a lot of impact and are visible to others. Whatever you do, maintain a record of your activities and work projects. Take good notes about what you encounter, either in journal form or in other ways that allow you to review and reflect on what you encounter and what you learn.

At various points in the year—and this should be at least twice a year—take a time-out to update your personal SWOT analysis. Refer to what I shared with you in Chapter 1, or how I described the technique in Chapter 8. This "state of you" snapshot is critical in the evaluation of the work you've completed and what you've contributed to the business. From this, the next steps on your journey should come into focus for you.

Once you're done with this exercise, I recommend that you rewrite your resume and update your LinkedIn profile. Yes. Rewrite to ensure that it's as up-to-date as possible. You may realize that your next step is not inside your current company, but perhaps in another firm where the opportunities (the *O* from SWOT) can be clearly set forth and become easier to communicate to a prospective employer.

The last part of this assignment is for you to, at a minimum of twice a year, write up your accomplishments or achievements to share with your manager. Most companies have a performance appraisal process that establishes goals and allows you and your manager to check in from time to time to assess your performance and to receive directional support. If you keep track of your accomplishments, it will hasten the performance appraisal process to focus on forward-facing work. It will also demonstrate that you care about your job and that you are focused on continuous improvement.

TEMPLATE TO CREATE YOUR PURPOSEFUL PROFESSIONAL DEVELOPMENT STRATEGY

Group 1: General Business

Characteristic	Goals	Action Plan
Managing		
Defining processes		
Making decisions		
Being a self-starter		
Managing time and being efficient		
Adapting to changing situations		

Group 2: Business and Market Environment

Characteristic	Goals	Action Plan
Deriving market insights		
Understanding products		
Evaluating the industry and domain		
Experiencing business on a global level		

Group 3: Mindset and Orientation

Characteristic	Goals	Action Plan
Critical thinking		
Strategic thinking		
Systemic thinking		
Solving problems		
Entrepreneurial thinking		
Developing organizational instinct		
Exercising political judgment		

Group 4: Communication

Characteristic	Goals	Action Plan
Listening attentively		
Observing actively		
Writing clearly and concisely		
Presenting persuasively		
Influencing others		

Group 5: Interpersonal Skills

Characteristic	Goals	Action Plan
Building positive relationships		
Developing customer relationships		
Developing external relationships		
Including others		
Helping or coaching others		
Being a reliable team player		
Negotiating		

Group 6: Business Performance

Characteristic	Goals	Action Plan
Being results oriented		
Evaluating business performance		
Improving business processes		
Taking action		
Assuming accountability		

Group 7: Yourself

Characteristic	Goals	Action Plan
Earning credibility		
Acting with integrity, ethics, and trust		
Being confident		
Exercising managerial courage		

YOUR APPLIED LEARNING PROJECT

To enhance your development, I suggest that you identify and proactively pursue applied learning projects. An applied learning project is one that builds a specific set of skills or capabilities. You may be able to carry out several of these each year. When this kind of work plan is integrated into your goal-setting or performance planning process with your manager, it helps you plan out and act on purposeful work activities. It also cultivates a good rapport with your manager. Use the following Applied Learning Project Template to articulate your project and negotiate with your manager.

Applied Learning Project Template

Name:

Project title:

Importance:

Skills and experience you plan to develop:

Project goals:

Techniques and methods you will apply:

People with whom you plan to work:

Requested support from management:

Evidence you will provide:

When you complete this applied learning work project, you should write a complete report. It should contain the following elements:

1. The challenge you took on.
2. The concepts, skills, techniques, models, or tools you used, and how you used them.
3. The process you followed.
4. The people with whom you worked.
5. The obstacles you encountered and how you overcame them.
6. The overall outcome of the project and the impact on the business.

SUMMARY

Successful business people are continuous learners. Sometimes the learning is purposeful, and sometimes it's serendipitous. My goal for this chapter has been to equip you with a simple methodology so that you can proactively focus your efforts on your own career development. The use of a structured, data-driven approach can be most helpful to you as you take the reins of your career in business. Just as performance metrics in business serve to steer the company, ongoing evaluation and reflection can result in purposeful action planning and focused applied learning projects. These put you at the helm, and with this, you can more easily steer the ship of your career.

My parting wish is that you have as many opportunities to learn and grow as you desire, and that you realize the potential you envision for yourself as a business professional. If you master what's contained in this book and you're able to optimize your overall business acumen, you will know that you are destined for business greatness!

APPENDIX A

THE BUSINESS ACUMEN ASSESSMENT

As mentioned in Chapter 1, this assessment will contribute to your understanding of your business acumen and your domain understanding. To evaluate your business acumen, insert an X in each cell to designate your response. To properly derive your score, use the following scale and point values for each response:

RATING	DEFINITION	POINTS
Limited	This means you haven't had many opportunities to focus on this skill or apply it in your work.	1
Intermittent	You have had some opportunities to use the skill intermittently and are developing more familiarity with its use.	2
Frequent	You frequently utilize this skill, yet encounter some challenging situations where you may need some guidance from your manager.	3
Consistent	You effectively and consistently utilize this skill and are able to coach others.	4

You can also go online to http://survey.sequentlearning.com/s3/business-acumen to take this assessment. Before you do, make sure you've studied the definitions provided in Chapter 1. The online assessment will provide you with a report of your scores, a comparison of your scores to others in the worldwide database, and some suggestions to help you along.

Group 1: General Business

CHARACTERISTICS	LIMITED	INTERMITTENT	FREQUENT	CONSISTENT	SCORE
I set goals and plan the work to be done to meet those goals.					
I understand and utilize key business processes to get work done.					
I make decisions based on facts and data.					
I define and initiate work without supervision.					
I dynamically prioritize work without wasting a lot of time and money.					
I adapt easily to changing situations at work.					
				GROUP TOTAL	

Group 2: Business and Market Environment

CHARACTERISTICS	LIMITED	INTERMITTENT	FREQUENT	CONSISTENT	SCORE
I derive market insights from information collected about customers and competitors.					
I know the products sold by my company and the benefits they bring to customers.					
I can explain the characteristics and trends associated with the industry in which my company operates.					
I have international business experience.					
				GROUP TOTAL	

Group 3: Mindset and Orientation

CHARACTERISTICS	LIMITED	INTERMITTENT	FREQUENT	CONSISTENT	SCORE
I think critically in my assimilation of information from the business, or from the situations I encounter at work.					
I synthesize business and market data that helps me create goals and strategies.					
I establish connections between disparate data that enable me to examine business from a holistic perspective.					
I logically evaluate situations to reveal and solve problems.					
I am entrepreneurial.					
I adapt my behavior to the climate and culture of the company.					
I carry out my work with diligence and care based on the political climate in the organization.					
				GROUP TOTAL	

Group 4: Communication

CHARACTERISTICS	LIMITED	INTERMITTENT	FREQUENT	CONSISTENT	SCORE
I pay close attention to what people say and reassure them that their points are understood.					
In my writing, I convey ideas and information in an organized manner, targeted to the reader.					
In my presentations, I inspire and persuade others using techniques that are appropriate for the targeted audience.					
I influence others by building strong relationships so that people devote what's necessary to produce agreed-upon outcomes.					
				GROUP TOTAL	

Group 5: Interpersonal Skills

CHARACTERISTICS	LIMITED	INTERMITTENT	FREQUENT	CONSISTENT	SCORE
I build positive relationships with others in my company.					
I develop constructive customer relationships that earn customers' loyalty and trust.					
I work effectively with suppliers and partners.					
I harness the perspectives of people from diverse backgrounds.					
At work, I offer support, guidance, or coaching to others who need help.					
I am a reliable, dependable team player, and I fulfill my commitments.					
When I negotiate with others, I'm able to obtain the best outcome from all interested parties.					
				GROUP TOTAL	

Group 6: Business Performance

CHARACTERISTICS	LIMITED	INTERMITTENT	FREQUENT	CONSISTENT	SCORE
I meet my commitments to the business, regardless of obstacles.					
I analyze financial information to evaluate business performance.					
I evaluate nonfinancial measures or key performance indicators to analyze aspects of business performance.					
I assess the effectiveness of business processes and look for opportunities to improve efficiency and save money.					
I proactively take action on challenges or opportunities that are outside my normal job description.					
I am accountable for the work I perform.					
				GROUP TOTAL	

Group 7: Yourself

CHARACTERISTICS	LIMITED	INTERMITTENT	FREQUENT	CONSISTENT	SCORE
I earn credibility by being perceived by others as a person to be counted on.					
I act with integrity and do the right things for people and the business at all times.					
I am confident in the work I do, with a can-do attitude.					
I courageously convince leaders to make business decisions based on my convictions and beliefs, even if those decisions seem unpopular.					
				GROUP TOTAL	

After you add up the "group total" scores in the preceding groups, insert those scores in the following table. Then, sum the scores in the table to derive your total business acumen score.

GROUP	TOTAL SCORE
General Business	
Business and Market Environment	
Mindset and Orientation	
Communication	
Interpersonal Skills	
Business Performance	
Yourself	
TOTAL BUSINESS ACUMEN SCORE	

Now you're ready for the second part—the domain assessment. This should only take a minute or so. First, review the information in the following two lists so that you can associate yourself with the "domain" that's closest to your expertise as shown in Table A.1. There are two contextual areas for domain. The first covers the industry or sector in which you work, and the second is related to the subject area (as in academic specialty).

Industry or sector—this is most closely associated with the 10 sectors set forth by the Global Industry Classification Standard established by MSCI (see www.msci.com):

- Financial services (bank, brokerage, insurance, asset management, real estate development)
- Industrial (aerospace, logistics, trucking, manufacturing, construction, mining, machinery, rail, etc.)
- Consumer products—discretionary (automobile, consumer electronics, homebuilding, appliances, apparel, broadcasting, hospitality, leisure, media, textile)
- Consumer products—staples (food, beverage, household, personal)
- Energy (equipment, oil, gas, power, etc.)
- Healthcare (medical products, biotech, life science tools & services, pharmaceutical, managed care)
- Information technology (software, hardware, IT services, networking, semiconductor, electronic equipment, office electronics, technology distributors)
- Materials (chemicals, construction, metals, containers, paper)
- Telecommunication services
- Utilities (electric, gas, water)

The subject area of expertise that you identify with the most:

- Science
- Technology
- Engineering
- Mathematics
- Liberal arts
- Not applicable

There is no right or wrong answer, and there could be shades of gray as you consider industry and subject area. Further, as you gain experience in different companies that operate in any number of sectors, your domain experiences will most certainly evolve. As a matter of fact, for me, when I worked in the software business unit for a telecommunications company, my expertise in these two areas developed (telecommunications and technology). Yet, when I went to work for a large software company, I gained more diverse levels of experience in software development within the business process automation field. While I wasn't a programmer, I was able to define and describe the functionality and features of the software. In the end, I would have earned, at best, a 3 in that corporate role. To make the best judgment call, try the exercise that follows so that you can make the best judgment for your domain rating based on the descriptions in Table A.1.

EXERCISE

Consider all of the work experiences you've had over the course of your career thus far. At first, write down some notes about these experiences. Next, consider where your interests have focused in terms of reading, research, and other activities that serve to broaden your perspectives. Finally, write a short story that you feel best reflects your past and present domain context, and then try to imagine your next steps in your career.

Table A.1 Rating for Domain Expertise

Level	Description
1	Some familiarity and cursory understanding due to casual interactions and light reading.
2	Studied in school and keep up to date on industry goings-on, but not involved professionally.
3	Establish and maintain connections to communities of practice and/or associations, and have garnered experience through work or other projects.
4	Contribute to the body of knowledge through writing and speaking. Earning a positive reputation in the industry.
5	Developed a solid industry reputation and are sought out by others for subject matter expertise. May participate in efforts to improve the profession through influence of work on standards bodies, working on patentable ideas or other inventions.

Your next step in the process is to summarize your Business Acumen Assessment score and match it to the level shown in Table A.2.

The last part of this is to plot your coordinates on the chart in Figure A.1.

Table A.2 Rating for Business Acumen

Level	Score on the Business Acumen Assessment
1	0–38
2	39–75
3	76–105
4	106–130
5	More than 131

Figure A.1 Business Acumen and Domain Matrix

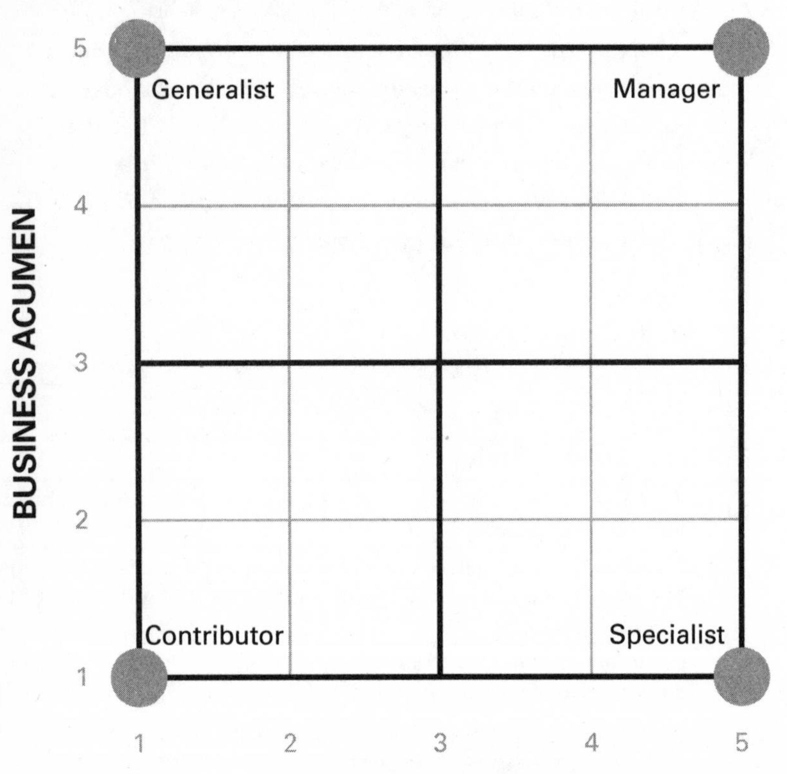

For example, if you associated yourself as a "2" for domain and a "3" for business acumen, you could plot your coordinates in the matrix as shown in Figure A.2. However, before viewing that figure, I'd like to provide some clarity around the descriptions for each quadrant of the matrix.

1. *Contributor*—a person with a preference to participate in projects as an individual contributor whose work is guided by a manager or supervisor. Employees may be newer in their career or new to an organization and may prefer a higher degree of support.
2. *Generalist*—demonstrates more experience in several areas of business acumen, but not all of them. May not have developed some industry or domain expertise. A business analyst may

Figure A.2 Business Acumen and Domain Matrix

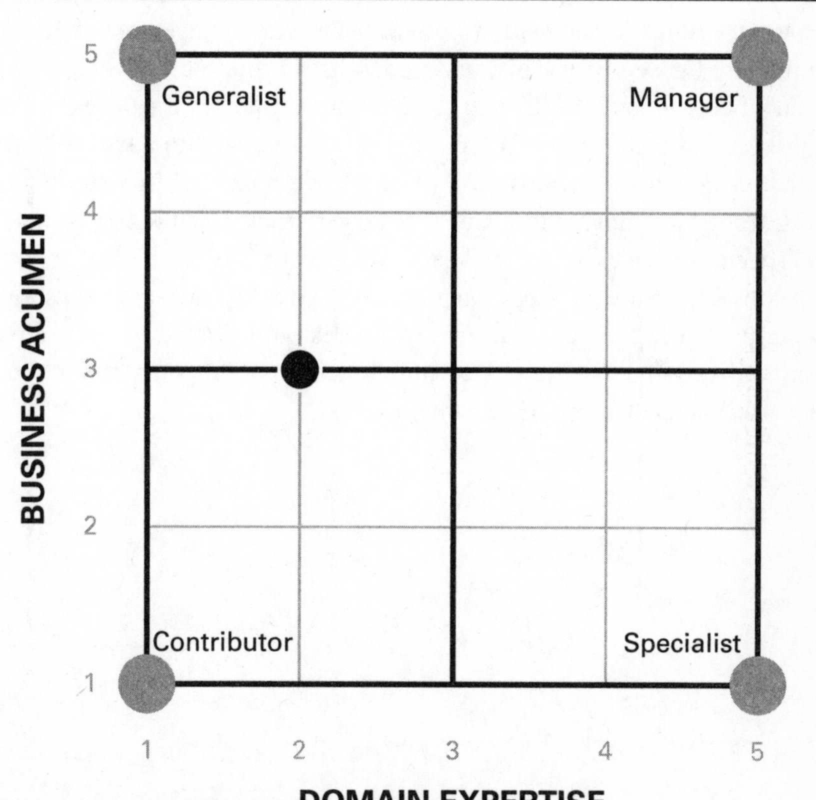

understand the financials but not have sufficient experience in working with customers.

3. *Specialist*—exhibits greater level of mastery of an industry or domain (e.g., computer programming) but has not expanded perspective sufficiently into areas associated with business acumen.
4. *Manager*—has developed a solid balance of business and domain expertise and is a trusted employee who can work independently and get things done, either with or without direct reports.

In organizations that need more from fewer people, business people who have both generalist and specialist skills will tend to do better, have more career opportunities, and get promoted into higher level managerial or leadership roles. However, depending on where you work, there is a back and forth between attaining more generalist skills and domain or specialty skills. In the field of human resources management (HR), this interplay between specialist and generalist is pronounced. People who start their careers in HR begin as generalists. Then, as they expand their interest and gain more experience, they may move into a specialty area such as benefits administration or employee relations. In a subsequent role, they may move into a higher-level generalist role or shift their area of specialty such as organizational development. The main idea for you is to consider your career as a journey where your business acumen should continue to expand as your area of interest and domain expertise may shift. The matrix in Figure A.2 can help you to point yourself in a direction that is most appropriate for you.

GLOSSARY

Accountable—The actions of a person who must ultimately deliver on a commitment is said to be accountable.

Accounts payable—The debts owed by a business, usually in relation to goods or services, inventory, or supplies.

Accounts receivable—The money owed to a business by its customers for products and services delivered to a customer.

Activity-based costing—A technique that logically allocates overhead to products based on actual usage of factory facilities or machinery.

Actuals—A term that is used to describe actual revenue earned or expenses incurred. In variance analysis, an actual is compared to the budget.

Allocation—The apportionment or assignment of a business function's expense to an income statement (P&L).

Amortization—The systematic write-off of costs incurred in the purchase of an intangible asset such as a patent or copyright.

Analysis paralysis—An expression used to describe the ongoing analysis of a problem without making a decision.

Assets—On the balance sheet, an asset is something owned that has value, including cash, marketable securities, accounts receivable, plant and equipment, and inventory.

Assumption—When used in a business case, forecast, or other planning document, an assumption is a statement that relates to a potential future state or future situation.

Attainable market share—The market share you could potentially or realistically achieve (attain) in volume and/or revenue.

Audit—An inspection of the plans, procedures, or records of a part of a business to determine whether or not a plan was followed and if a desired outcome was achieved.

Balance sheet—A financial statement that provides a snapshot of a company's overall financial health. The balance sheet is composed of assets, liabilities, and owner's equity (or net worth).

Barrier to entry—A condition that exists in a market that makes it difficult for another business to establish a foothold. A barrier can include intense competition, governmental regulation, a shortage of skilled labor, or other obstacles.

Benefit—Something of value as perceived by a customer.

Best practice—A business practice that has been codified, endorsed, and improved over time and is proven to contribute to positive business outcomes.

Brainstorming—A creative technique used to come up with ideas or concepts. In business, brainstorming can be used for general problem solving, thinking up new innovations, or improving processes.

Budget—An estimate of sales, prices, costs, and expenses over a specified time period, which is typically a year. Another way to think of a budget is to refer to it as a spending road map.

Business acumen—A term used to describe a person's understanding of various dimensions of a business that are "in play" as situations arise. It's a business common sense that enables a business person to see how a business operates from a holistic, systemic perspective.

Business case—A formal document used to justify business investments and make decisions. These could include new facilities, products, or capabilities. Business cases also support decisions required to enter new markets, to create marketing campaigns, and even to evaluate a possible acquisition.

Business model—How a company makes money based on its goals and strategy, and how it organizes itself to achieve those goals.

Business-to-business (B2B)—A business model where a company (a business) sells its products to other businesses.

Business-to-business-to-business (B2B2B)—A business model where a company (a business) sells its products to other businesses, which in turn sell those products to other businesses.

Business-to-business-to-consumer (B2B2C)—A business model where a company (a business) sells its products to other businesses, which in turn sell those products to consumers.

Business-to-consumer (B2C)—A business model where a company (a business) sells its products directly to consumers.

Buyer—A customer type in a business who serves as the purchaser of a product or service (e.g., a procurement manager).

Capital expenditure (CAPEX)—An investment in equipment, facilities, or other tangible asset that is used in the business.

Cash flow—a measure of a firm's liquidity. Cash flow considers net income (from the P&L) and required expenditures to operate the business.

Cash flow statement—A financial statement showing the inflows and outflows of money. Cash flow is the basis for deriving discounted cash flow (DCF).

Closed system—A way to describe an organization that is solely focused on internal operations.

Competitive advantage—The relative advantage that one product or product line has over products offered by other companies.

Competitive positioning—Ensuring that your product (or your company) can be favorably compared with your competitor's product (or company)—especially when attracting or retaining a customer.

Competitor profile—A document that characterizes a competitor, its products, and other competitive attributes.

Consumer—Typically used in defining an individual or household that will benefit from using a product or service (e.g., B2C).

Cost of goods sold (COGS)—The total cost of raw materials, labor, and overhead used in the creation of a tangible product.

Cross-functional team—A team of people who bring their functional expertise to work together on a project.

Customer experience management—An element of the strategy of an organization that seeks to bring about favorable perceptions across every type of interaction a customer may have with a company and/or product.

Customer focus—The extent to which a company, division, or product team seeks to fully understand the needs, motivations, and way of life of customers.

Customer insights—That which is discerned from understanding a variety of customer needs and behaviors. Insights can be used to influence strategies, guide product development, and validate segmentation models. Insights are also used for guiding the creative process, which is used to drive advertising and promotional activity.

Customer loyalty—The degree to which customers continue to buy or recommend products from the same company. A tool commonly used to measure loyalty is the net promoter score.

Customer type or customer target—In segmentation, many people may be considered the "customer," and may therefore be involved in a purchasing decision. This can include a buyer, a user, an influencer, and a decision maker.

Customer visit—A formal structured excursion to a customer's location, or to a location where it is feasible to observe customers carrying out activities that may provide clues as to their needs.

Cycle time—The speed with which an operation takes place from beginning to end. In product development, cycle time is often the time it takes from concept to product launch.

Decision criteria—A set of formally established and agreed-upon parameters used to make a decision.

Decision matrix—A tool or method used to weight and rank multidimensional choices and to prioritize work.

Deliverable—The tangible or intangible work product from one person or team to someone else, either inside or outside of the company.

Demographic—The characteristics of a market segment, or population. Most often, demographic characteristics include age, gender, income, educational level, etc.

Dependency—When one business function needs another business function to complete a task, series of tasks, or deliverables before completing its own work or fulfilling its commitments.

Depreciation—The value that an asset loses over time—typically, the asset's useful life. An example could be a machine used to produce a product that may have a useful life of five years; therefore, it loses 20 percent of its value each year. That 20 percent appears on the profit and loss statement (P&L) as depreciation.

Development—This term is used in two ways. First, it is the functional department in an organization responsible for designing and building products. Second, it is a term ascribed to the actual creation of the product.

Differentiation—The act of setting the product apart from competitors in ways that are most meaningful to targeted customers.

Discount rate—The cost of funds (cost of capital) to the company that is used to discount future cash flows to the present (see *Discounted cash flow*).

Discounted cash flow (DCF)—A financial expression that considers all future cash inflows and discounts those cash flows to the present (using the discount rate). This acknowledges the fact that money received sooner has more value than money received later.

Distribution channel—A mechanism that allows a product to be moved from its source of supply to the end customer. This could include via direct salespeople, indirect methods (as in wholesalers and retailers), or via the web. *Channel* is the expression that encompasses one of the four Ps of the marketing mix: place.

Documentation—A term that refers to documents or artifacts produced by people who work in a company, which might include process work flows, analytical techniques, etc.

Duration (task)—The amount of time it takes to complete a task, from the time it begins until the time it is finished.

EBITDA—Earnings before interest, taxes, depreciation, and amortization is the money realized (earned) by a business or a product before taxes, depreciation, and amortization are deducted from those earnings.

Entrepreneur—An individual who passionately operates a new venture or new business, accepting all risks for the business. Some leaders expect business people to exhibit entrepreneurial characteristics.

Equity—In a balance sheet, equity is what remains after liabilities are subtracted from assets.

Execution—The act of carrying out planned work.

Feature—A product capability or attribute that fulfills a specific customer or market need and provides an appropriate benefit.

Financial planning—The process of evaluating the income and expenditures of a business in an effort to forecast future cash inflows and outflows.

Financial ratio—The relationship of one financial measure to another, usually expressed as a percentage.

Forecast—The outcome of a series of exercises and analyses that helps a business predict the number of units it might sell or produce, or the market share it could attain.

Functional area—A business department in a company.

Functional project team—A project team staffed by people from a single business function.

Functional silo—An individual business function that tends to act as a stand-alone function, often formulating its own strategies and work plans in parallel with other business functions.

Functionality (of a product)—Typically, the product's functionality enables the product to do what it's supposed to do. In other words, a product's functionality enables it to address customers' needs.

Future method of operation (FMO)—An envisioned or possible set of procedures, processes, and methods that might be employed by a company, division, or organization to accomplish business objectives that is different than the present method of operation (PMO).

Gantt chart—A project planning and scheduling technique. It uses horizontal bars to portray a project's tasks and depicts each task's start date, end date, and duration. It also can show dependencies on other tasks being carried out within the overall project.

GICS—Global Industry Classification Standard managed by MSCI and Standard & Poor's (S&P) to provide a way to classify different sectors and industries. These classifications can be helpful to business people who carry out industry analysis.

Gross margin—A financial calculation that subtracts cost of goods sold (COGS) from revenue. Gross margin also provides a broad measure of business profitability.

Holistic—An expression applied to looking at an organization or a process completely and systemically.

Inbound marketing—The efforts devoted to securing data and information from a variety of sources so that it can be used to guide marketing plans and programs.

Income statement—See *Profit and Loss statement (P&L).*

Industry—A set of companies that focus their businesses on customers who operate in similar market segments. (e.g., oil and gas production companies within the Energy sector, or retail banks within the Financials sector).

Industry analysis—The methodology employed in determining the activities and trends of a set of organizations that bring about business and economic activity by selling and marketing products to similar market segments or customer types. Industry analysis is a vital element of overall market research and analysis. (See *PRESTO.*)

Informal organization—A network of contacts and relationships between people that is not usually represented on a formal organization chart.

Interface—An interface exists between different systems or between systems and networks when considered within the context of computer technology. An interface can also refer to the way in which people interact with a computer or other type of device (a user interface or graphical user interface). An interface can also have an organizational connotation where one organization works closely with (interfaces with) another.

Inventory—A collection of or listing of products that are held in storage (in stock) by a business.

Inventory turnover—A measurement of how many times the inventory is refreshed because of ongoing sales.

IT—Refers to the functional department known as information technology that deals with computer systems and software.

Key performance indicators (KPIs)—An important set of nonfinancial metrics (see *Metrics*) used to determine how well various parts of a business operate and to properly steer a company.

Knowledge sharing network—An informal community that is established to gather and share data, information, and knowledge among people with common interests.

Liabilities—Financial obligations that are represented on the balance sheet.

Make-versus-buy analysis—A structured analytical technique used to determine the optimal manner in which to produce a product. The alternatives include developing and building a product in-house versus having it developed by another company.

Market analysis—The activity involved in translating data gathered from market research to yield information on which business strategies can be formulated.

Market attractiveness—The appeal of a market area based on the customer types in that market area or market segment or by the ease of access (limited competitive activity).

Market focus—A strategic orientation of an organization or product team that holistically considers the dimensions of the industry, the dynamics of the competitive environment, and customers' needs in determining the appropriate business strategies and product portfolio investments.

Market penetration—The degree to which a product is being sold in a given market area. Higher penetration means that more people in a currently pursued market area are purchasing the product, or that the product is being sold in other market areas.

Market pricing—Pricing strategies that consider customer needs, the value proposition, the strength of the brand, and other market forces.

Market research—The formal and informal methods used to learn about the industry, competitors, and customers, enabling an organization or product team to achieve the optimal market focus. Also the activities related to the systematic, ongoing efforts aimed at gathering and capturing data about industries, competitors, and customers.

Market segment—A group of customers (or potential customers) that share common needs or buying behaviors.

Market segmentation—The classification method that helps managers identify customer types based on specific categories such as common needs or similar buying behaviors.

Market share—The amount of market demand that can be captured by a product or product line. Market share is expressed as a percentage of the total addressable market (TAM).

Marketing mix—A combined set of strategic or tactical tools—often referred to as the four Ps. The mix elements include the product itself, its pricing, the advertising and promotional programs that support the product, and place (meaning distribution channel).

Mentoring—A technique used to help less skilled or experienced people learn from more experienced people. The mentor is the experienced person and the protégé is the person who is guided.

Metrics—A metric is a measurement. When a plan is put into place, a way to measure the outcome is needed. When a market share forecast is created and the outcomes are measured at a future date, the planned metric is compared with the actual metric to determine the degree to which the forecast was met.

Motivational state—That condition (or need) existing in the mind of a customer that drives the customer to purchase a product. (See also *Need state*.)

Need—As defined for markets, a specific, recurrent requirement experienced by a given market segment or group of target customers. Needs are sometimes complex and not easily related to primal or basic human needs as defined in Maslow's hierarchy of needs.

Need state—A basic human need or requirement, at a specific point in time. Basic needs can focus on safety or security. However, need states (or motivational states) are generally transient. For example, when a consumer's car is beyond repair, she enters a new need state that motivates her to evaluate different types of new cars to purchase that will help her achieve her objectives (commute to work, shuttle children to sports activities, or transport passengers).

Net income—Excess (or deficit) obtained when total expenses are subtracted from total revenue. Generally computed over a standard accounting period, such as a month, quarter, or year.

Net present value (NPV)—The value of some future financial outcome stated in today's dollars, taking into account the fact that a dollar (or other unit of currency) today is worth more than a dollar in the future, accounting for the effect of the cost of those funds, typically computed by compounding using a stated discount rate.

Net promoter score (or NPS)—A measurement used by a company to determine the willingness of a customer to recommend your company or its products.

Net worth—Assets, less debts and obligations (liabilities). Also referred to as *owner's equity* or just *equity*.

New product development (NPD)—NPD is a process to evaluate ideas and opportunities for products and innovations and includes the methodology to fund, develop, validate, and launch a product.

North American Industry Classification System (NAICS)—The NAICS is a highly granular, standard numerical classification system that assigns six-digit codes and standard titles to every possible business type.

Open system—A reference to an organization that is set up to reflect influence by external market factors.

Operating expenses (OPEX)—Refers to ongoing, usually variable costs of operating a business; contrasted with capital expenses, which refers to the plant and equipment needed to support operations.

Optimization—A state in which all inputs, components, elements, and processes are working together to produce the most desirable, viable, and sustainable outcome possible given the current operating conditions.

Organization chart—An illustration that portrays the structure of any organization (business, not-for-profit, university, etc.).

Organizational connection chart—An organization chart that visually shows how information can move between people or departments listed on an organization chart.

Organizational culture—The collective set of attitudes, activities, and behaviors that, collectively, tend to give an organization its personality.

Organizational instinct—A business person's intuitive understanding of goings-on in a company.

Overhead—Expenses incurred in the production of a product that are indirectly related to the cost of the product. Overhead might include rent, electricity, fuel, and similar expenses. Overhead in service businesses relates to similar types of expenses and is often categorized as "general and administrative" expenses.

Payback period—The amount of time it takes to recover an investment's initial outlay.

Persona—A customer archetype or model created to represent a common set of characteristics or motivations, as with a customer type within a market segment or demographic. It is typically a representation of a group of people as opposed to a single individual.

Place—See *Distribution channel.*

Plant and equipment—The physical production assets of a manufacturing company.

Platform—The underlying foundations, technology frameworks, base architectures, and interfaces upon which products are built.

PMBOK (Project Management Body of Knowledge)—A standard approach to project management espoused and promoted by the Project Management Institute. For the most current details, see www.pmi.org/Resources/Pages/Global-Standards-Program.aspx.

Policy—A general, usually strategically focused statement, rule, or regulation that describes how a particular activity, operation, or group of operations will be carried out within a company.

Political capital—The goodwill earned by a business person through the relationships made, positive visible results obtained, and confidence earned by others.

Positioning statement—The document used to competitively position a product in the market by identifying the target customer or market segment, clarifying the product's benefits, describing its unique characteristics, and comparing it to equivalent competitive products.

Present method of operation (PMO)—In essence, the current way of doing things, that is, the collection of procedures, processes, and methods currently employed by a company, division, or organization to accomplish business objectives.

PRESTO—A useful, macroscopic view of a market, segment, or market area, constructed by examining the political, regulatory, economic, social, and technological factors affecting that market (or geographic area) as well as other factors that do not easily fit into one of these categories.

Price—The amount of money charged for a product, or the amount a customer is willing to pay for the perceived benefit received one of the four Ps of the marketing mix.

Process—A structured series of activities that are organized and sequenced to achieve a goal.

Product—Something that is offered for sale, which may be either tangible or intangible.

Product elements—Components, subassemblies, or parts of a tangible product. A product element could be a feature or term of use for an intangible product.

Product life cycle—A term to describe a product, from its conception to its discontinuance and ultimate market withdrawal.

Product line—A grouping of products focused on similar markets or on solving a particular type of problem.

Product mix—The combination of all products sold within a given portfolio. Very often, the term *product mix* is used for budgeting or portfolio tracking because it describes how many of each product are to be sold or are actually sold.

Product portfolio—Several products or product lines may be grouped into a related collection called a product portfolio. Portfolios may be organized based on segments targeted, their underlying architecture, or even the specific source or manufacturing method used.

Product positioning—The way in which a product or service is presented or communicated to a particular market or market segment such that a specific perception can be created in the minds of the desired customer types within that segment. Product positioning is important because it asserts a product's differential advantage over competitors' products.

Profit and loss statement (P&L)—A periodic financial statement that compares income and expenses to determine if a business produces a profit or a loss. The most important elements are *revenue* (units sold × price charged), *cost of goods sold* (material, labor, and overhead), and *gross margin* (total revenue minus cost of goods sold).

Project—A group of related activities and tasks associated with accomplishing a specific goal or objective. As referred to in this book, projects usually produce a deliverable from a person or person in a functional department.

Project management—The act of planning and managing a series of tasks and agreed-upon deliverables. (Refer to Project Management Institute at PMI.org for a complete definition.)

Promotion—One of the four Ps of the marketing mix that involves a variety of methods used to communicate to select customer types within desirable market segments.

Rational ignorance—A flaw in the decision-making process built on the assumption that no decision will produce an acceptable result, and thus, any decision can be made without the need for reasonable consideration.

Regulatory requirements—Requirements that are imposed by an outside (usually governmental) agency that must be met by a company operating in a given market.

Responsible person—One who commits to fulfilling the purpose of a task. The "doer" of work.

Results—A business outcome that is produced as a consequence of specific or purposeful actions.

Return on investment (ROI)—Any method of comparing the amount of money invested in a given initiative with the profitability or financial results of the initiative. ROI calculations are generally very subjective.

Revenue—The amount of money obtained from the sale of products or services. Revenue is calculated by multiplying the number of units of the product sold by the price per unit.

Risk—The consideration of a situation that might arise that would tend to prevent a strategy or objective from being successfully achieved.

Risk mitigation—The act of developing advance plans or taking immediate actions to minimize or prevent known or unknown events (risks) from adversely impacting a strategy or business objective.

Scalability—The capability of a business or a product line to be readily enlarged or expanded to handle greater capacity.

Scenario—A specific sequence of hypothetical events and contingencies, used for planning and forecasting purposes. A scenario can be thought of as a possible story about the future. Scenarios are useful when preparing business cases, budgets, and forecasts.

Segment—See *Market segment.*

Segmentation—See *Market segmentation.*

Sensitivity analysis—The practice of changing a variable in a financial model or forecast to determine how a change in that variable affects the overall outcome. For example, to consider the way in which a change in price might affect the gross margin in a product forecast, one might vary the price in small increments and recompute the figures to see how gross margin changes.

Share—See *Market share.*

Socialize—Building support for ideas, plans, and strategies by sharing them with various interested and/or influential members of the organization. Socializing is based on the observation that people will tend to show more interest in ideas that are more widely discussed.

Solution—A combination of products, services, and other elements that solve complex problems, have a high degree of integration across disparate elements, and usually require customization for a specific customer type or industry.

Stock-keeping units (SKUs)—A standardized numbering system for uniquely labeling products so that there is no confusion at any point along the value chain.

Stock-out—When a company does not have product available to fill existing orders.

Storytelling—A narrative way of describing a scenario, product idea, or strategy intended to provide a real-world context to promote decision making and better understanding.

Strategy—A game plan that establishes parameters for achieving competitive advantage. Strategies are built on the goals of what's to be done along with the activities and actions that spell out how it's to be done.

Strengths—The attributes or characteristics of a product or service that tend to give it a natural competitive advantage.

Suppliers—External companies that provide subassemblies, components, or other product elements.

SWOT—A general method used as an element of strategic planning. SWOT is an acronym for strengths, weaknesses, opportunities, and threats. SWOT is used to synthesize the many elements of the business environment so that a current state of the business can be captured and future strategies considered.

Synergy—Any relationship between two persons or entities in which the combined effort produces a more useful result than the individual efforts of those entities would produce on their own. Sometimes described by the phrase, "the whole is greater than the sum of its parts."

Target customer—Within a given market segment, those customers with common needs are likely to benefit from a given product. Some also use the term *customer target.*

Target market—The grouping of target customer types (by geography, demographic, or other segment definition) who exhibit a common set of needs.

Threats—With respect to SWOT, threats are represented by the competitive products or their characteristics that offer the competition the best opportunity to damage your reputation.

Turnover—A ratio that refers to the number of times the inventory is replenished in a given time period. Higher turnover is preferred because it indicates that products are selling rapidly. (In countries other than the United States, turnover may refer to sales revenue.)

Upsell—The practice of convincing a customer to purchase a higher-value product or service than the version currently owned.

User—A person, customer type, or target customer that is identified to primarily use the product or application. A user could also be the ultimate consumer of the product.

User experience (or UX)—An expression that encompasses the feelings, beliefs, emotions, or attitudes of customers (as users) in their interaction with a product or service. In the world of digital products, UX is a term used to describe a desirable, meaningful human-computer or human-machine interaction.

Value-added—Refers to the addition of something else of value to a customer as a vendor attempts to solve a customer's business problem. Value-added services, for example, might include the addition of consulting services or customizing a product explicitly for a customer.

Value proposition—Defines the need and proves the economic or qualitative benefit to a specific customer, based on the benefit perceived by that customer. Value propositions must be expressed clearly in language that the customer understands.

Variance—The difference between a plan or budget and an actual result.

Variance analysis—The evaluation of a number of variances to determine root causes. Product managers will examine a variety of variances in order to create narratives or explanations as to what transpired and the remedies that will be undertaken to improve performance.

Vertical markets—Market segments focused on a specific industry, such as pharmaceuticals, telecommunications equipment, or fast food. Often referred to as industry verticals.

Vision—The envisioned end state or optimal future situation. A leader envisions a firm's position in the market at a point in the future.

Voice of the customer (VOC)—A technique that captures customer needs through either explicit or direct interactions with customers using surveys, focus groups, or observations made on a visit to a customer's location.

Volume—The quantity of units or amount of money associated with a particular product; can be applied to sales, inventory, production rates, or any product-related quantity.

Weaknesses—With respect to SWOT, the attributes of a product that cause the product to be less than competitive.

Work breakdown structure (WBS)—A structured list of all activities and tasks required to complete a project.

Work flow—The entire sequence of steps, activities, processes, and tactics carried out in order to transform a given input into a desired output.

Working capital—The amount of liquid assets (generally, cash) that are available to operate or run a business.

BIBLIOGRAPHY

Allen, David, *Getting Things Done: The Art of Stress-Free Productivity*, New York: Penguin, 2001.

Berman, Karen, and Joe Knight, *Financial Intelligence: A Manager's Guide for Knowing What the Numbers Really Mean*, Boston: The Harvard Business School Press, 2013.

Blanchard, Kenneth H., *Empowerment Takes More Than a Minute*, San Francisco: Berrett-Koehler Publishers, 2001.

Blank, Steve, *The Four Steps to the Epiphany*, K&S Ranch, 2013.

Bossidy, Larry, and Ram Charan with Charles Burck, *Execution: The Discipline of Getting Things Done*, London: Random House, 2002.

Caporale, Bob, *Creative Strategy Generation: Using Passion and Creativity to Compose Business Strategies that Inspire Action*, New York: McGraw-Hill, 2015.

Cardona, Pablo, and Paddy Miller, *The Art of Creating and Sustaining Winning Teams*, Boston: Harvard Business School Publishing, 2000.

Christensen, Clayton M., *The Innovator's Dilemma: When New Technologies Cause Great Firms to Fail*, Boston: Harvard Business School Press, 1997.

Cohen, Allen, and David L. Bradford, *Influence Without Authority*, Hoboken, NJ: John Wiley & Sons, 2005.

Collins, Jim, *From Good to Great: Why Some Companies Make the Leap . . . and Others Don't*, New York: Harper Business, 2001.

Collins, Jim, and Porras, Jerry I., *Built to Last: Successful Habits of Visionary Companies*, Harper Collins, 2004.

Drucker, Peter, *The Practice of Management*, New York: Harper & Row, 1954.

Drucker, Peter, *On the Profession of Management*, Boston: Harvard Business Review Book, 2003 (a collection of articles from 1963–2003).

Drucker, Peter, et al., *Harvard Business Review on Decision Making*, Boston: Harvard Business School Publishing, 2001.

Duarte, Deborah L., and Nancy Tennant Snyder, *Mastering Virtual Teams: Strategies, Tools, and Techniques that Succeed*, San Francisco: Jossey-Bass, 2000.

Edwards, Helen, and Derek Day, *Creating Passionate Brands*, London: Kogan Page, 2005.

Farris, Paul W., Bendle, Neil T., Pfeifer, Phillip E., and Reibstein, David J., *Marketing Metrics: The Definitive Guide to Measuring Marketing Performance* (2nd ed.), Upper Saddle River, NJ: Pearson Education, 2014.

Fisher, Tony, *The Data Asset: How Smart Companies Govern Their Data for Business Success*, Hoboken, NJ: John Wiley & Sons, Inc., 2009.

Fuld, Leonard M., *The New Competitor Intelligence: The Complete Resource for Finding, Analyzing, and Using Information About Your Competitors*, New York: John Wiley & Sons, 1995.

Galbraith, Jay R., *Designing Organizations: Strategy Structure, and Process at the Business Unit and Enterprise Levels*, San Francisco: Jossey-Bass, 2014.

Gladwell, Malcolm, *Tipping Point: How Little Things Can Make a Big Difference*, New York: Little, Brown and Company, 2002.

Gladwell, Malcolm, *Blink: The Power of Thinking Without Thinking*, New York: Little Brown and Company, 2005.

Haines, Steven, *Managing Product Management: Empowering Your Organization to Produce Competitive Products and Brands*, New York: McGraw-Hill, 2012.

Haines, Steven, *The Product Manager's Survival Guide*, New York: McGraw-Hill, 2013.

Haines, Steven, *The Product Manager's Desk Reference*, 2nd ed., New York: McGraw-Hill, 2014.

Hooks, Ivy, and Kristen Ferry, *Customer Centered Products: Creating Successful Products Through Smart Requirements Management*, New York: Amacom, 2001.

Jacobs, Robert W., *Real-Time Strategic Change: How to Involve the Entire Organization in Fast and Far-Reaching Change*, San Francisco: Berrett-Koehler, 1997.

Kahaner, Larry, *Competitive Intelligence: How to Gather, Analyze, and Use Information to Move Your Business to the Top*, New York: Touchstone, 1997.

Kanaga, Kim, and Michael E. Kossler, *How to Form a Team: Five Keys to High Performance*, Greensboro, NC: Center for Creative Leadership, 2004.

Katzenbach, Jon R., and Douglas K. Smith, *The Wisdom of Teams: Creating the High-Performance Organization*, Boston: Harvard Business School Press, 1993.

Kim, W. Chan, and Renee Mauborgne, *Blue Ocean Strategy*, Boston, MA: Harvard Business School Press, 2005.

Koestenbaum, Peter, *Leadership—The Inner Side of Greatness—A Philosophy for Leaders*, San Francisco: Jossey-Bass, 1991.

Kotler, Philip, *Principles of Marketing*, Upper Saddle River, NJ: Pearson Prentice Hall, 2007.

Kotonya, Gerald, and Ian Sommerville, *Requirements Engineering: Processes and Techniques*, West Sussex, UK: John Wiley & Sons, 1998.

Leherer, Jonah, *How We Decide*, New York: Houghton Mifflin Harcourt Publishing Company, 2009.

Lencioni, Patrick, *The Five Dysfunctions of a Team*, San Francisco: Jossey-Bass, 2002.

Levit, Alexandra, *They Don't Teach Corporate in College*, 3rd ed., Pompton Plains, NJ: Career Press, 2014.

Lewis, Bob, *Bare Bones Project Management: What You Can't Not Do*, Eden Prairie, MN: IS Survivor Publishing, 2006.

Maxwell, John, *How Successful People Think: Change Your Thinking, Change Your Life*, New York: Street Center, 2009.

Mills, D. Quinn, *E-Leadership: Guiding Your Business to Success in the New Economy*, Upper Saddle River, NJ: Prentice Hall, 2001.

Mootee, Idris, D*esign Thinking for Strategic Innovation: What They Can't Teach You at Business or Design School*, Hoboken, NJ: John Wiley & Sons, Inc., 2013.

Nagle, Thomas T., and Reed K. Holden, *The Strategy and Tactics of Pricing: A Guide to Profitable Decision Making*, Upper Saddle River, NJ: Prentice Hall, 2002.

Nonaka, I., and H. Takeuchi, *The Knowledge Creating Company*, New York: Oxford University Press, 1995.

Osterwalder, Alexander, *Business Model Generation: A Handbook for Visionaries, Game Changers, and Challengers*, Hoboken, NJ: John Wiley & Sons, Inc., 2010.

Parmenter, David, *Key Performance Indicators (KPI): Developing, Implementing, and Using Winning KPIs*, Hoboken, NJ: John Wiley & Sons, Inc., 2007.

Pfeffer, Jeffrey, and Robert I. Sutton, *The Knowing-Doing Gap: How Smart Companies Turn Knowledge into Action*, Boston: Harvard Business School Press, 2000.

Porter, Michael E., *Competitive Advantage*, New York: The Free Press, 1985.

Project Management Institute, *A Guide to the Project Management Body of Knowledge (PMBOK® Guide)*, 3rd ed., Newtown Square, PA: Project Management Institute, 2000.

Ramsey, Dave, *EntreLeadership; 20 Years of Practical Business Wisdom from the Trenches*, New York: Howard Books, 2011.

Ries, Al, and Jack Trout, *Positioning: The Battle for Your Mind* (twentieth anniversary ed.), New York: McGraw-Hill, 2001.

Sandberg, Sheryl, *Lean In: Women, Work, and the Will to Lead*, New York: Alfred A. Knopf, 2013.

Schein, Edgar H., *The Corporate Culture Survival Guide*, San Francisco: Jossey-Bass, 2009.

Senge, Peter, *The Fifth Discipline*, New York: Doubleday, 1990.

Sun-Tzu, *The Art of War (The New Translation)*, New York: William Morrow and Company, 1993.

Treacy, Michael, and Fred D. Wiersema, *The Discipline of Market Leaders*, Reading, MA: Addison-Wesley, 1995.

Trout, Jack, *Differentiate or Die: Survival in Our Era of Killer Competition*, New York: John Wiley & Sons, 2000.

Tseng, Mitchell M., and Frank T. Pillar, *The Customer Centric Enterprise: Advances in Mass Customization and Personalization*, Berlin: Springer-Verlag, 2003.

Ursiny, Tim, *The Coward's Guide to Conflict: Empowering Solutions for Those Who Would Rather Run Than Fight*, Naperville, IL: Sourcebook, Inc., 2003.

Whiteley, Richard, and Diane Hessan, *Customer Centered Growth: Five Proven Strategies for Building Competitive Advantage*, Reading, MA: Addison-Wesley, 1996.

INDEX